ENCYCLOPEDIC DICTIONARY
OF SCHOOL LAW

Richard D. Gatti
and
Daniel J. Gatti

Parker Publishing Company, Inc.
West Nyack, New York

Library of Congress Cataloging in Publication Data

Gatti, Richard DeY
   Encyclopedic dictionary of school law.

   1. Educational law and legislation—United States
—Dictionaries. I. Gatti, Daniel Jon
joint author. II. Title.
KF4117.G3   344'.73'0703   74-22415
ISBN 0-13-275859-8

TO OUR MOTHER

ALSO BY THE AUTHORS

The Teacher and the Law

Foreword

Anyone pursuing a career in education will likely, at sometime, be involved in a lawsuit or legal proceedings. In recent years there have been many thousands of court cases involving educators and school-related issues. We are now witnessing a vast proliferation of school laws. The inevitable result has been serious confusion and misunderstanding on the part of "school people."

Consequently, this book should be in the hands of every teacher and administrator, and in every school library. The authors have successfully compiled and set forth in easy-to-understand language every aspect and issue of public school law with which the teacher or administrator must be concerned. What's more important, the authors give concrete answers and guidelines that the teacher or administrator can easily follow when confronted with a legal problem.

For educators concerned with legal issues, *Encyclopedic Dictionary of School Law* is one of the most comprehensive books ever published. This book clearly discusses such things as student rights, teachers' and administrators' constitutional rights, tenure, collective bargaining, contracts, powers of the local school boards, dismissals and dismissal procedures, negligence, and teacher and administrator liability for injuries to students or school personnel.

In addition to covering broad areas of concern for teachers and administrators, this book answers everyday questions arising from daily schooling activities. How does one go about building a personnel file that will stand up under intense cross-examination? How does one build a file, to be used as evidence against another file, in a future hearing? What about hair length, payment during maternity leave, paternity leave, elections, reorganization, slander, assault, evaluations, transfers, offensive language or obscene materials, and many, many other areas?

5

The authors are among the nation's leading authorities in public school law. Their first book, *The Teacher and the Law,* was one of the first books written directly for teachers in helping them to understand their liability, responsibility, and rights in the day-to-day aspects of working within a school.

My staff and I have had considerable contact with Richard and Daniel Gatti. Not only are they lawyers expert in this field, but they are lawyers who have extensive experience in teaching in the elementary and secondary schools. Their competence and desire to make education a better experience for teachers and administrators makes them eminently qualified to write this book. The task was indeed great, and they have accomplished that task with skill and clarity that is seldom matched in books of this kind.

Dale Parnell
Chancellor
San Diego Community College District

How to Use This Book

The *Encyclopedic Dictionary of School Law* provides the professional educator with practical material that fills the need for an easily accessible, comprehensive reference book covering all major aspects of school law. With a clear understanding of their legal rights, liabilities, and responsibilities, administrators and teachers will be more aware of the legal factors that affect their own future, the well-being of their students, and the educational system. When problems arise that relate to school law, the key issues and practical guidelines can be found in this book, all presented in a comprehensive, clearly organized manner.

Hundreds of legal subjects are thoroughly explained, among them: constitutional rights of teachers, administrators and students; liability of teachers for student injuries; contract rights and responsibilities; collective bargaining and related employee organizational activities; parochial school aid; tenure laws and the protections they provide; teacher dismissals and hearing procedures; required student expulsion procedures; compulsory attendance laws; discrimination; school board powers and duties. These subjects and all of the other school-related legal topics are covered in a manner which not only explains the law, but provides specific guidelines for action on a day-to-day basis.

To illustrate how this book is used, assume a question arises regarding a teacher's liability for negligence. By looking under "Negligence," one can quickly find the elements that are necessary if liability is to be imposed. Examples are given and guidelines for the prevention of negligent injuries are set forth. The most relevant issues with reference to negligence are explained under this section. However, other areas do relate, and these are cross-referenced so that the reader who wants a more thorough understanding can quickly turn to other sections. For example, "Rules" and their effect on one's liability for negligence are cross-referenced. A teacher's "Absence From Class" is sometimes very relevant to the imposition of liability for negligence

7

and is therefore cross-referenced. These, and other areas, give the reader a comprehensive understanding of the law on negligence, and as a result, injuries may be prevented and liability avoided.

To enhance the usefulness of this book, the topics have been arranged in alphabetical order and a Categorical Index has been provided. As an additional aid to the reader:

> When a subject cannot be found in the alphabetically arranged articles, consult the Index which contains a complete listing of entries.

> For a fuller account of many topics, follow the cross references from entry to entry. For example, "Corporal Punishment" refers you to "Governmental Immunity" or "Battery" and these entries contain important information that can be utilized when formulating guidelines on the subject of discipline.

> If a comprehensive explanation of a major field of education law is desired, consult the Category Index, in which many of the topics are listed under broad general categories.

The law is designed to provide teachers, administrators and students with the safeguards they need to make the educational system a safe, enjoyable, exciting place to work or study. This book provides educators with a functional knowledge of school law, which will benefit them in their everyday experiences both in the school and in the community in which they live.

Richard DeY Gatti
Daniel Jon Gatti

Categorical Index

ADMINISTRATION OF SCHOOLS AND SCHOOL PERSONNEL

Accountability
Administrative agencies
Automobiles
Bus drivers
Chief State School Officer
Commissioner of Education
Curriculum
Elementary and Secondary Education Act of 1965
Kindergartens
Music
Non-residents
Personnel records
Police

Principal
Residence
Safe Place Statutes
School calendar
School closures
Smoking
Special education
Summer school
Superintendent
Textbooks, free
Transportation
Tuition
Vice-principals
Workshops

CHURCH AND STATE RELATIONSHIPS

Bible reading
Compulsory education
Child-benefit theory
External benefit theory
Fundamental interest theory
Prayers
Private and parochial school aid

Private schools
Released time
Religion
Sex education
Shared-time
Vaccination
Vouchers

COLLECTIVE BARGAINING AND SCHOOL NEGOTIATIONS

Agency shop
Arbitration
Collective Bargaining
Dues checkoff
Factfinding

Meet and confer laws
Sanctions
Scope of bargaining
Strikes
Union security

CONSTITUTIONAL RIGHTS OF SCHOOL PERSONNEL

Academic freedom
Anti-evolution statutes
Anti-subversive laws
Appearance
Assembly, right of
Association
Constitutional law
Constitutional rights of teachers
    and administrators

Homosexuals
Loyalty oaths
Obscenity
Outside employment
Privacy
Religion
Self-incrimination
Silent, right to remain

CONSTITUTIONAL RIGHTS OF STUDENTS

Appearance
Assembly, right of
Athletics
Commencement exercises
Conscientious objectors
Constitutional law
Diplomas
Flag salute
Married students

Newspapers
Pledge of allegiance
Pregnant students
Religion
Search and seizure, unreasonable
Secret societies
Self incrimination
Student rights

CONTRACTUAL DUTIES AND PROTECTIONS

Agreement
Annual contracts
Assignments
Capacity
Certificate
Certification
Continuing contracts
Contracts
Damages
Evaluation
Express authority
Implied authority

Implied contract
Leaves of absence
Mass resignation
Maternity leave
Military leave
Moral turpitude
Offer
Paternity leave
Peace Corps
Sabbatical leave
Salary schedules
Sick leave

DISCIPLINE AND CONTROL OF STUDENTS

Absence
Assignments
Automobiles
Corporal punishment
Express authority
Implied authority

In loco parentis
Parental authority
Parental liability
Rules
Supervision

DISMISSALS, GRIEVANCES, AND TENURE

Abolition of positions
Damages
Decertification
Demotions
Grievances
Probationary teachers

Reinstatement
Renewal
Severance payments
Tenure
Transfers
Witnesses

EQUAL PROTECTION AND DUE PROCESS

Achievement tests
Athletics
Civil Rights Act of 1871
Civil Rights Act of 1964
Cross-examination
Desegregation

Discrimination
Due process
Equal protection
Expulsion
Intelligence testing
Mental examinations

INJURIES TO STUDENTS AND STAFF

Absence from class
Agent
Allocation of liability
Assault
Assumption of risk
Battery
Comparative negligence
Contributory negligence
Damages
Defamation
False imprisonment
Foreseeability
God, act of

Imputed negligence
Intentional tort
Medical services
Medication
Mental distress
Negligence
Omissions
Playgrounds
Reasonable and prudent
Supervision
Trespass to personal property
Vocational programs

JUDICIAL CONSIDERATIONS

Burden of proof
Certiorari, writ of
Common law
Contempt of court
Courts, organization
Defendant
Enjoin
Exhibits
Felony
Hearsay
Injunction

Malice
Mandamus
Mechanic's lien
Misdemeanor
Plaintiff
Preponderance of evidence
Presumptions
Question of fact
Question of law
Quo warranto
Search warrant

JUDICIAL CONSIDERATIONS (cont.)

Self-defense   Subpoena
Stare decisis   Substantive law
Statute of Limitations   Waiver
Statutes   Witnesses

SCHOOL ORGANIZATION, PROPERTY, FUNDS, AND FINANCING

Activity funds   Fees
Bonds   Funds, school
Buildings   Property
Common schools   Reorganization
Construction

SCHOOL BOARD POWERS AND LIABILITIES

Conflicts of interest   Open hearing
Discretionary acts   Public office, right to hold
Donations, acceptance of   Quorum
Express authority   Ratification
Governmental immunity   Removal from office
Malpractice   Save-harmless statutes
Ministerial acts   School boards, structure
Municipal corporation

A

Ability Grouping. See INTELLIGENCE TESTING.

Abolition of Positions. As the population growth rate decreases and as school districts consolidate in an effort to provide greater services at less expense, the issue of whether or not certain teaching or administrative positions may lawfully be abolished comes into more increasing prominence.

As a general rule, a teacher or administrator has no legal right to a position which is being abolished for bona fide reasons. This is true even if the teacher or administrator is tenured, and even though the applicable state statutes make no reference to abolition of position as a grounds for dismissal. However, three main legal arguments may arise:

1. Were the reasons bona fide?
2. Was the position abolished in fact?
3. Was DISCRIMINATION involved?

If any one of these three arguments is sustained, the teacher or administrator has a right to retain his or her position. The following examples provide an explanation of some of the issues.

The school district cannot dismiss a tenured teacher whose position is abolished, and retain a nontenured teacher in a similar position. Also, several cases have held that when two or more districts are consolidated, teachers who had TENURE in the old district retain their tenure status in the new district. However, several cases have resulted in a contrary decision and hold that the school board of the consolidated district must remain free to exercise discretion in the initial staffing of the new district, and therefore, the tenure rights do not continue. This split of authority remains unresolved and whether or not tenure rights will continue in the new district is dependent upon the individual state courts' decisions.

Sometimes there is one new school constructed to replace two older schools, and at times there are two persons who have approximately equal rights to a new position which is being created to replace their two old positions. There are no easy general rules which apply to this situation, but several applicable cases provide an insight into the kind of factors the COURTS are likely to consider in deciding who is entitled to the new position. In one case, a new, enlarged school was constructed to replace two older schools. Although the principal of one of the schools had attained tenure, the court held that it was proper for the school board to assign the principal to a teaching position at the same salary she had been receiving as a principal. The court said that since the *old school no longer was in existence,* the school board was under no duty to appoint the woman as principal of the new school.[1] In a case involving REORGANIZATION, two principals were involved. The board decided to have one principal for grades 7 to 12, and abolished the junior high school principalship. The junior high school principal initiated a court case to compel the board to grant him the "new" principalship instead of the high school principal. The court held for him, because the two principals were equally qualified but he had seniority as well as a secondary school principal's CERTIFICATE.[2]

Where an old school is torn down and several new schools are built to replace it, problems sometimes arise. For example, one case involved a principal of a school having grades 7 to 12. When two new schools, a new junior high school and a new senior high school, were built to replace the torn down school, the principal was assigned to the junior high school. He sued, contending that he had a right to the principalship of the senior

---

[1] *Jantzen v. School Committee of Chelmsford,* 124 N.E.2d 534 (Mass. 1955).

[2] *Jadick v. Board of Education of the City School District of Beacon,* 204 N.E.2d 202 (Ct. of App., N.Y. 1964).

high school. The court found that this was not a demotion, and the board had acted properly in assigning the principal to the junior high school.[3]

Absence. See COMPULSORY EDUCATION; LEAVES OF ABSENCE.

Absence from Class, Teacher. At times, when a teacher is absent from the classroom, the students feel inclined to become more rowdy, and occasionally a student is injured. In an effort to recover DAMAGES for the injuries sustained, the student may sue the teacher, contending that the teacher was negligent.

A teacher who absents himself or herself from the classroom is not negligent as a matter of law. NEGLIGENCE is a QUESTION OF FACT which will be determined by looking at all of the facts and circumstances surrounding the absence. The teacher is not an insurer of his or her students' safety, but liability will exist where injuries result from the teacher's failure to exercise reasonable care.

Reasonable care requires that in supervising students, the teacher must act as the REASONABLE AND PRUDENT teacher would act under the same or similar circumstances. For example, while the reasonable and prudent first grade teacher would not normally leave his or her classroom for ten minutes without providing for some substitute supervision, such a teacher might do so in an emergency situation. As a result, whether or not the teacher is acting in a reasonable and prudent manner and is therefore free from negligence must be examined in light of the following factors:

1. The purpose for the absence;
2. The age and maturity of the students;
3. The activities being conducted in the classroom at the time of the absence;
4. The propensity of the students to become "rowdy";
5. The length of the absence;
6. Whether or not the students are aware of RULES and regulations governing their conduct while the teacher is gone; and
7. The precautions taken by the teacher.

---

[3] *Verret v. Calcasieu Parish School Board,* 103 So.2d 560 (La. 1958).

Academic Freedom. The concept of academic freedom originated in the German universities in the 19th century and provided professors a freedom to teach on any subject they deemed educationally relevant or beneficial. The professors were not limited to a prescribed course of study.

As embodied in the American concept, academic freedom allows a teacher freedom to inquire and question, but the universities and public schools are allowed to prescribe the general subject matter. Academic freedom is an interest which the COURTS will endeavor to protect. As the Supreme Court of the United States has stated:

> Our nation is deeply committed to safeguarding academic freedom, which is of transcendent value to all of us and not merely to the teachers concerned. That freedom is therefore a special concern of the First Amendment, which does not tolerate laws that cast a pall of orthodoxy over the classroom.[4]

In giving legal status to academic freedom, the Supreme Court recalled Justice Learned Hand's words:

> The classroom is peculiarly the "marketplace of ideas." The Nation's future depends upon leaders trained through wide exposure to that robust exchange of ideas which discovers truth "out of a multitude of tongues, [rather] than through any kind of authoritative selection." [5]

University professors have the right to lecture without fearing dismissal or NONRENEWAL based on the prejudices or idiosyncracies of their employers. The COURTS have recognized that failure to safeguard this right would impose a straitjacket on our intellectual leaders and "would imperil the future of our Nation." The schools must remain open as a place for freedom of inquiry, study, and evaluation.

The concept of academic freedom and the classroom as a "marketplace of ideas" is also applicable to public elementary and secondary schools. This is well explained in the words of a federal district court:

> Most writing on academic freedom has dealt with the universities. In *Sweezy v. State of New Hampshire* . . . for example, the Court spoke of the "essentiality of freedom in the community of American universities." Yet the effect of procedures which smother grade-school teachers cannot be ignored. An environment of free inquiry is

---

4 *Keyishian v. Board of Regents*, 385 U.S. 589, 603 (1967).
5 *Ibid.*

necessary for the majority of students who do not go on to college; even those who go on to higher education will have acquired most of their working and thinking habits in grade school and high school. Moreover, much of what was formerly taught in many colleges in the first year or so of undergraduate studies is now covered in the upper grades of good high schools . . .

The considerations which militate in favor of academic freedom—our historical commitment to free speech for all, the peculiar importance of academic inquiry to the progress of society in an atmosphere of open inquiry, feeling always free to challenge and improve established ideas—are relevant to elementary and secondary schools as well as to institutions of higher learning.[6]

This concept of academic freedom is applicable in issues surrounding teachers' and administrators' constitutional rights: their freedom of speech both within and outside the classroom and their freedom of association. The extent of such freedom will depend upon the grade being taught, and the age, intelligence, and experience of the students. In addition, academic freedom tends to be more limited in the public elementary and secondary schools than in colleges and universities because a great deal of what is taught at the elementary and secondary level of education is prescribed by the state board of education, local school board policies, statutory provisions, constitutional provisions, and court decisions.

See also: CONSTITUTIONAL LAW; CONSTITUTIONAL RIGHTS OF TEACHERS AND ADMINISTRATORS; STUDENT RIGHTS.

Acceptance of Contracts. See CONTRACTS.

Acceptance of Donations. See DONATIONS.

Accidents. See NEGLIGENCE.

Accountability. Accountability and assessment laws first were introduced and enacted in a few states in 1970. Now, nearly every state has examined, evaluated, or enacted some form of accountability legislation. The contents of such laws are as widely different as the number of laws enacted. The effectiveness of such legislation also remains to be determined.

Accountability legislation is basically aimed at seeking a method to:

---

[6] *Albaum v. Carey,* 283 F.Supp. 3, 10-11 (U.S. Dist. Ct. N.Y. 1968).

(1) evaluate professional employees; (2) assess the achievement of students; and (3) evaluate and assess management methods. Whether or not the laws themselves will be effective remains to be seen. However, educators are responding to the concern demonstrated and are seeking methods which will eventually result in a greater accountability of professional employees and in the management of schools.

See also: ACHIEVEMENT TESTS; EVALUATIONS; MALPRACTICE; MERIT PAY.

Achievement Tests. In 1972, a teacher found herself being dismissed from her teaching position because her students failed to perform well on several student achievement tests ("Iowa tests"). In the suit initiated to compel reinstatement, the court held that a teacher's professional competence could not be based solely on his or her students' performance on achievement tests. Such a reason for dismissal is arbitrary and capricious, and violates DUE PROCESS. *Scheelhaase v. Woodbury Central Community School District,* 349 F.Supp. 988 (U.S. Dist. Ct. Iowa, 1972).

See also: ACCOUNTABILITY; INTELLIGENCE TESTING; TEACHER, dismissals.

Acquisition of Property. See BUILDINGS; PROPERTY.

Activity Funds. Income received from student activities such as athletic events and school plays are legally considered to be school FUNDS, subject to the control and under the responsibility of the school board. As a result, activity funds are subject to audit and disposal in the same manner as other school funds. The authority to administer and dispose of school funds is governed by the state statutes, and local school officials must comply.

Administrative Agencies. State and federal governments create administrative agencies to carry out the laws, policies and provisions enacted by the legislative branch of government. State and local SCHOOL BOARDS are among these agencies. The legislature must prescribe standards for the agency: it must prescribe what is to be done, by whom, and it must specify the scope of authority which is granted.

Legal problems frequently arise in this area because the Constitution requires a separation of executive, legislative and judicial powers. The legislature cannot delegate its powers to an administrative agency like the state board or local boards of education, but the COURTS will allow some delegation of authority where the legislature has specified required guidelines or standards which act as checks or balances on the administrative agency's actions. There are instances where the legislature may not delegate certain powers. On the other hand, where the legislature has delegated to a specified agency the responsibility for administering certain actions, that agency has no authority to delegate its responsibility to still another agency or person. For example, in most states, only the local school board has the authority to expel students. If the local board were to attempt to grant that power to the superintendent, the district's individual principals, or even to individual members of the board, it would amount to an unauthorized delegation of powers, and any action taken would be improper.

Broad, general guidelines are sufficient and the courts will uphold them, particularly in the case of specialized agencies like boards of education. For example, a lawsuit was initiated in a case where the Illinois legislature delegated to the state superintendent the power to specify minimum standards to protect the health and safety of students. The court found that such a delegation was not unconstitutional because the legislature had supplied guidelines as to the kinds of standards to be formulated—such as those relative to heating, seating, plumbing, and other specified items which were relative to protecting the health and safety of students. However, in this case, although the delegation of authority was upheld, the superintendent had gone beyond the powers granted to him and had set standards far more stringent than those "minimum" standards necessary to assure protection of the students. *Board of Education of the City of Rockford v. Page,* 211 N.E.2d 361 (Ill. 1965).

The courts will not substitute their judgment for a decision which is made within an agency's designated authority and which is in compliance with proper procedures. The wisdom or merit of the agency's act cannot be questioned. However, if the agency acts in an arbitrary, capricious, or unreasonable manner, or its actions are in violation of an individual's constitutional rights, the court will not uphold the agency's acts. The extent of judicial review can be explained in the words of the Supreme Court of Wisconsin:

> ... [A] court in reviewing the action of an administrative board or agency ... will go no further than to determine: (1) whether the board kept within its jurisdiction, (2) whether it acted according to

law, (3) whether its action was arbitrary, oppressive or unreasonable and represented its will and not its judgment, and (4) whether the evidence was such that it might reasonably make the order or determination in question. *State v. Board of School Directors of Milwaukee*, 111 N.W.2d 198, 205 (Wis. 1961).

Administrators. See CONSTITUTIONAL RIGHTS OF TEACHERS AND ADMINISTRATORS; PRINCIPAL; SUPERINTENDENT; VICE-PRINCIPAL.

Agency Shop. An agency shop is an arrangement whereby all employees must either belong to the employee organization or must pay a fixed monthly sum, usually the equivalent of the employee organization's dues and fees, as a condition of employment, to help defray the organization's expenses in acting as a bargaining agent for the group. Some arrangements provide that payments may be allocated to the organization's welfare fund or to charity, rather than to the organization's treasury. Agency shop agreements may violate a public employee's constitutional rights. In addition, state statutes generally prescribe the grounds for dismissal of a teacher, and no state statutes include refusal to join a labor organization or refusal to grant authority for DUES CHECKOFF as a lawful grounds for dismissal.

Agent. An agent is a person who acts on behalf of another, often termed a principal. An agent has the power to bind the principal so long as he (the agent) is acting within the scope of his authority.

Agreement, collective bargaining. A COLLECTIVE BARGAINING agreement is the written contract between the employer and the employee organization, usually for a definite term, defining the conditions of employment and the procedures to be followed in settling disputes or handling issues that arise during the term of the contract. The following items form the basic skeletal outline of a typical collective bargaining agreement:

1. A recognition statement. (This is a statement whereby the employer agrees to recognize a designated employee organization as the exclusive bargaining agent and representative of specified employees.)
2. Definition of supervisory personnel.

3. Statement of supervisory personnel rights.

4. Employee organization security. (This is a statement of the rights of the organization and its members, i.e. DUES CHECKOFF rights, organization business leave, non-discrimination, etc.)

5. Working conditions. (Hours, number of days, meal periods, etc.)

6. Leaves. (SICK LEAVE, LEAVES OF ABSENCE, MATERNITY LEAVE, PATERNITY LEAVE, SABBATICAL LEAVE, etc.)

7. Termination of employment. (This is a statement of the grounds for dismissal and the procedures which the school board agrees to or is obligated to follow.)

8. Fringe benefits. (This is an explanation of any fringe benefits, such as medical insurance dental insurance, retirement provisions, etc.)

9. Evaluation. (Some agreements set up provisions for EVALUATION of teachers or administrators.)

10. Vacations, promotions, and transfers. (These statements will explain who is eligible, maximum accrual of vacation time, if seniority is to be considered in transfers, etc.)

11. Grievance procedures. (These are the procedures which are available for processing GRIEVANCES relating to the internal operations of the school.)

12. Salary provision. (This includes ranges and increment patterns.)

13. Participation in policy development. (Some agreements specify whether or not teachers or administrators are eligible to participate in the development of policy recommendations affecting CURRICULUM, budget, personnel, etc.)

14. Job descriptions. (Some agreements specify what is expected of administrative employees, but do not describe the duties of the teachers.)

15. Duration of agreement.

16. Bargaining procedure. (MEDIATION, FACT-FINDING, binding ARBITRATION, etc.—when applicable.)

17. Applicability of state laws.
18. Administrative and teacher behavior prior to, during and
    following a work stoppage.

Not all collective bargaining agreements will follow this pattern or include
each of these provisions. However, some agreements may even be more
inclusive.

See also: MEET AND CONFER BARGAINING LAWS; SCOPE
OF BARGAINING.

Aides, teacher—liability. See NEGLIGENCE.

Allocation of Liability. If a student is injured while engaging in required
school activities, and the injury is the result of the teacher's NEGLI-
GENCE, who will be liable for the DAMAGES?

School districts have what is termed a "sovereign status," and therefore, they are immune from liability for the tortious acts of their employees
unless the state STATUTES or COURTS have abrogated such immunity.

Superintendents and other school administrators are liable for their
personal torts, but some states grant them immunity from liability when
they are engaged in the performance of official acts.

Teachers have no sovereign status and will be liable for injuries students
sustain as a result of the teacher's negligence. Whether or not such personal
liability will result in the teacher's being forced to pay will depend upon
the state's position in regard to GOVERNMENTAL IMMUNITY and
SAVE-HARMLESS STATUTES.

Amish. See COMPULSORY EDUCATION.

Annual or Long-Term Contracts. In several of the states which do not
have TENURE laws, annual or long-term contracts are authorized. These
specify the permissible length of the contract term. In other words, annual
or long-term contract laws specify the period in which a contract may be
entered into between the school board and the teacher.

See also: CONTINUING CONTRACT LAWS; CONTRACTS,
teachers.

Anti-Evolution Statutes. The theory of evolution, Darwinism, has been
the subject of several legal suits in the 1900's. Anti-evolution statutes were

enacted to prohibit teaching in the public schools of the theory of evolution, which denies the story of the divine creation of man as taught in the
Bible, and teaches instead that man descended from a lower order of
animals. These statutes, frequently called "monkey laws," were upheld in
the celebrated 1927 case involving John Scopes. *Scopes v. State,* 289 S.W.
57 (Tenn. 1927). However, by 1968, only a few states still had "monkey
laws." One such law, in Arkansas, was challenged by a young biology
teacher. In that case, the Supreme Court declared anti-evolution statutes
unconstitutional and said that the state has the right to prescribe CUR-
RICULUM, but does not have the right to prohibit the teaching of a
scientific theory or doctrine where such a prohibition is in violation of
freedoms of speech and RELIGION. *Epperson v. Arkansas,* 393 U.S. 97
(1968).

Under this ruling, it would also seem logical that since Darwinism is
not a proven scientific theory, it might be unconstitutional to prohibit the
mentioning of the possibility of the divine creation of man as taught in
the Bible.

See also: CONSTITUTIONAL RIGHTS OF TEACHERS AND
ADMINISTRATORS.

Anti-Subversive Laws. Anti-subversive laws were enacted during World
War II in an effort to prevent infiltration of Communists and other persons
who advocated the unlawful overthrow of the government by force and
violence. New York's Feinberg Law received the most attention. This
law was designed to rid the school system of "subversive teachers." The
Board of Regents, which controlled the New York schools, was given
the power to designate which groups were subversive, and to provide that
membership in such organizations constituted prima facie evidence for
disqualification for a position in the school system. This law was upheld
in 1952, but it was challenged again in 1967.

Three instructors from the University of New York refused to sign a
LOYALTY OATH saying that they were not Communists, or that if they
had ever been Communists, they had communicated that fact to the president of the university. New York's Feinberg Law was used as a basis for
not renewing the contract of one of these instructors, Harry Keyishian.
Keyishian appealed to the courts, and in 1967 the Supreme Court of
the United States invalidated the part of the law which provided for
removal of any teacher who belonged to any organization which advocated

unlawful overthrow of the government. The Court said that mere membership in a subversive organization is insufficient to justify dismissal of a teacher. However, if the teacher can be shown to have the intent to bring about the illegal objectives of the organization, he or she may be removed from the public schools. *Keyishian v. Board of Regents*, 385 U.S. 589 (1967). In other words, the Court is saying that "guilt by association" will not be allowed. Subversive teachers and administrators may be removed from their public school positions, but persons are to be considered subversive only if they can be shown to have the intent to bring about the illegal objectives of the organization of which they are members.

Whether or not a teacher may refuse to answer questions concerning his or her membership or activities in an alleged subversive organization is controlled by the courts' interpretation of the teachers' right to freedom from SELF-INCRIMINATION. (See SILENT, right to remain).

See also: CONSTITUTIONAL RIGHTS OF TEACHERS AND ADMINISTRATORS; STRIKES.

Appearance. Dress codes for faculty and students must yield to the requirements of the Constitution. Many state and federal COURTS have held that a person's appearance is frequently an expression of his or her personality, heritage, race, or culture, and as such is entitled to the protection of the Constitution. In addition, the courts are willing to question the *reasonableness* of such school RULES. However, there are also many cases upholding school dress codes. As a result, the validity of appearance regulations will depend upon the individual state court decisions.

Dress codes will be upheld by the majority of courts only where the appearance restrictions are found to be reasonable. Such restrictions are reasonable only where they are necessary for the protection of health, safety, or welfare, or are necessary to protect the school from a material and substantial disruption. Under this test of reasonableness, consider the following examples:

1. Health: A rule requiring students to keep their hair clean is reasonable because it helps to prevent lice and other health hazards.

2. Safety: Elaborate jewelry can be dangerous. As a result, students could be prohibited from wearing large rings, etc. in a physical education class.

3. Disruption: Students wearing a beret or turban may be required to sit in the back of the classroom in order to not block other students' view of the blackboard, etc. However, where appearance is regulated on the basis of disruption, the response of the other students is the key concern. Therefore, if the appearance does not disrupt the other students' schoolwork, it is not disruptive.

See also CONSTITUTIONAL RIGHTS OF TEACHERS AND ADMINISTRATORS; STUDENT RIGHTS.

Arbitration. Arbitration is a method of settling disputes through recourse to an impartial third party whose decision is usually final and *binding*. However, *advisory* arbitration is sometimes utilized, but here the arbitrator's decision is not binding and therefore, this method of resolving disputes is closer akin to FACT-FINDING.

Binding arbitration is frequently resorted to in the interpretation of *existing* contract terms or provisions of memorandums of understanding. This is often termed "grievance arbitration," and there is widespread support for this type of arbitration.

On the other hand, binding arbitration, as a means of settling disputes over the negotiation of the provisions of a *new* contract (sometimes termed "contract arbitration"), is not as widely accepted. Arbitration is *voluntary* when both parties, of their own volition, agree to submit a disputed issue to arbitration, and *compulsory* if required by law to prevent a work stoppage. Several states have authorized voluntary arbitration of new contract provisions as a part of the COLLECTIVE BARGAINING rights of public employees. In addition, a few states have taken the initiative and mandate arbitration of teachers' CONTRACTS.

Compulsory binding arbitration is an adequate substitute for the right to STRIKE. Nevertheless, many critics argue that:

1. Where the arbitrator settles the dispute, the school board is not making the final decision, and public sovereignty is infringed upon.
2. Genuine collective bargaining is discouraged.
3. Strikes are not completely eliminated.
4. Arbitrators sometimes ignore or do not adequately understand municipal fiscal difficulties.

The validity of some of these arguments is questionable, but even if all of the critics' arguments are well-founded, binding arbitration has a great many desirable aspects which outweigh all objections. As a result, it is gaining wide acceptance. This is particularly true where binding arbitration is used as a means of settling disputes which do not involve the expenditure of money.

The arbitrator is generally chosen in one of three ways:

1. The school board and the employees each pick a representative, and a neutral third representative is chosen.
2. A professional arbitrator is chosen by agreement.
3. An outside body selects the arbitrator.

The arbitrator then holds a hearing and takes evidence. Sometimes the arbitrator conducts an independent investigation. After completion of the hearing and the investigation, the arbitrator makes a decision as to how the dispute shall be settled, and this decision is binding on both the school board and the employees.

Architects. See BUILDINGS; CONSTRUCTION; FUNDS.

Armbands. See CONSTITUTIONAL RIGHTS OF TEACHERS AND ADMINISTRATORS; STUDENT RIGHTS.

Assault. An assault is (1) an offer to use force, (2) causing the apprehension of (3) immediate, (4) harmful, or offensive bodily contact. The wrongdoer must have the apparent ability to carry out the threat. An assault is an intentional tort.

As with all torts, each of the elements in the definition of an assault must exist before the tort has been committed. Therefore, one must analyze the elements carefully before he or she can totally understand what this tort means.

An assault is a tort committed against another's mind. A person has been assaulted when he or she is put in *fear* for his or her immediate personal safety. No physical contact is necessary. If there is physical contact, then a BATTERY has been committed in addition to an assault.

The offer to use force can be verbal or through actions. If one intentionally threatens immediate harm, or acts in a menacing menner, an assault has occurred if fear reasonably results. If the person being assaulted is overly paranoid, and if the offer to use force would not put the reasonable man in fear, then no assault has occurred. For example, if a third grader threatened to strike his six-foot tall male teacher, there probably would be no assault because the actions would not ordinarily cause apprehension.

In addition to the offer to use force, there is the necessary element of "immediacy." There must be apprehension of *immediate* harmful or offensive contact. This means that if a student threatens to "get you," his teacher, the next time you do something, or threatens you harm "after school," no assault has been committed. Certainly the teacher can discipline the student for the threat alone; however, the tort of assault has not yet occurred.

As previously mentioned, a student can be disciplined for making the threat. Even though an assault has not been committed, there is no necessity for the teacher to put up with threats or insubordination. This is because threats and assaults are often the forerunners to batteries, and such harmful student conduct should be curtailed at the earliest possible time.

In establishing that an assault has occurred, one must not only show the offer to use force, the reasonableness of the apprehension, and the fact that the fear was immediate, but it is also necessary to show that the offer to use force was directed toward one's person. A threat to slash the tires on a car or to ransack a house is not an assault. This is a threat for which the student can be disciplined, but there is no actual assault.

Threats and assaults are commonplace within schools. Students threaten teachers and administrators, and students threaten other students. Student liability can at least compensate for some of these things; however, educators should clearly understand that it is their duty to prevent an assault or battery where it is reasonably foreseeable. If a student comes to his or teacher and reports that he or she has been assaulted, it is the teacher's duty to see that the wrongdoer is disciplined. The teacher must do this before a more serious problem results.

All schools seem to have students who are known as "bullies." If a student comes to his teacher and says that he is afraid to go home because another student is going to "get him" after school, the teacher has the duty to investigate. If the teacher believes the report to be true, he or she has the duty to do something about it. Neither proof beyond a reasonable doubt or even clear and convincing evidence is required before the teacher can legally take action to protect a student. If the teacher, relying on his or her experience with children and the particular children involved, in good faith takes action, such action will relieve the teacher from potential liability and may prevent serious injuries from occurring.

Assembly, right of. This right is protected through the First Amendment provision which states in part that Congress shall make no law abridging "the right of the people peaceably to assemble, and to petition the government for a redress of grievances." Freedom of association is deemed to be a right existing in the Constitution as a "right of assembly," and as such is protected against unreasonable state action by the DUE PROCESS clause of the Fourteenth Amendment. The right of assembly is also contained in the state constitutions of all but four states: Maryland, Minnesota, New Mexico, and Virginia.

The right of assembly exists only so long as it is peaceable. Therefore, if a material and substantial disruption is caused, the assembly is no longer protected. Under this test, various demonstrations may be restricted. In addition, the right of assembly is subject to reasonable rules.

See also: ANTI-SUBVERSIVE LAWS; CONSTITUTIONAL RIGHTS OF TEACHERS AND ADMINISTRATORS; LOYALTY OATHS; STUDENT RIGHTS.

Assignments, non-classroom. Assignment of "extra" teaching duties outside the classroom has been the subject of dissatisfaction and often litigation, particularly when no extra compensation is paid for performance of the extra duties. The question of whether or not a teacher may legally refuse to perform extra duties depends on the *reasonableness* of the requirement. One court suggested guidelines to be considered in determining reasonableness of extra duty assignments; and the following items were among the suggestions:

1. A teacher may be required to take over a study hall.
2. A teacher may be expected to supervise student organizations in the area of his or her teaching field.
3. English and social science teachers may be requested to coach or supervise plays.
4. Physical education teachers may be expected to coach intramurals.
5. Teachers may be required to supervise field trips. *Parrish v. Moss*, 106 N.Y.S.2d 577, 584-585 (N.Y. 1951).

Even in considering the above suggested guidelines, legal issues may still arise:

1. Is an excessive number of hours involved in the assignments?
2. Are the students benefited?
3. Are the extra assignments distributed evenly among the teachers? i.e. is DISCRIMINATION involved?
4. Are the assignments professional in nature?
5. Do the assignments relate to the teacher's field of CERTIFICATION and interests?

Two cases may help to point out that the COURTS will accept challenges to schools' extra assignments based on the above questions. For example, question four asks if the assignment is professional in nature. This is important, because teachers may not be required to perform menial tasks. As a result, one case held that a teacher could not be forced to collect tickets at a football game because this is a task any adult can perform, and the requirement was motivated by a desire to cut expenses. *Todd Coronway v. Lansdowne School Dist. Number 785,* Court of Common Pleas of Delaware County, Penn., June Term (1951).

In another case, the question of whether or not the assignment related to school was important. In this case, a social studies teacher refused to supervise a bowling club which met once a week at a local bowling alley. He was dismissed by the board for incompetence and willful violation of school RULES. The Supreme Court of Pennsylvania said that the important question was whether or not the activity the teacher was assigned to was "so related to the school program" as to justify the assignment. In holding that it was *not,* the court said that classroom duties do not constitute all of the duties teachers may be required to perform, but SCHOOL BOARDS are not given unlimited authority to assign teachers to extra-curricular duties. The court said that the activity assigned must relate to the school program, and the assignments "must be fairly and reasonably made." *Pease v. Millcreek Township School Dist.,* 195 A.2d 104, 108 (Penn., 1963).

Reasonable extracurricular assignments which meet the requirements stated above, are considered implied duties under teachers' CONTRACTS and therefore, extra compensation is not required. However, such items are generally negotiable, and the teachers' employee organization can bargain for extra compensation for extra duties, as well as for restriction of such duty assignments.

Association, freedom of. See ANTI-SUBVERSIVE LAWS; ASSEMBLY; CONSTITUTIONAL LAW; CONSTITUTIONAL RIGHTS OF TEACHERS AND ADMINISTRATORS; LOYALTY OATHS; STUDENT RIGHTS.

Assumption of Risk. Assumption of risk is often used as a defense to NEGLIGENCE. If a person knows of a dangerous condition or activity, but voluntarily ignores the danger, he or she is said to assume the risk of any injury which results.

Assume that a 13-year-old student is left unsupervised with other students on the playground. Also assume that a ball somehow lands on the top of a building. If the student starts to climb up the side of the wall, knowing that such an activity is dangerous, he will be responsible for any injury he sustains if he falls. The defense in a suit of negligence for failure to properly supervise the playground is that the student assumed the risk. This defense is very similar to CONTRIBUTORY NEGLIGENCE.

It should be noted that, in order for one to assume a risk, he or she must know of the risk. In other words, a person only assumes the risk of dangers which are reasonably expected to be inherent in the activity. For example, in baseball, one would assume the risk of "sliding" or being hit by the baseball once he or she has been instructed in how the game is played. On the other hand, if, for example, the teacher does not instruct the students how to hold the bat properly, and if, as a result, a student hits at the ball and lets the bat fly, thereby injuring the pitcher, the teacher could be held negligent. The pitcher did not assume the risk of being injured by the bat because the risk is not an inherent danger of the game once the students have been properly instructed.

It must also be noted that the assumption of the risk must be voluntary. For example, if a teacher forces a student to climb up a rope to the top of the gymnasium, after the student has expressed his fear of heights and reluctance to climb, the student could not be ruled to have assumed the risk of an injury if he falls off the rope.

Athletics, funds. See ACTIVITY FUNDS; FUNDS.

Athletics, required participation in. See CURRICULUM.

Athletics, sex discrimination in. Sports programs which provide for competitive athletics for male students, but fail to provide an equal opportunity for female students to compete, came under fire in the early 1970's.

For example, a 1972 case examined a school program which did not allow female students to participate on the boys' golf team. The court held that this was unconstitutional, and stated:

> The issue is not whether Debbie Reed has a "right" to play golf; the issue is whether she can be treated differently from boys in an activity provided by the state. Her right is not the right to play golf. Her right is the right to be treated the same as boys unless there is a rational basis for her being treated differently. *Reed v. Nebraska School Activities Association*, 341 F.Supp. 258, 262 (U.S. Dist. Ct. Neb., 1972).

Where no rational basis for the DISCRIMINATION can be shown, the failure to provide equal opportunity is a denial of the students' right to EQUAL PROTECTION.

Another of the leading sex discrimination in sports cases involved two Minnesota high school girls who desired to compete in varsity sports at their respective schools. One of the girls was an excellent tennis player, and the other was a highly qualified skier and cross-country runner. No comparable alternative programs to the boys' varsity teams were sponsored by the schools for girl athletes. The court upheld the argument that the state interscholastic rule which prohibited girls from participating in the boys' interscholastic athletic program was arbitrary and in violation of the equal protection clause. *Brendon v. Independent School District 742*, 342 F.Supp. 1224 (U.S. Dist. Ct. Minn., 1972). As a result, the rule was established that girls may not be barred from participating on varsity athletic teams where they are as qualified as male members of the team, and where no comparable program exists for girls.

The initial cases suggest three possible ways in which school boards can meet the demands of equal protection with regard to sports programs:

1. Individualized try-out should be used as the basis for determining which students are eligible to compete on athletic teams; or
2. Establish a comparable girls' team; or
3. Eliminate the boys' team.

Most of the challenges to sports programs have involved "non-contact" sports, such as tennis, golf, skiing, cross-country, and swimming. With regard to contact sports, no precedent has been clearly established. If it can factually be shown that extreme physical-type contact sports such as football would be unduly jeopardizing the safety of a girl athlete, preventing girls from competing against boys would be reasonable. But, physical characteristics are not the only, or even the main, requirement for success in sports. Athletes themselves say that determination, intelligence, sensory perception, constant practice, etc. are the keys to success. Therefore, the courts will look closely at the facts on a case-by-case basis, if necessary, to determine whether or not a rational basis exists for denying female students the right to an equal opportunity to participate in sports programs.

Until society recognizes the true value athletic competition provides for girls and society as a whole, equality is more likely to come about through a division of funds. If a school has X amount of dollars budgeted for sports programs, one-half X should be spent on girls' sports programs. If football is an available sport for the boys, the school should establish a comparable sport such as soccer or field hockey for the girls.

As a final note, the courts will not demand an *immediate* establishment of equal sports programs. The courts will not require hasty action, but will demand that a proposed plan for equal opportunity for girl athletes must be immediately made, and that this plan be carried out within a reasonable period of time. The time for some form of affirmative action has arrived, however, and this is mandated by federal law. The U.S. Education Amendments of 1972 include an adjunct labeled Title IX, which forbids sex discrimination in any institutions using federal funds. If you feel that such discrimination exists in your local schools, you can get action to have it rectified by writing to: Director, Office for Civil Rights, Department of HEW, Washington D.C. 20201.

In 1974, Department of HEW proposed rules implementing the provisions of Title IX. Under these rules, coed intramural athletics and physical education classes will be required, but integration of inter-scholastic competitive teams will not be mandated. Separate athletic teams will be allowed where women would be effectively discriminated against if they had to compete with men for the same positions. The proposed rules will result in greater opportunity for women in the field of sports, and also will require equal admission and treatment of students applying for admission into various classes and graduate schools. The final draft of the rules is expected to take effect in the spring of 1975.

See also: MARRIED STUDENTS; STUDENT RIGHTS.

Attendance of Pupils. See COMPULSORY EDUCATION.

Authority, parents. See PARENTAL AUTHORITY.

Authority, teachers. See IN LOCO PARENTIS; RULES.

Authority, school board. See SCHOOL BOARDS.

Automobiles. Reasonable school RULES regarding student use of automobiles will be upheld, particularly where they are necessary to protect
the safety of the students. For example, a female high school student who
drove to school, parked her car one block from the school, and went home
for lunch every day, challenged a school rule which required that students
who drove automobiles to school must park them in the parking lot and
could not move them until school was over for the day. The court rejected
the student's challenge to the rule, and said that in the interests of safety
and the necessity of preventing hazardous traffic conditions from occurring,
such a rule was reasonable. *McLean Independent School District v.
Andrews*, 333 S.W.2d 886 (Tex. 1960).

Auxiliary Services and Materials. See PRIVATE AND PAROCHIAL
SCHOOL AID; RELIGION; TRANSPORTATION; VOUCHERS.

B

Band Uniforms. See FUNDS.

Bargaining. See COLLECTIVE BARGAINING; MEET AND CONFER
   BARGAINING LAWS.

Battery. A battery is the (1) unpermitted, (2) unprivileged, (3) contact with
another, in a (4) rude or angry manner. This is an intentional tort.

   Unlike an ASSAULT, a battery involves contact. This is a tort against
one's person and not against one's mind. People often hear of "assault and
battery" as if commission of a battery is also commission of an assault, and
vice versa. Assault and battery are often tied together as one crime, but in
civil cases, an assault is a tort which is distinct and separate from a battery.

   An assault is generally the forerunner to a battery. However, rather
than hearing about assaults, we normally hear about batteries because
they tend to be more violent and serious. Unfortunately, they occur far too
frequently in the schools. Teachers, administrators, and students are
battered, and the wrongdoers must be severely disciplined.

   Students are liable for their own torts, both financially as well as for
disciplinary purposes (See STUDENTS, liability). If a student batters a
teacher or another student, he or she is liable. There are times, however,
where teachers and administrators are also liable for batteries committed

by one student on another, as well as for committing their own acts of aggression on students. The liability of a teacher for battery of one student upon another generally happens where students are not properly supervised, or when it is foreseeable that one student is going to injure another and nothing is done about it. Some students are more dangerous than others, and if such a student has been identified within the school, he or she must be carefully supervised, and possibly removed if he or she poses a threat to others.

As with all torts, each element of the definition of a battery must be met before liability can be imposed. First of all, the contact must be unpermitted. If two students both voluntarily agree to enter into a fight, permission for contact is granted. In other words, one student would generally not be liable to the other for battery. (Nevertheless, the teacher or administrator might be negligent if he or she fails to try to stop the fight.)

In addition to lack of permission, in order to constitute a battery, the contact must be unprivileged. There are certain times when one person will have a legal "privilege" to batter another. For example, one may defend himself or herself without being liable for battery. However, this self-defense privilege is limited by the rule that a person may only use the kind of force required to repel the attack. Once the attack has been effectively stopped, one cannot continue battering the assailant. Also, a person may only use force calculated to kill or permanently disable when it is necessary to repel the attack. In other words, a person may meet deadly force with deadly force. However, if the assailant is using force which is not likely to result in permanent or fatal bodily injury, deadly force in self-defense exceeds the privilege and would not be condoned.

As a general rule, there is no duty to come to the defense of another person unless there is some special relationship between the parties which imposes such a duty. In other words, if a stranger saw that another person was being beaten, he or she would not be obligated to attempt a rescue. On the other hand, teachers have a duty to protect the safety of the students. Therefore, if a teacher observes that a fight is taking place or that a student is in danger, the teacher would be obligated to render any possible aid. The teacher would not be required to subject himself or herself to grave personal danger, but must render any possible aid. For example, if a petite female teacher observed two husky male students battling it out, she would not be obligated to throw herself in between the students, but she would have an obligation to tell them to stop fighting and to seek other help if necessary to force the students to stop. If a teacher or administrator acts to defend a student, he or she will be privileged to commit a battery upon the attacker if it is necessary to prevent further injury.

Teachers and administrators have certain privileges that students do not. As a general rule, teachers and administrators have a privilege to use CORPORAL PUNISHMENT and make other necessary "contacts" with students. Without this privilege, lawsuits involving school-related batteries woud be filed regularly. Removing a student from the classroom, grabbing a student's arm in a rude manner, and searching a student could all be classified as batteries without this privilege. Of course, the privilege only allows the teacher or administrator to exercise contact which is reasonable and necessary under the circumstances.

In order for a battery to occur, there must be contact. It should be noted that the contact could not only be with a person's body, but also with what the person is wearing or carrying. For example, if a shirt is torn off of a person's back, a battery has occurred. (See also TRESPASS TO PERSONAL PROPERTY.)

An additional element of battery is the requirement that the contact must be made in a rude or angry manner. Even though the perpetrator is not angry, he or she does not have the right to rudely touch another person. For example, if a student kisses his teacher, much to the teacher's dismay and without her consent, a battery has occurred. On the other hand, if the touch is not made in a rude or angry manner, and is merely a touch upon the arm or shoulder in a reasonable manner, a battery has not occurred, and there would be no grounds for either discipline or liability.

Remember that in order for there to be a battery, there must be the intent to have contact with the other person. If a student is running down the hall and accidentally knocks someone down, that is negligence and not battery. It is important to note that the "act" must be intended, not necessarily the result. It is said that one intends the natural foreseeable consequences of his or her acts. For example, if a student throws a rock through a window, he or she would be liable for any injury resulting from broken glass falling. Even though the student only intended to break the window, it is foreseeable that someone could be injured as a consequence of the falling glass.

"Intent" can also be transferred. This means, for example, that if a student throws a rock at one student and misses, but hits another, he or she could not defend on the grounds that there was no intent to injure the victim. The intent to injure the first student is "transferred," and thus liability can be imposed for battery.

Batteries can be very serious. A battery can be both a crime and a tort at the same time. The fact that a student is criminally punished by the state for committing a battery does not prevent the school from punishing the student, and it does not prevent civil liability from being imposed.

Beards. See APPEARANCE; CONSTITUTIONAL RIGHTS OF TEACHERS AND ADMINISTRATORS; STUDENT RIGHTS.

Bible Reading. A Pennsylvania statute required the reading of Bible verses at the opening of school. Several members of the Unitarian faith brought suit to enjoin enforcement of the statute, because specific doctrines as written in the Bible verses were contrary to their religious beliefs. The district court ruled against the statute, and the Pennsylvania legislature amended it to allow any child to be excused upon written request. However, the case was still appealed to the U.S. Supreme Court, and the Court declared the statute unconstitutional. The Court explained that the statute gave a preference to the Christian RELIGION because it specified the Bible. Justice Clark said:

> [I]t is no defense to urge that the religious practices here may be relatively minor encroachments on the First Amendment. The breach of neutrality that is today a trickling stream may all too soon become a raging torrent and, in the words of Madison, "it is proper to take alarm at the first experiment on our liberties." *School District of Abington v. Schempp*, 374 U.S. 203, 225 (1963).

As a result of this decision and several subsequent cases, the rule has been firmly established that state statutes or local school or school board policies prescribing Bible reading are unconstitutional as violative of the First and Fourteenth Amendments of the Constitution. Bible reading is prohibited even if students are allowed to be excused during the time the verses are read.

See also: CONSTITUTIONAL LAW; CONSTITUTIONAL RIGHTS OF TEACHERS AND ADMINISTRATORS; RELIGION; STUDENT RIGHTS.

Bids. See BUILDINGS; CONSTRUCTION.

Bill of Rights. See CONSTITUTIONAL LAW; CONSTITUTIONAL RIGHTS OF TEACHERS AND ADMINISTRATORS; STUDENT RIGHTS.

Bonds. School districts sometimes are forced to go into debt in order to finance capital CONSTRUCTION or to provide for the day-to-day operation of its schools. The authority of local school boards to incur debt is governed by state STATUTES and state constitutions. If no express authority exists in the state statutes, the board is not authorized to incur any indebtedness. However, in all states, authority to incur some debt is expressly granted by state statutes. The extent of such authority varies greatly from state to state, and since the state statutes will be strictly construed, school board members should learn exactly what is required under the statute with respect to:

1. The *purposes* for which indebtedness may be incurred;
2. The *procedures* which must be followed; and
3. The maximum *amount* of allowable indebtedness. (The maximum amount is generally based on a percentage of taxable property in the district.)

Most school indebtedness is incurred through the issuance of bonds. Express statutory authority is required before a district may issue bonds. If the bonds are issued without authority or for an unauthorized purpose, the bonds are void. Since powers of the school board are matters of public record, persons dealing with the board are deemed to be on notice of the board's restrictions, and therefore, innocent purchasers of void bonds or bonds which prove to be invalid may still get hurt. However, holders of invalid bonds do have two methods of recourse:

1. Recovery of money given for the bonds. This method of recourse is available only where the money has not been spent, and is identifiable.
2. Recovery of property purchased with the proceeds of the invalid bonds. This recourse is available only where the property will not be harmed and the district will not be hurt.

Some states require that the question of whether or not bonds shall be issued must be submitted to the voters. If the voters approve of the bond issuance, they may not later revoke their approval. Unless limited by statute, the board may repeatedly submit the bond question to the voters. Where voter approval is given, the bonds may be issued only for the purpose or purposes for which they were voted.

Defects in bonds due to failure of the board to follow the required proper procedures may sometimes be cured by ratification or legislative action.

Short-term loans for emergency or day-to-day operation of the district, until tax levy proceeds are obtained, may be negotiated only where there exists express or implied legislative authority. If no such authority exists, any notes issued are void.

Performance and payment bonds—see BUILDINGS, construction.

Borrowing. See BONDS.

Boundaries. See REORGANIZATION.

Budgets. See FUNDS, school.

Buildings. 1. *Construction;* 2. *Use;* 3. *Disposal.*

1. *Construction.* CONSTRUCTION of school buildings is governed by state STATUTES. Where the state statute grants construction authority, local boards have the power to exercise their discretion and can construct buildings which they deem necessary or beneficial to any education program. They also have the implied power to employ architects to design the buildings.

Some statutes require the board to employ contractors on the basis of competitive bidding. Where this is the case, these statutes must be strictly complied with; if they are not, any contract entered into will be void. Where bidding is not required by statute, the board has discretionary authority and may or may not choose to contract by submitting the construction contract to competitive bidding.

Where bidding is required by statute, or voluntarily agreed to by the board, bidders must be given sufficient data to allow them to ascertain a fairly precise estimate of the cost. Their bids are accompanied by a bond, and if they fail to enter into the contract after their bid is accepted, the board will be entitled to the value of the bond plus interest *or* the amount of the difference between that bid and the next lowest. Correction of a bid is allowed if done prior to opening of the bids, and in a few special instances where the mistake is extremely large or obvious. If not prohibited by statute, the board can reject all bids. In all other instances, where the board is required to accept one of the bids, it must give the contract to the lowest, *responsible* bidder. The board is allowed to consider the bidder's reputation, financial stability, etc., to determine the bidder's responsibility.

The contractor will be liable for poor workmanship, defects in the building, and for a reasonable penalty for delays in completion where such a penalty is specified in the contract. An architect's certificate is generally required to be given upon satisfactory completion of the work.

Various performance and payment BONDS are often required by statute to be obtained from the contractor. Since a lien is not allowed by law to attach to school property, the contractor's employees have only the payment bond as protection if the contractor goes bankrupt or fails to pay them. Consequently, some cases have held that where a payment bond is required to be given by the contractor, and if the school board is negligent in failing to obtain such a bond, the board members will be personally liable for any loss. This is particularly true in those states in which the statutes specifically provide for such liability.

2. *Use.* School buildings are the PROPERTY of the state, and the state legislature has the power to control the use of school facilities. However, for the most part, state STATUTES generally do not make any mention of the possible uses of the property, and therefore, use is within the discretion of the local SCHOOL BOARDS. On the other hand, California is one of a few states which does specifically attempt to control use of school property, and the California statutes equate schools with "civic centers" and provide that the schools shall be available for public meetings relating to the educational, artistic, political, and moral interests of the citizens.

Three main rules control the use of school property for activities which are not school functions:

1. Neither the state nor local school boards may authorize the use of school facilities for any purpose which is in violation of the state or federal constitution.
2. The use cannot interfere with the school program.
3. Uses which may foreseeably result in damage to school property cannot be allowed.

Subject to these three rules, the school board generally is granted the discretionary authority to use school property for other than educational purposes.

The board does not have to allow school buildings to be used by the public for meetings or entertainment, in the absence of a state statute compelling such use. However, where the board decides to open school buildings for public use, it cannot administer this in an arbitrary or discriminatory fashion. Nevertheless, though the schools may be opened for certain uses, the board may deny a particular group permission to use the buildings *if* the board can show that a clear and present danger and possible damage to the building will result if the use is allowed.

As a result, the board in its discretion can allow the school buildings to be used for anything which does not interfere with the educational programs, and may allow the charging of an admission fee, so long as the fee is incidental to the purpose and not the main reason for the authorized use. (The board also has the power to invite the public to school-related functions, and can even charge admission.)

At times, particular uses of school buildings raise legal questions. If the legislature authorizes use of school buildings for political purposes, the board may allow groups to conduct such activities on school property. The board cannot allow use of school buildings for religious services or instruction, *but* short-term use by such organizations for educational, cultural, or even some religious purposes have been held by some courts not to be in violation of the establishment of the RELIGION clause of the First Amendment. However, the board can, of course, bar *all* uses of a religious nature if it chooses to do so.

Cafeterias and school stores may be established within the school, as long as the reason for such use is not primarily for commercial gain.

The school board has the authority to purchase insurance for school buildings, and in most states this is mandated by statute.

3. *Disposal.* The public owns the school property, and therefore, disposition of such property is controlled by state statutes. Local school officials must comply with these statutory requirements in disposing of school property or a conveyance will be declared invalid. Local school officials have no authority to sell school property unless the authority is specifically granted by statute. Where such authority is not granted, the legislature has complete control of disposal. When the power to dispose is granted, the disposal is subject to the three following rules:

1. The disposal must be for the benefit of the district;
2. School property may not be given away; and
3. School property must be sold for its fair market value, and
   may not be sold for merely a nominal consideration.

A split of authority exists as to whether or not school property may be leased. A majority of COURTS hold that school property may be leased for a reasonable period of time where the use is not entirely foreign to public policy. However, if the period of the lease is for an excessively long time, the majority of courts will not allow it.

If the school district ceases to use school property for school purposes, there is a possibility that the land may in some cases revert to the original owner. However, the property will not revert where there have been no provisions for reversion made in a deed granting the property to the school. In such cases, the board may dispose of the property in the manner authorized by statute. Reversion provisions are strictly construed by the courts. Nevertheless, in the absence of statutes to the contrary, land acquired through condemnation which is no longer used for school purposes, will revert to the original owner. (See PROPERTY).

Burden of Proof. Burden of proof is having the duty to go forward with the evidence to prove disputed facts. In a trial or administrative hearing, each side has certain things they must prove. If the initial proof is made, the other side has the burden of rebutting the other party's evidence. In a lawsuit, the PLAINTIFF has the burden of showing a prima facie case. In other words, the plaintiff must show all of the elements of his or her cause of action. If the plaintiff shows these elements, the burden of proof shifts, and it becomes the DEFENDANT'S duty to rebut the plaintiff's prima facie evidence. If either side does not meet its burden, there is either a directed verdict or a summary judgment for the other side. On the other hand, if one side proves its prima facie case but the other side presents reliable evidence to dispute it, then it is for the jury to weigh the evidence and reach a decision.

Some burdens of proof are heavy, and some are light. In a criminal case, the prosecutor must prove the prima facie elements of a crime and the fact that the defendant committed that crime "beyond a reasonable doubt." That is the heaviest burden in our court system.

In many other types of cases, the burden of proof must be "clear and convincing." This is somewhat less than beyond a reasonable doubt, but more than a preponderance of the evidence. This burden is easier to meet, but is still heavy.

In most civil cases, the plaintiff is only required to prove his case by a "preponderance of the evidence." This means that if there is a 51 percent chance to a 49 percent chance he has met his burden. Again, this is a heavy burden. It is certainly not as heavy as the others, but it must be met before liability will be imposed.

The easiest burden of proof to meet is "rational basis in fact." Generally, this burden relates to administrative decisions and discretionary acts. For ADMINISTRATIVE AGENCIES to exercise their discretion in a valid manner, there must be some rational basis in fact. In other words, if there is some basis for the decision, and if that basis is rational, any exercise of discretion based upon the facts in question would be considered proper.

Bus Drivers. State STATUTES generally set forth the minimum requirements for school bus drivers, and frequently include standards of character, physical condition, and special licensing. Minimum and maximum ages are prescribed, and some states require school bus drivers to have had first-aid training.

Busing. See DESEGREGATION; DISCRIMINATION; TRANSPORTATION.

Buttons. See APPEARANCE; CONSTITUTIONAL RIGHTS OF TEACHERS AND ADMINISTRATORS; STUDENT RIGHTS.

C

Cafeteria. See BUILDINGS, use.

Campaign Activities. See CONFLICTS OF INTEREST; CONSTITUTIONAL RIGHTS OF TEACHERS AND ADMINISTRATORS; PUBLIC OFFICE.

Capacity. Capacity as used in this context is intended to mean the "legal ability" to enter into CONTRACTS. Insane persons and minors are examples of those persons who do not have the legal ability to enter into a contract and make it binding.

SCHOOL BOARDS and educators must have the capacity to enter into a contract with one another. In order for a school board to have capacity, it must be acting at a properly convened MEETING. An individual board member lacks the capacity to enter into a contract on behalf of the entire board. This means that a teacher's contract should be signed while the board is in session, and if it is not, it must at least have been agreed to in a proper session. If a contract with the board has not gone through the proper procedures, it is void.

The teacher or administrator also must have legal capacity to sign. This means that the teacher or administrator must have a valid CERTIFICATE or else he or she is not a competent party to be paid under the contract.

Some states say that there must be legal capacity (certificate) at the time of entering into the contract, and other states say there must be legal capacity before one commences his or her duties. Either way, there must be capacity before one can demand payment for the services he or she performs. For example, if one teaches without a proper certificate, but later obtains one, he or she generally will only be able to obtain payment for those days in which he or she had the required legal capacity to teach.

See also CERTIFICATION, teacher.

Censorship. See ACADEMIC FREEDOM; NEWSPAPERS; OBSCENITY; STUDENT RIGHTS.

Certificate. A certificate is a license granted by the state, and it enables a teacher to enter into a lawfully binding contract to teach.

In order to be paid for teaching in the public schools, a person must have a teaching certificate. This certificate is issued by the state, and it must be granted where minimum requirements for CERTIFICATION have been met by the applicant. Generally, the requirements include: (1) The necessary college preparation; (2) physical capability; and (3) moral character.

Whether or not one meets these requirements is discretionary with the state. However, this direction is not absolute. The COURTS require some measures or standards under which the applicant is judged. For example, if the board is trying to determine moral character, it must have basic guidelines which are capable of objective scrutiny. The primary inquiry into a person's moral character must be related to his or her fitness to teach and to the protection of students. This means that the measures and standards must be relevant and appropriate to the teacher-pupil relationship. If they are not, and a person is denied a certificate as a result, the denial would de deemed arbitrary and capricious, and the license would be granted. (See also CONSTITUTIONAL RIGHTS OF TEACHERS AND ADMINISTRATORS.)

Acts which have been upheld in the denial of a certificate include: (1) commission of a FELONY; (2) conviction of a crime involving MORAL TURPITUDE; (3) repetitive patterns of committing MISDEMEANORS; and (4) fraud in obtaining the certificate. No doubt there are many other acts which would constitute grounds for denial of a certificate. Nevertheless, these grounds must relate to the position being sought and cannot violate the applicant's constitutional rights, or be arbitrarily or discriminatorily enforced.

When talking about a teaching certificate, one should note that the states are divided as to just when a teacher must possess the certificate. Some states say that the teacher must have the certificate when the contract is signed, or else the contract is void. The better view, and the majority of states, says that the teacher must have the certificate before any teaching duties are performed. Either way, a teacher cannot demand payment for his or her services unless he or she is certified to teach in the public schools. Without this license, the teacher lacks legal CAPACITY.

It should also be noted that setting up minimum requirements for certification is a state function and is not up to local boards. In other words, the state determines who may be certified. This does not mean that one who is certified has a right to a teaching position. Local boards have the right to make other reasonable requirements. For example, a local board has the right to require continuing education requirements for its teachers. These new requirements are within the discretionary powers of the local boards, so long as they are not discriminatory or totally irrelevant.

See also: CERTIFICATION, teacher; DECERTIFICATION.

Certification, teacher. A teacher's CERTIFICATE is a document which specifies that the named individual has met the legal requirements of the particular state to teach school in that state. A certificate is required before a person can enter into a valid teaching contract, but this certificate does not give the person the right to demand a teaching position. Without a certificate, a person performing teaching services is deemed to be a volunteer, and as such is not entitled to payment for services performed. Furthermore, many states have laws which forbid school boards from employing persons to perform teaching duties who do not have valid teaching certificates. The penalty for violation is generally a loss of the state funds which are normally contributed to help finance the costs of the particular teaching position.

Qualifications for teaching certificates vary to some degree among the individual states. Most states require that the person complete an approved course of teacher preparation at an approved teacher education institution, and that the person meet various character standards. Approval of the course of study and of the institutions' programs is generally within the power of the state board of education. The state board also is generally granted the power to set the minimum standards required for approval.

However, an interesting law was enacted in Oregon, which grants the power of approval for certification and DECERTIFICATION of teachers to what is termed the Teacher Standards and Practices Commission. This commission is mainly composed of educators, the majority of whom are teachers. It also has the power to prescribe minimum standards for approval of teacher education programs and institutions.

Local SCHOOL BOARDS are frequently allowed to prescribe standards and qualifications for employment which go beyond the minimum state requirements for certification, and these are upheld unless they are unreasonable, arbitrary, or capricious. For example, one school board policy required that in order to be employed, teachers must achieve a minimum score on the Graduate Records Examination (G.R.E.) or fulfill one of several various other alternatives. This policy had the effect of disqualifying a disproportionate number of black teachers, nine of whom sued on the alleged grounds of denial of EQUAL PROTECTION and DISCRIMINA-TION. The court did not rule on the discrimination issue. It held, however, that the G.R.E. requirement was arbitrary because such a test was not designed to, nor could it adequately measure teacher competency. The rule eliminated good teachers and had no reasonable relation to the purpose for which it was designed. However, the court suggested that the alternative requirements of teachers having an AA Teaching Certificate or Master's Degree could perhaps be justified. *Armstead v. Starkville Municipal Separate School District*, 461 F.2d 276 (5th Cir. 1972).

Certiorari, writ of. A writ of certiorari is an original writ commanding judges or officers of inferior COURTS to certify or to return records of proceedings in a cause for judicial review. Frequently, a party wishing to appeal a case to the U.S. Supreme Court will request the Supreme Court to issue a writ of certiorari. If the Supreme Court does not wish to review the case, it denies the writ.

See also: COURTS.

Chief State School Officer. The chief state school officer is called several different names in different states: State Commissioner of Education; State Superintendent of Public Instruction; or the State Superintendent of Public Schools. The chief state school officer's relationship to the State Board of Education depends upon the Board's policies and rules. The title used to describe this relationship also varies: Executive Secretary to the Board; Chief Administrative Officer; and others.

In nearly one-half of the states, the chief state school officer is selected by the State Board of Education. This is often felt to be the superior method of selection, because it helps to prevent politicians who have little or no experience in education from becoming the chief officer. In most of the remaining states, selection is by popular vote.

Few qualifications, and in many states no qualifications, are required by state statutes for the person who will be selected as the chief officer. In the states which do prescribe qualifications, the most common is that the chief officer must be able to qualify for a teaching certificate.

The term of office varies. Some 19 states have no specific term specified, and most of these provide that the Superintendent remains in office at the pleasure of the board. Most of the other states prescribe a specific number of years, the most common being four-year terms.

The salaries of the chief state school officer also vary a great deal, and in some states, the salary is clearly insufficient to assure the public that the most competent person will be selected as the head of the state school system.

See also: COMMISSIONER OF EDUCATION; STRUCTURE OF THE SCHOOL SYSTEM.

Child-Benefit Theory. The child-benefit theory is occasionally applied by the COURTS to uphold certain forms of aid to children attending private or parochial schools. This theory originated out of a case involving a Louisiana statute which provided for free TEXTBOOKS to *all* students, even if they attended PRIVATE SCHOOLS. The Court upheld the law by saying that the statute provided free books for the children and was enacted for their benefit, as well as the resulting benefit to the state. The aid to the private schools was seen as being merely incidental. *Cochran v. Louisiana State Board of Education,* 281 U.S. 370 (1930).

Under the child-benefit theory, use of public funds for busing children to nonpublic schools was also held not to violate the United States Constitution. *Everson v. Board of Education,* 330 U.S. 1 (1947). However, there is a strong possibility that the child-benefit theory could violate individual state constitutions, and if so, it would be invalid under state rather than federal law.

The child-benefit theory depends on a two-part test: (1) What is legislative intent? and (2) Who receives the aid—the school or the parent and child? This theory has lost much of its support in recent years.

See also: PRIVATE AND PAROCHIAL SCHOOL AID; RELIGION.

Church-State Relations. See BIBLE READING; PRAYERS; PRIVATE AND PAROCHIAL SCHOOL AID; RELIGION; SHARED-TIME.

Cigarettes. See RULES; TRESPASS TO PERSONAL PROPERTY.

Civil Rights Act of 1871. A federal statute enacted in 1871 is frequently used as the legal basis for seeking DAMAGES or other remedies for infringement on individuals' constitutional rights. This statute, 42 U.S.C. § 1983 (Act April 20, 1871, chap. 22, § 1, 17 Stat. 13), reads as follows:
    § 1983. Civil action for deprivation of rights.

> **Every person who, under color of any statute, ordinance, regulation, custom or usage, of any State or Territory, subjects, or causes to be subjected, any citizen of the United States or other person within the jurisdiction thereof to the deprivation of any rights, privileges, or immunities secured by the Constitution and laws, shall be liable to the party injured in an action at law, suit in equity, or other proper proceeding for redress. (R.S. § 1979).**

This act makes school personnel liable to persons suing for injunctive relief and damages for violation of the person's constitutional rights. When suing on the basis of this federal act, reinstatement, back pay, compensation for financial loss, damages for loss of promotion in career, damages for loss of reputation and professional status, damages for physical or mental suffering, and even punitive damages have been found to be available as remedies in appropriate instances.
    See also: CONSTITUTIONAL RIGHTS OF TEACHERS AND ADMINISTRATORS; STUDENT RIGHTS.

Civil Rights Act of 1964. Although education is primarily a state function, the federal government may impose various restrictions on state action by conditioning federal grants on compliance with prescribed conditions. The Civil Rights Act of 1964, 74 Stat. 86 (Title 28, § 1447; Title 42 §§ 1971, 1975a-1975-d, 2000a-2000h-6) was designed to provide federal financial aid for various educational programs, in such a manner as to ensure individuals' freedoms and equal opportunity.
    Initially, no guidelines for implementation or interpretation of this act were published; however, several sets of guidelines have since been issued by the Equal Employment Opportunity Commission (E.E.O.C.). Some of the interpretive guidelines were necessary to clarify § 601 of Title VI, which provides that:

> No person in the United States shall, on the ground of race, color,
> or national origin, be excluded from participation in, be denied the
> benefits, or be subjected to discrimination under any program or
> activity receiving federal financial assistance.

As a result, discriminatory practices are prohibited: e.g. SEGREGATION,
DISCRIMINATION in quality, quantity, or manner of benefit given; discriminatory requirements for participation; discrimination in employment;
discrimination on the basis of sex, etc.

If a person believes he or she has been discriminated against, the person
should file a complaint with the chairman of the E.E.O.C. in Washington
D.C., consult an attorney, or preferably do both. In some instances, violations of the provisions of the Civil Rights Act will not necessarily amount
to a violation under the EQUAL PROTECTION clause of the Constitution.
Nevertheless, decisions of the E.E.O.C. and the reasoning behind those
decisions will be of some significance in future court cases as well as in
decisions of the E.E.O.C.

Several of the more novel complaints registered with the E.E.O.C. have
involved PATERNITY LEAVES and sex discrimination in ATHLETICS.
The ELEMENTARY AND SECONDARY EDUCATION ACT OF
1965 provides federal aid to schools, and is, therefore, also subject to the
Civil Rights Act of 1964. In addition, cases involving pregnant teachers
have at times been brought under this act. The E.E.O.C. guidelines say
that it is a violation of Title VII to exclude employees "from employment . . . because of pregnancy . . ." 29 C.F.R. § 1604.10(a), 37 Fed.
Reg. 6837 (1972). These guidelines also provide that disabilities due to
pregnancy, miscarriage, abortion, childbirth, and recovery from these
"disabilities" are to be treated under the employee's health plan insurance
and under any applicable plan sick leave. As a result, cases involving
pregnant teachers clearly have a better chance of success by filing under
the Civil Rights Act than by merely raising constitutional issues. (See also
MATERNITY LEAVE.)

Closed Shop. See UNION SECURITY.

Collective Bargaining. Prior to the Civil War, STRIKES for higher wages
were treated as criminal conspiracies, but in the following fifty years, the
United States witnessed a tremendous growth in industry, and a consequent
growth in the organization of laborers. By 1900, labor organizations were

not considered to be criminal, but many of their activities, including strikes and picketing, were prohibited. With the aid of various federal acts, many of these restrictions gradually were removed. Enacted in 1935, the National Labor Relations Act (the Wagner Act) has become the major piece of legislation which formed the basis for authorizing bargaining and strike rights for private employees.

The organization rights of public employees lagged far behind their counterparts in the private business sector. However, in the mid-1900's, the ranks of public employees began to swell as the public demanded more and more services. On the education side of public employment, teachers were in great demand as the "baby boom" seubsequent to the Second World War necessitated more schools and more educators. In addition, the 1950's and 1960's were times which witnessed a large increase in the number of men joining the teaching profession.

As the number of public employees began to grow, so did the desire for greater bargaining rights. These employees wanted to form employee organizations and bargain over wages and other employment relations. Public employees watched persons employed in private business strike and bargain with their employers, and they demanded equal rights.

The legislatures of many states made efforts to pacify public employees by granting them some employment rights; and the COURTS also were called upon to define to what bargaining rights public employees were entitled. It is now clearly recognized that public employees have the right to organize and to be represented by an employee organization. Moreover, beginning in the 1960's many states enacted special laws necessary to grant bargaining rights to public employees. Some of these laws granted a more limited form of bargaining rights in what are termed "MEET AND CONFER" BARGAINING LAWS. Several of the more enlightened states enacted laws granting collective bargaining rights to public employees. Many states are looking closely at these laws, and each year several more states extend collective bargaining rights to persons engaged in public employment. More than half of the teachers and administrators in the United States are in states which provide some form of collective bargaining rights, and all teachers and administrators are affected by these laws.

Collective bargaining laws are still in their formative stages. The scope of negotiable issues, the use of binding ARBITRATION, and the right to strike are all issues which have not been uniformly resolved at the present time. These issues will continue to be experimented with for a good many years to come. However, the basic form of collective bargaining laws and the procedures utilized in the required manner of bargaining and settling labor disputes will eventually be fairly similar throughout the states, and will be patterned around issues and their solutions, as explained in the following description of collective bargaining laws.

Collective bargaining is a method of determining conditions of employment through *bilateral negotiations* between representatives of the employer and the certified employee organization. These parties are required by law to reach a settlement which is mutually binding. This settlement is then set forth in a written AGREEMENT. Collective bargaining, as defined by the National Labor Relations Act and several state laws, is:

> **. . . the performance of the mutual obligation of the employer and the representative of the employees to meet at reasonable times and confer in good faith with respect to wages, hours, and other terms and conditions of employment, or the negotiation of an agreement, or any question arising thereunder, and the execution of a written contract incorporating any agreement reached if requested by either party, but such obligation does not compel either party to agree to a proposal or require the making of a concession. . . .**

Note that the parties meet as equals and determinations are made pursuant to bilateral negotiations. This differs considerably from pure "meet and confer" statutes in which the employees are given the right to discuss employment relations, but management retains the right to act unilaterally. Also, meet and confer statutes are distinguishable in the range of legally permissible topics about which the parties may "confer" as opposed to "negotiate." Under collective bargaining, the SCOPE OF BARGAINING is considerably more extensive.

Collective bargaining laws do not compel the public employer to give up its sovereign authority to make decisions. These laws only require that a technique of bargaining procedures must be followed. The requirements are that the employer must bargain in good faith and in so doing must negotiate with its employees. After a reasonable period of good faith bargaining, if a settlement has not been reached, the parties can each make a final offer which they will take to impasse.

An impasse occurs when the parties are unable to reach an agreement. Impasse machinery is designed to help the parties reach a settlement on their own. MEDIATION and FACT-FINDING are found in all collective bargaining laws, and these are utilized to aid the parties in resolving their dispute. If these procedures are unsuccessful, some of the laws provide that a third party shall settle the dispute through what is known as binding ARBITRATION. A few laws allow the public employees to STRIKE at this point in the impasse.

In order for collective bargaining to truly work effectively, there must exist impasse machinery which provides both parties with equal bargaining power if the dispute is submitted to impasse. In this way, the parties will theoretically bargain in good faith during the earlier stages of the negotiations, in the hope that they will achieve a more advantageous settlement. Binding arbitration provides the parties with an equal chance of obtaining a favorable settlement in the event of an impasse. Many states have recognized this, and the trend is toward greater utilization of binding arbitration in settling public employee labor and contract disputes.

The following flow chart, found on page 54, briefly outlines the collective bargaining process.

Commencement Exercises. SCHOOL BOARDS have the authority to enact reasonable RULES governing student conduct and operation of the schools. Requiring that students who wish to participate in commencement exercises must wear caps and gowns has been held to be a reasonable rule. *Valentine v. Independent School District of Casey,* 183 N.W.434 (Iowa, 1921). This requirement would seem to be unreasonable, however, if no provision were made for providing caps and gowns to students who could not afford them. In such cases, it would seem that the school would either have to provide the caps and gowns or would have to allow the students to participate without them. In 1974, a federal district court upheld the right of a school district to hold PRAYERS at a high school graduation ceremony.

The school may not condition granting of the DIPLOMA upon participation in the commencement exercises. Such a rule would be arbitrary because it is not reasonably related to the educational process.

Commissioner of Education. (For an explanation of the commissioner's legal status, qualifications, etc., see CHIEF STATE SCHOOL OFFICER.) In several states, the judicial authority to handle grievances over routine educational issues has been delegated to certain ADMINISTRATIVE

COLLECTIVE BARGAINING

Selecting Negotiating Team
Public employes choose a negotiating team, which is informed of the necessary facts and information. Parameters of positions are established.

Selecting Negotiating Team
Public employer chooses a negotiating team, which is provided the necessary facts and information. Parameters of positions are established.

Good Faith Bargaining
The negotiating teams meet and discuss their proposals. If good faith bargaining occurs, the parties should be able to reach an agreement. If so, collective bargaining process stops here.

Agreement
Once an agreement is reached by the negotiating teams, it is submitted for approval.

Impasse
If the parties cannot reach an agreement even though they should be able to if they have engaged in good faith bargaining, the dispute is submitted to impasse. These impasse procedures follow below.

Employe Organization Approval
The public employes vote as to whether or not the agreement is acceptable to them. If not, the parties are forced into negotiations again.

Voter Approval
If the agreement reached involves the expenditure of money, voter approval is generally required in order to obtain the necessary funds. If the required approval is not granted, the agreement is broken and the negotiations begin again.

Mediation
An impartial third party tries to get the parties negotiating again. If the mediator is successful, the parties once again enter good faith bargaining. If not, the impasse procedures require factfinding.

Factfinding
A factfinder listens to both sides of the dispute, makes findings of facts and recommends a solution. If the parties accept the recommendations, agreement is reached. If not, the factfinder's findings and recommendations are made public.

If factfinding fails to encourage the parties to reach an agreement, the laws vary in their approaches to the final step on impasse. The most common approach is arbitration, but strikes are allowed in some states.

Strike
Several states authorize public employes to strike at this point. Strikes generally will get the negotiations started again. Most laws provide that injunctive relief is available in the event that the strike creates a clear and present danger to the public health, safety or welfare.

Binding Arbitration
A third party holds a hearing, listens to both sides of the dispute, investigates the facts, and recommends a solution. The arbitrator's recommendations are binding.

Advisory Arbitration
This process is much like that used in binding arbitration but the arbitrator's recommendations are advisory and not binding. As a result, this step is closer akin to factfinding and it is an added expense. Therefore, it is not widely adopted.

AGENCIES. For the most part, this puts the GRIEVANCE out of the COURTS, where time and expense is often more excessive. New York and New Jersey have been the leaders in utilizing this method of handling school disputes. The Commissioners of Education of these two states have extensive authority to render decisions on school disputes.

Common Law. Common Law is the general universal law of the land. This law is not derived from state STATUTES, but is developed through court decisions over hundreds of years. Common law prevails in England and in the United States, and is the controlling law unless abrogated or modified by state or federal statutes.

For example, NEGLIGENCE involves the elements of: (1) duty; (2) violation; (3) cause; and (4) injury. This concept is not generally defined by statute, but has developed through the years with court decisions. It is because of the "common law" that one can generalize about the law over all of the United States without having to specifically search each state's statutes. Only where states modify or abolish the common law is it necessary to look at individual states specifically. For example, most states have statutes changing the common law status of TENURE or GOVERN-MENTAL IMMUNITY. On the other hand, the concept of IN LOCO PARENTIS still prevails to some extent in the majority of states. The limits of *in loco parentis*, therefore, are generally defined by court decisions and not by state statutes.

See also: COURTS; STARE DECISIS.

Common Schools. Many state constitutions and statutes provide that the state shall establish and maintain common schools. Common schools are schools which may be attended by any school-age child residing within designated boundaries. Such schools are supported by public funds and must be provided free of charge to any attending students.

The extent of education required to be provided by the state depends upon the wording of applicable state constitutions and statutes. High schools, junior high schools, and elementary schools are common schools.

However, in some states, KINDERGARTENS are not considered to be common schools which the legislature must establish. Schools for adults and community or junior colleges are also not required. These additional education programs may be established by the legislature, but common school funds may not be expended on them without the necessary constitutional or statutory amendments.

Communists. See ANTI-SUBVERSIVE LAWS; LOYALTY OATHS.

Comparative Negligence. Comparative negligence is the doctrine by which acts of the opposing parties are compared in the degrees of NEGLI-GENCE. Some states use degrees of "slight," "ordinary," and "gross," but the trend has been to allow juries to determine the percentage of negligence each party was responsible for.

Comparative negligence is a relatively new concept that is being enacted in a number of states. This type of law eliminates the defense of CONTRIBUTORY NEGLIGENCE in many situations, and replaces it by requiring the jury to find and compare the negligence of both parties. Under the concept of comparative negligence, if one party has contributed more to an injury than another, that party will have to pay his or her proportionate share. If the parties are equally negligent, neither party pays any DAMAGES. For example, if you are driving down the street at an excessive rate of speed, you are negligent. If another person collided with you because he was under the influence of liquor, he would also be negligent. The jury then decides who contributed what percent to the injury. If your excessive speed contributed 20 percent, and the other person's drunk driving contributed 80 percent, you would be entitled to recover 80 percent of your damages under the main system of comparative negligence laws. However, the other party, being 80 percent negligent, would not be allowed to recover 20 percent of his damages because, under most negligence laws, if a party is more than 50 percent at fault, he or she is not allowed to recover.

As our COURTS and laws are improved to meet the needs of the times, comparative negligence should become more prevalent as opposed to a strict negligence law where the least bit of negligence by one not primarily at fault would preclude that person from recovery. Many Bar Associations throughout the United States are making a recommendation to adopt the law of comparative negligence. Presently, Wisconsin, Maine, Oregon, Nebraska, South Dakota, Arkansas and Mississippi are among the states which have comparative negligence laws. More states will no doubt be added as each legislature convenes.

Competitive Bids. See BUILDINGS; CONSTRUCTION.

Compulsory Education. Compulsory education laws were enacted in the years 1852-1918 in an effort to protect children from widespread labor abuses, and to ensure that the enormous number of immigrants who had come to America would learn the English language and American customs.

The extent of this state's right to compel school attendance has been challenged many times in the 1900's. In 1972, the Supreme Court of the United States reversed its earlier stand and said, "However strong the state's interest in universal compulsory education, it is by no means absolute to the exclusion or subordination of all other interests." *Wisconsin v. Yoder*, 406 U.S. 205 (1972). This case involved a challenge to Wisconsin's compulsory education statute which required children between the ages of seven and sixteen years of age to attend school regularly. The parents of one such school age child who was not yet sixteen years old refused to send the child to school after the eighth grade. They felt that continued education violated the tenets of their AMISH religion. The parents were convicted of violating the Wisconsin compulsory education statute. They appealed the conviction, saying that the compulsory education statute infringed upon their free exercise of RELIGION, and was therefore unconstitutional.

The Wisconsin Supreme Court agreed with the parents' argument. The U.S. Supreme Court affirmed this decision and held that the establishment of religion clause of the First Amendment, made applicable to the states through the Fourteenth Amendment, prohibits state action which needlessly interferes with a parent's right to control the religious training of his or her children.

This case was the first major inroad on compulsory education. The Court explained the new test for compelling attendance at school beyond an education providing minimum literacy:

> ... [I]n order ... to compel school attendance beyond the eighth grade against a claim that such attendance interferes with the practice of legitimate religious belief, it must appear either that the State does not deny the free exercise of religious belief by its requirement, or that there is a state interest of sufficient magnitude to override the interest claiming protection under the Free Exercise Clause. (406 U.S. at 214.)

This certainly does not invalidate laws requiring students to attend school beyond the eighth grade. This case merely suggests that although minimum literacy is a compelling state interest, high school education is not. Nevertheless, only those students having strong religious beliefs against higher education are allowed to be free of compulsory attendance beyond the eighth grade. However, it is clear that compulsory attendance laws are in for more challenges. Although it is not likely such laws will be abolished entirely, it is likely that some modification is in order. The state's commitment to education will continue, but its form and timetable may change.

Many state laws provide that particular individuals are declared exempt from compulsory attendance: e.g. severely physically or mentally handicapped students. Also, MARRIED STUDENTS are emancipated from being compelled to attend school against their will. In addition, it should be noted that the State is not required to establish compulsory attendance laws. For example, in the 1950's, Mississippi abolished its compulsory education law in an effort to avoid the Supreme Court's DESEGREGATION directive of 1954.

To comply with compulsory attendance laws, parents or guardians may elect to send their children to the assigned public school, or to a private school of their choice, so long as such schools meet the requirements of the state education CERTIFICATION law. The minimum standards for such PRIVATE SCHOOLS vary from state to state. In some states, the statutes permit or court decisions have held that instruction at "home schools" complies with that state's compulsory education laws.

The minimum standards for home schools vary depending upon the individual state's compulsory education law or the court decisions interpreting the law. The minimum instructional programs (i.e., number of days, hours, courses, etc.) is most often prescribed by the state laws or state board of education rules, and these minimum requirements must be met by the home school. Where the requirements are not prescribed by the state laws, the COURTS are left to decide whether or not approval of the home school shall be granted. Where the state's compulsory education law does not allow alternatives for attendance "at a school" and instead demands attendance at a public or formally organized private school, home instruction has not been allowed.

Condemnation. See PROPERTY.

Conflicts of Interest. Local school board members and other school personnel are not allowed to hold offices which present a conflict of interest. Typical conflicts of interest arise where a member of a school board has a contract with that same school board to provide services or materials. Generally, this is not allowed. Also, a school board member may not be employed as a teacher or administrator in the same district.

In addition, it has been held that a person cannot hold two PUBLIC OFFICES at the same time where the offices might present direct conflicting interests. Where one office is directly subordinate to the other, acceptance of the superior office is at times an automatic vacation of the subordinate office. As a guideline:

> . . . Where one office is not subordinate to the other, or the relations of the one to the other such as are inconsistent and repugnant, there is not that incompatibility from which the law declares that the acceptance of the one is the vacation of the other. The force of the word, in its application to this matter is that from the nature and relations to each other, of the two places, they ought not to be held by the same person from the contrariety and antagonism which would result in the attempt by one person to faithfully and impartially discharge the duties of one, toward the incumbent of the other . . . The offices must subordinate, one to the other, and they must, per se, have the right to interfere, one with the other, before they are incompatible in common law. *People v. Green*, 58 N.Y. 295 (1874).

Some offices are declared by statute to be in conflict. However, there are also some offices which are normally deemed to be legally in conflict but which are allowed by special statutes or constitutional amendments. For example, Oregon amended its constitution to allow teachers to serve as members of the state legislature.

Conscientious Objectors. A case arising out of World War II held that a teacher who had stated that he was a conscientious objector and would not serve the United States as a combatant or noncombatant in its involvement in the war could lawfully be removed from his teaching position. *State v. Turner*, 19 So.2d 832 (Fla. 1944). Today, this case would have been decided to the contrary. Now, the law clearly provides that a teacher may not be dismissed or refused employment because he is a conscientious objector.

See also: CONSTITUTIONAL RIGHTS OF TEACHERS AND ADMINISTRATORS.

Consolidation. See REORGANIZATION.

Constitutional Law. The Constitution of the United States was completed on September 17, 1787. In 1789, the first ten amendments were submitted to Congress and ratification of them was completed on December 15, 1791.

These amendments constitute what is frequently called the Bill of Rights. The framers of the Constitution feared that the new Constitution had created a system of government which, if its powers were not restricted, might someday have the power to unduly infringe upon the civil rights of individual citizens. The Bill of Rights was designed to ensure individuals certain basic personal safeguards and freedoms.

Before the Civil War, the Supreme Court of the United States was not often called upon to interpret these guaranteed freedoms. However, when it was called upon, the Supreme Court felt that the intent of the Bill of Rights was to protect personal freedoms against federal action, but not against state action. This meant, for example, that if one were arrested by a state police officer for a state crime, the Constitution did not protect his individual freedoms. However, if that same person were arrested by a federal officer on a federal charge, those freedoms enumerated in the Constitution were guaranteed.

Following the Civil War, the Thirteenth Amendment was ratified, thereby giving constitutional sanction to President Lincoln's wartime Emancipation Proclamation. Nevertheless, the rights of black people continued to be severely limited by the "black codes" of some states. In an effort to protect black people's rights, Congress adopted the Civil Rights Act of 1866. The Fourteenth Amendment was designed to sustain this Act, and it was ratified in 1868. However, the language of this Amendment was not limited to DISCRIMINATION based on race, color, or previous condition of servitude.

Following the enactment of the Fourteenth Amendment, during the period from about 1875 to 1900, two major new concepts were conceived:

1. The Fourteenth Amendment's "due process clause" could be used to invalidate federal and state statutes which arbitrarily or unreasonably curtail or interfere with the individual's right of liberty and property.

2. Furthermore, the states' police power could be exercised only in areas promoting health, morals and safety.

These concepts led the way; and now, the United States Supreme Court has interpreted the broad language of the Fourteenth Amendment to mean that nearly each and every one of the individual freedoms and rights guaranteed to the people by the Bill of Rights are protected against infringement by state action as well as against unnecessary federal action.

The First Amendment has had a tremendous effect on education. A majority of the cases brought by, or which affect, teachers or schools involve this amendment. The First Amendment says that:

> **Congress shall make no law respecting an establishment of religion or prohibiting the free exercise thereof; or abridging the freedom of speech or of the press; or of the right of the people peaceably to assemble, and to petition the government for a redress of grievances.**

Although this amendment specifically refers to Congress, as previously stated, the Supreme Court of the United States has held that this restriction also applies to the states.

The First Amendment protects four freedoms: (1) religion; (2) speech; (3) press; and (4) assembly. In the past, the first clause, respecting establishment of RELIGION, had the greatest effect on schools. In recent years, however, teachers and administrators have brought an increasing number of suits to the COURTS concerning their rights to freedom of speech and association. Many changes in the law resulted from these late 1960 and early 1970 cases.

The Fifth Amendment provides certain other protections for individuals accused of crime, and also prevents the state from taking property without just compensation. It reads as follows:

> **No person shall be held to answer for a capital or otherwise infamous crime, unless on a presentment or indictment of a grand jury, . . . nor shall any person be subject for the same offense to be twice put in jeopardy of life or limb; nor shall be compelled in any criminal case to be a witness against himself, or be deprived of life, liberty, or property, without due process of law; nor shall private property be taken for public use, without just compensation.**

Several aspects of this amendment have had an effect on the schools. Teachers and administrators have at times sought to use the privilege against SELF-INCRIMINATION in instances involving LOYALTY OATHS and possible connections with subversive organizations. (See SILENT, right to remain.) School districts are affected by the last clause of this amendment in that they are required to pay just compensation in condemnation proceedings. (See PROPERTY).

The Fourteenth Amendment of the Constitution is often referred to as the DUE PROCESS clause and the EQUAL PROTECTION clause. Section 1 of this amendment defines citizenship and specifies that citizens have certain privileges:

. . . No State shall make or enforce any law which shall abridge the privileges and immunities of the citizens of the United States; nor shall any State deprive any person of life, liberty, or property, without due process of law; nor deny to any person within its jurisdiction the equal protection of the laws.

Both the equal protection and due process clauses have been extremely important in establishing the CONSTITUTIONAL RIGHTS OF TEACHERS AND ADMINISTRATORS. (See also STUDENT RIGHTS.)

Constitutional Rights of Teachers and Administrators. (For a preliminary introduction, see CONSTITUTIONAL LAW.) Laws governing employees of the public school system come from three major sources: (1) the COMMON LAW; (2) state constitutions and STATUTES; and (3) the United States Constitution.

The Fourteenth Amendment of the U.S. Constitution provides in part that: ". . . No state shall make or enforce any law which shall abridge the privileges or immunities of citizens of the United States; . . ." In the Bill of Rights, the Constitution specifically states that individual citizens have certain fundamental rights and freedoms. Through the Fourteenth Amendment, the Supreme Court of the United States has ruled that the rights and freedoms as enumerated in the Bill of Rights are protected against infringement by the State.

The State has the responsibility of establishing and maintaining the public schools. Even though local school boards do the actual hiring, the State is the employer of public school teachers and administrators. The school board acts as an agent of the state, as do the school district employees when they are performing their governmental duties. As the Supreme Court has said, the State may not enact any laws or engage in any activities which are in violation of an individual's constitutional rights. It follows, therefore, that local SCHOOL BOARDS and school officials are also prohibited from enacting any RULES or regulations which substantially infringe on an individual's constitutional rights.

This means that teachers and administrators have certain constitutional protections assuring them of such liberties as:

1. Freedom of speech outside the school environment.
2. Freedom of speech within the classroom.
3. Freedom from undue restrictions on their personal APPEARANCE.

4. Freedom to lead their lives in PRIVACY.
5. Freedom of association.
6. Freedom of RELIGION.
7. Protection from arbitrary, capricious, or discriminatory actions or dismissals on the part of the local board, and
8. DUE PROCESS.

These protections are substantial. Nevertheless, it must be stressed that these rights are not absolute. *Reasonable* restrictions may be placed upon one's constitutional rights because the COURTS must weigh the constitutional rights against the need for effective school management and operation. Therefore, certain restrictions may incidentally curtail the teacher's or administrator's constitutional rights. That is, they may do so if these restrictions are necessary to promote the efficient operation of the school. When that is the case, such restrictions will be upheld. The problem lies in balancing the teacher's or administrator's protected rights against the state's right to maintain the schools free from actions or persons which pose a material and substantial threat to the order and efficiency of the school system.

Keep in mind that the United States' system of democracy is built upon a foundation which stresses the importance of freedom and openness. Certain rights such as freedom of speech necessitate close protection because threat of dismissal from employment clearly has a chilling effect on free speech. The public has an interest in protecting all individual's rights, and this interest must be considered in the balancing process.

Note—Most of the cases involve teachers, but the principles enumerated in these cases apply to administrators as well as teachers. For simplicity, the term "teachers" will be used throughout this section, and it is meant to include administrators as well as other certificated personnel.

FREEDOM OF SPEECH—OUTSIDE THE SCHOOL ENVIRONMENT

Today, while outside of the school building, teachers should feel free to discuss topics which are of interest and concern to them as individuals. This has not always been so. In the past, statements which had no relationship to the teacher's fitness to perform his or her duties were frequently used as a basis for that person's dismissal. As stated by Howard Beale in 1941, "In theory . . . [a teacher] is freer to advocate unpopular causes outside class than inside, but in practice the advocacy of unpopular causes in the community gets him into trouble more quickly than doing so in school." [7]

Beale's statement proved to be painfully correct. In a 1944 case, a Florida court upheld the dismissal of a teacher whose sole indiscretion had been his statement that he was a CONSCIENTIOUS OBJECTOR and that he would not aid the United States in either a combat or a noncombat status.[8] In another World War II case, a female teacher wrote a letter to a former student who had refused to register for the draft. In the letter she congratulated him on his "courageous and idealistic stand," and she stated that "you and the others who take the same stand are the hope of America." The court upheld the dismissal.[9]

Such cases were based on the premise that the public must be protected from unfit teachers. This concept remains unquestioned; but can it be said that a person who is conscientious, experienced, well-qualified, and performs the teaching duties in a capable, competent manner is unfit because he or she challenges accepted opinions? In addition, the early cases failed to recognize that the public also has a strong interest in encouraging free and unhindered debate on issues of public importance. The individual's freedom of speech must be protected in order for such open debate to flourish.

In 1968, the Supreme Court of the United States rendered a decision in a case called *Pickering v. Board of Education*.[10] In this case, Pickering, a teacher, was dismissed for writing a letter to a local newspaper which the school board believed was detrimental to the efficient operation of the schools. In this letter, Pickering stated, among other things, that (1) the school board had misinformed the public about allocation of finances in a proposed school bond issues; and (2) the superintendent had threatened to discipline any teacher who refused to support the school bond. Although some of Pickering's statements proved to be untrue, the Supreme Court held that teachers have constitutional rights and that Pickering had been denied his First Amendment right of free speech. In considering the fact that several of Pickering's statements were incorrect, the Supreme Court said:

---

[7] Beale, H. K. *A History of Freedom of Teaching in American Schools*, Charles Scribner's Sons, p. 237 (1941).

[8] *State v. Turner*, 19 So.2d 832 (Fla. 1944).

[9] *Joyce v. Board of Education*, 60 N.E.2d 431 (Ill. 1945), cert. denied, 327 U.S. 786 (1946).

[10] 391 U.S. 563 (1968).

> ... Absent proof of false statements knowingly or recklessly made
> by him, a teacher's exercise of his right to speak on issues of public
> importance may not furnish the basis for his dismissal from public
> employment.[11]

For teachers, this was a giant step forward. Prior to this time, teachers could be fairly certain to find themselves seeking new employment if they publicly criticized local businesses or accepted mores of the community. It was out of the question to even consider criticizing the school system.

In 1968, the teacher was seen to have constitutional rights and the Supreme Court said that before a teacher's freedom of speech may be restricted, there must be a showing that: (1) the statements harm a substantial public interest; or (2) render the person unfit to teach. The problem arises in trying to determine what a "substantial public interest" is. In the *Pickering* case, the Supreme Court provided guidelines to be considered in making a determination of whether or not a substantial public interest has been harmed. These guidelines are:

Pickering Guidelines to Consider

1. Disruption of superior-subordinate relationships;
2. Breach of loyalty or confidentiality;
3. General disruption of the public service;
4. Indication of unfitness from content of the statement; and
5. Failure to comply with established grievance procedures.

What the Supreme Court has said is that the teacher has a right of free speech, but where his or her statements have harmed a substantial public interest, he or she may be disciplined. In determining whether or not a substantial public interest has been harmed, the above guidelines must be considered. The extent of the harm must also be considered. To help point out how these guidelines are applied, consider the following situation.

What if a teacher publicly criticizes school officials and the school system —can the teacher be disciplined? The answer is not always yes or no; it will depend on whether or not a substantial public interest has been harmed. In this circumstance, the answer to this question will depend on whether or not the statements have disrupted superior-subordinate relationships, or

---

[11] Ibid at 574.

have disrupted the public service. Superior-subordinate relationships are these close-working relationships which are necessary to enable the teacher to fully perform the required duties. This is meant to mean those relationships in which the persons frequently meet and work together. In most schools, teachers are in a superior-subordinate relationship with the principal, but no close-working relationship exists between the superintendent or the school board and the teachers. On the other hand, a close-working relationship generally exists between the superintendent and the school principals.

Disruption of the public service occurs where the statements *materially and substantially interfere* with the order and efficiency in the operation of the school. Some minor disruption frequently will occur, but it must be tolerated. The teacher's criticisms need not be couched in mild, ineffective terms, and the use of profanity is not always fatal.

Where the teacher's comments are related to issues of public importance, they enjoy even stronger protections than statements related to the internal operation of the school. Although such comments may at times call into question the teacher's fitness to teach, they may not alone constitute an independent basis for dismissal. The statements may be used as evidence of general unfitness, but the school board would be forced to demonstrate how the statements have in actuality rendered the teacher unfit to teach.

Where criticisms relating to the internal operation of the school are concerned, the teacher may be required to exhaust the school's established internal GRIEVANCE procedures prior to making the grievance public. However, this is true only where the grievance procedures are capable of providing a solution to the alleged problem. For example, if the criticism is related to textbook selection, unsafe facilities or equipment, or selection of field trips, potential solutions are available within school channels, and the complaint should first be handled within them. Where established grievance procedures do not exist or are not made known to the teachers, the teachers are not required to comply.

In addition to the right to talk freely, a teacher has a right to demonstrate so long as the demonstration is constitutionally protected. If the demonstration becomes violent or interferes with scheduled school classes or activities, the demonstrators cannot expect or demand the protection of the Constitution even if they did not encourage or participate in the actual disruption. When a person joins in speaking with a group, he or she must bear the consequences of any splintered voices.

FREEDOM OF SPEECH WITHIN THE CLASSROOM

The protections of freedom of speech within the classroom stem from the concept of ACADEMIC FREEDOM. Through this doctrine and the First Amendment of the Constitution, the classroom is recognized as a marketplace of ideas—a place where old and new concepts may be questioned and examined. Challenging students to think on their own and to question their beliefs is bound to lead to some unpleasantness or discomfort. The courts recognize this, and the Supreme Court of the United States has said:

> **Any word spoken, in class, in the lunchroom, or on the campus, that deviates from the views of another person may start an argument or cause a disturbance. But our Constitution says we must take this risk. . . .**
>
> **In order for . . . school officials to justify prohibition of a particular expression . . . [they] must be able to show that [their] action was caused by something more than a mere desire to avoid the discomfort and unpleasantness that always accompany an unpopular viewpoint.[12]**

The Supreme Court has provided the test for determining whether or not justification exists for school officials to prohibit particular kinds of expression within the classroom:

> **Freedom of speech may be restricted only where it materially and substantially interferes with the requirements of appropriate discipline in the operation of the school.**

However, this does not confer upon teachers the authority to say whatever they wish or to use any materials they alone deem desirable. The teacher must be able to show that the statements or materials serve an educational purpose which is supported by a substantial segment of the teaching profession.

Statements made or materials used must be relevant to the topic being taught in order for them to serve an educational purpose. If the teacher attempts to use the classroom as a forum to express his or her personal political views which are completely irrelevant to the topic being taught, he or she may be disciplined. For example, school officials can require and expect teachers of mathematics to confine their classroom teaching to

---

[12] *Tinker v. Des Moines Independent Community School Dist.*, 393 U.S. 503, 508-509 (1969).

topics relevant to that subject. If the teacher desires to discuss race relations, politics, or sex, he or she should seek employment as a social science teacher or a similar position which lends itself to discussions of a more controversial nature.

On the other hand, teachers have a right to present scholarly, non-pornographic material in their classes. The age, intelligence, and experience of the students will be an important consideration in determining the appropriateness of the material. However, censorship of materials based merely on the fact that some parents are offended should not be allowed because parent views are not the measure for determining what is proper education.

As previously suggested, a teacher's authority to discuss controversial topics may depend on the nature of the subject being taught. In one case, a high school civics teacher who had taught a six-day unit on race relations and who, in response to a student's question, replied that he was not personally opposed to interracial marriage, became the object of disgruntled parents' demands for his removal. In the case initiated to compel reinstatement, the court held that the teacher should be reinstated because he had treated both sides of the topic fairly and the administration was aware of what was being taught.[13]

In another case, an English teacher used the word "fuck" in a lecture concerning taboo and socially acceptable words. The court reinstated the teacher, but said that school officials who wish to forbid certain types of classroom discussions or teaching methods, such as this one, will be upheld in doing so *IF* they give the teachers *clear and specific* guidelines showing what types of classroom discussions or assignments are prohibited.[14] Whether or not the teacher's right of free speech is unconstitutionally infringed upon can only be determined on a case by case inquiry, the court added.

Several cases have held that a teacher has the right to wear an armband, but this is, of course, subject to the requirement that such "speech" does not cause a material and substantial disruption of the order and efficiency in the operation of the school.

Teachers cannot be forced to subscribe to a certain idea which conflicts with their freedom of speech. On this basis, teachers may not be required

---

[13] *Sterzing v. Ft. Bend Independent School Dist.*, 376 F.Supp. 657, vacated 496 F.2d 92 (5th Cir. 1974).
[14] *Mailloux v. Kiley*, 448 F.2d 1242 (1st Cir. 1971).

to lead the PLEDGE OF ALLEGIANCE or engage in a FLAG SALUTE. However, the teacher is obligated to remain sitting or standing respectfully, and may be required to make arrangements to have a student or another teacher lead such exercises.

FREEDOM FROM UNDUE RESTRICTIONS ON PERSONAL APPEARANCE

What is "acceptable" in the manner of APPEARANCE changes with the times. There always seem to be people whose appearance attracts attention. Whether their manner of dress is several years behind or ahead of the times is not always readily ascertainable, but one thing is certain, the school is not the safe place for fashion trend setters.

The school system has traditionally attempted to prevent persons from appearing in a manner which is contrary to the accepted norm. Howard Beale wrote in a book in 1936[15] in which he related that in 1924 a Santa Paula, California teacher was dismissed for bobbing her hair. In 1928, some teachers in West Virginia were forced to sign contracts in which they promised to "fasten their galoshes up all the way." In still another instance, a teacher was dismissed because the wives of some of the more affluent citizens in the town objected to the poor quality of dresses the teacher purchased with her forty dollars a month salary. And, in 1915, some teaching contracts prohibited teachers from wearing "bright colors," required the wearing of two petticoats, and prohibited teachers from wearing dresses which were more than two inches above the ankle.

Times have not changed school efforts to prescribe uniform manners of appearance, but time has resulted in changes of the battleground areas. Now, the fight is over dresses two inches above the knee, the wearing of bras and pants suits, and the wearing of hair on the chin or extending down around the shoulders. These cyclical changes in values do present some strange anomalies. For example, one army reservist who was ordered in 1970 to shave the Van Dyke beard he had worn for five years was amazed when he uncovered an 1842 general army order *requiring* officers to wear beards.[16]

---

15 Beale, H. K. *Are American Teachers Free?* Charles Scribner's Sons, pp. 390-391 (1936).
16 *Los Angeles Times,* July 21, 1971, sec. 1, p. 5, col. 6-7.

In the late 1960's and early 1970's, the schools found their dress codes and appearance regulations being challenged from every direction—principals, teachers, and students. By 1975, the majority rule was clearly established that school rules regulating appearance can only be justified by a showing of reasonableness. Rules which prohibit appearance which causes an *actual substantial disruption* or rules which are *necessary for health, safety or morals* will be upheld. Rules going beyond these bounds will not be upheld.

Rules regulating the length of a person's hair are unreasonable because such rules control a person's appearance 24 hours a day, seven days a week, whereas the person is within the school less than eight hours a day. Moreover, when a person's appearance is an expression of his personality, heritage, race, or culture, and it does not impair the educational process, such appearance warrants protection under the Constitution.

Besides the many cases involving hair, rules prohibiting certain forms of dress have also been challenged. Rules prohibiting the wearing of pants suits have been struck down as being unreasonable where evidence was presented which shows that such dress can even aid a teacher, particularly in the elementary grades.[17] In 1971, a New York teacher who had been dismissed for wearing a bikini while giving swimming instructions to male and female students was ordered reinstated.[18]

It is clear that all courts recognize that teachers should be free from unreasonable rules regulating their appearance. However, what is seen as being unreasonable varies to some extent from state to state and with changing times. As a result, it must be suggested that school personnel who are asked to shave, cut their hair, or otherwise conform to appearance regulations, should consult an attorney for advice on the position the courts of that state take with regard to a teacher's freedom of appearance.

A TEACHER'S FREEDOM TO LEAD A LIFE OF PRIVACY

The Supreme Court's decision in the *Pickering* case has lent support to the argument that a teacher's private life may form the basis for his or her dismissal only where it affects his or her fitness as a teacher. Prior to the 1960's, teachers' personal affairs were subject to close scrutiny by their employers, and frequently were used as the basis for dismissal.

17 In re *School District of Kingsley and Kingsley Educ. Assn.*, 56 Lab. Arb. 1138 (1971).
18 In re *Heather Martin*, #8156 (N.Y. Commissioner of Educ., Aug. 3, 1971).

In 1936, Howard Beale described the restrictions placed on teachers. He explained that in 1928, in North Carolina, teachers were forced to sign contracts in which they promised "not to fall in love" and "not to go out with any young men except in so far as it may be necessary to stimulate Sunday-school work." This was quite liberal compared to several 1915 contracts in which teachers promised "not to loiter in ice cream stores," "not to go out with men," and "to be home between the hours of 8 P.M. and 6 A.M." The dismissal cases are even more enlightening. In one case, for example, a high school principal was dismissed for walking home from school every day with a high school teacher. In 1927, a science teacher found that going riding one afternoon with two of his girl students subjected him to removal from the public schools.

As Mr. Beale relates:

> Often petty social restrictions or offenses against them come in combination, because the teacher who is a non-conformist is likely to get into trouble on several scores. A young South Carolina history teacher, now happier in a better school system, almost gave up teaching because of his first experience. He was not allowed to dance or to have "dates." He had to teach a Sunday school class. Then he got into trouble for saying that Negroes had as much right to an education as whites. In three hour faculty meetings the superintendent dictated every detail of the teachers' lives. Even before he got into evolution difficulties, John Scopes was criticized in Dayton for smoking cigarettes and for dancing. In an Iowa town a woman was recently dismissed because she invited boy students to her apartment and because she was known to smoke and to drink. One young teacher writes, "How I conduct my classes seems to be of no great interest to the school authorities, but what I do when school is not in session concerns them tremendously. My contract requires me to refrain from keeping company with young men in the community. Yet I must live in the school district and remain here three weekends out of four during the entire school year. I mustn't dance, play cards, or be out late on week-day nights; in fact, they want me to be an old maid.[19]

The courts have now recognized that teachers' constitutional rights includes the right to live their lives in privacy. The key to the question of

---

[19] Beale, H. K. *Are American Teachers Free?* Charles Scribner's Sons, (1936), pp. 394-395.

whether or not a person's acts or life style may form the basis for his or her disappearance from public employment depends on whether or not such conduct renders the teacher unfit to teach. There must exist some nexus between the conduct complained of and the teacher's ability to perform his or her necessary duties. As one court explains what may form the grounds for dismissal:

> The private conduct of a man, who is also a teacher, is a proper concern to those who employ him only to the extent it mars him as a teacher. . . . Where his professional achievement is unaffected, where the school community is placed in no jeopardy, his private acts are his own business and may not be the basis of discipline.[20]

Under this "fitness as a teacher" test, the deleterious effect on the teacher's services must be capable of being objectively ascertainable. Cases in which a teacher was convicted of possession of marijuana and "hit and run" driving[21] have held that their fitness as teachers was not adversely affected and they could not be dismissed.

Sex has caused many teachers of the past to seek new employment. Living with a person of the opposite sex has been the subject of several court cases. The modern judicial attitude toward removing a teacher from the classroom based merely on his or her private sex life was expressed quite well by one court in 1969.

> Surely incidents of extramarital heterosexual conduct against a background of years of satisfactory teaching would not constitute "immoral conduct" sufficient to justify revocation of a life diploma without any showing of an adverse effect on fitness to teach.[22]

Where having relations with members of the same sex is concerned, no controlling court decision has as yet been rendered. However, one court has held that a teacher who had engaged in a limited non-criminal HOMOSEXUAL relationship could not have his teaching CERTIFICATE revoked.[23] In addition, another court, confronted with a case involving the dismissal of a homosexual, held that "immorality" as a grounds for dismissal was unconstitutionally vague, and suggested that in order to lawfully dismiss a person who happens to be a homosexual, there must exist some

20 *Jarvella v. Willoughby-Eastlake City School Dist.*, 233 N.E.2d 143, 146 (Ohio, 1967).
21 *Hale v. Bd. of Education, City of Lancaster*, 234 N.E.2d 583 (Ohio, 1968).
22 *Morrison v. State Bd. of Education*, 461 P.2d 375, 383 (Cal., 1969).
23 *Ibid.*

nexus between the conduct complained of and the person's fitness to teach.[24]

In 1974, a New Jersey court held that a tenured male teacher who underwent sex-reassignment surgery to change his external anatomy to that of a female could be dismissed from a public school on the sole ground that his retention would result in potential harm to the students. Paul(a) Grossman taught students aged ten to 12. The court specifically stated that its decision was limited to Mrs. Grossman's fitness to continue teaching in the Bernardo Township school system. No opinion with respect to her fitness to teach in a district where her presence would not create such sensation and notoriety was expressed by the court.[25]

What these cases and the many others like them are saying is that teachers are not required to live their private lives under the close scrutiny of their employers. While it is true that school officials are rightfully allowed to consider a teacher's conduct outside the classroom as well as within, in order to lawfully justify dismissal on the grounds of the teacher's personal conduct there must be a showing that such conduct has a deleterious effect on the teacher's ability to perform his or her necessary duties. Where no such interference can clearly be shown, the courts cannot and will not uphold the dismissal.

FREEDOM OF ASSOCIATION

The First Amendment of the U.S. Constitution provides that individuals have the right to peacefully assemble. Within this guarantee of a "right of ASSEMBLY" is freedom of association. This means that people have a right to associate with the people or groups of their choice, and they may not be punished for doing so. This was not always true. In the early 1900's, white teachers in small towns were not allowed to have black friends, entertain them, or be seen in public with them. On the other hand, in many parts of the South, it was fatal for black teachers to have white friends. At one time, being a member of the Ku Klux Klan was grounds for dismissal in some communities, while refusing to join was grounds for removal in some others.[26]

---

24 *Burton v. Cascade School District*, Union High School #5, 353 F.Supp. 254 (U.S. Dist. Ct. Ore., 1973).

25 In re *Grossman*, 316 A.2d 39 (N.J., 1974).

26 Beale, H. K. *Are American Teachers Free?* Charles Scribner's Sons, p. 402 (1936).

Employee Organization Activity

In the past, participation in any form of labor activity, especially attempts to organize a labor organization, was particularly frowned upon. As one writer relates: "In Cleveland there was a fight in 1914 over the teachers' attempt to organize a union. The teachers were beaten, forced to disband the union, and sign a 'yellow-dog' clause in their new contracts promising not to join." [27] As late as 1920, St. Louis ordered that any teacher who joined a union was to be dismissed.

Now, the courts clearly hold that teachers, which includes administrators, are free to join an employee organization, assume leadership in it, actively attempt to increase its membership, negotiate with the school board on behalf of the organization, and advocate the organization's viewpoints. The teacher may not be punished for engaging in such activities even though such activity may become quite vigorous. However, should the teacher's activities cause material and substantial harm to the educational process, the First Amendment protections may be lost. In addition, mere membership in an organization which conducts unlawful STRIKES is not grounds for dismissal. The employee must be shown to have the intent to bring about the illegal objectives of the organization. For practical reasons, however, school boards do not dismiss teachers even where they actively engage in unlawful strikes. (See also COLLECTIVE BARGAINING.)

Political Activity

Teachers and other public employees have often been prevented from engaging in various forms of political activity. However, court cases decided in the 1960's and early 1970's clearly established that teachers cannot be punished for engaging in peaceful civil rights activities during non-school hours. In addition, it has been established that other forms of political activity can be restricted only where a countervailing state interest exists.

Under this countervailing state interest test, laws which attempt to ban public employees from engaging in *all* types of political activities have been found unconstitutional. Similarly, *non-partisan* political activity which does not affect the teacher's fitness or classroom performance may not be prohibited.

---

[27] *Id.* at 397.

Where *partisan* political activity is concerned, the COURTS came to a split of authority, some holding that partisan political activity could be curtailed, and some holding that it could not. Finally, in mid-1973, the U.S. Supreme Court settled the issue. In upholding the validity of the Hatch Act, the Supreme Court held that federal and state governments *can* bar public employees from engaging in partisan political campaigns. Justice White suggested that the reasoning behind this ruling was the belief that:

> [I]t is in the best interest of the country, indeed essential, that federal service should depend on meritorious service rather than political service, and that the political influence of federal employees on others and the electoral process should be limited.[28]

The Supreme Court's decision means that laws are constitutional which prohibit state employees in the classified service from:

1. Soliciting or receiving funds for a partisan political purpose;
2. Being a member of a political party committee; or
3. Being a candidate for any political office.

However, keep in mind that while the Supreme Court said that the state *can* prohibit its employees from engaging in the previously mentioned partisan political activities, the state is *not* forced to do so.

Although some state laws require the teacher to resign if he or she is a candidate for PUBLIC OFFICE, some states have special laws which specifically allow teachers to run for the legislature or hold other public offices. Some laws also allow a teacher to be a candidate, but require that he or she take a LEAVE OF ABSENCE without pay during the campaign; and some require the teacher to resign if elected. The Supreme Court's 1973 decision would clearly uphold these more limited restrictions on the teacher's partisan political activity as well as the laws which totally prohibit partisan political activity.

In addition, though some state laws may not specifically provide that teachers are prohibited from engaging in various political activities, certain legal principles would be a sufficient basis for upholding reasonable restrictions. For example, depending on the state's constitution and the nature of

---

[28] *United States Civil Service Commission v. National Association of Letter Carriers*, 93 S.Ct. 2880, 2886 (1973).

the position, a teacher elected to certain public offices may be required to relinquish his or her teaching position when the two positions threaten to present a CONFLICT OF INTERESTS. Also, in campaigning for or against school board members or superintendents, the teacher may lawfully be subjected to restrictions which are necessary to prevent a material and substantial disruption in the order and efficiency of the school system. For example, rules preventing teachers from campaigning during school hours or campaigning against their immediate superiors would be upheld.

Subversive Organizations

"Guilt by association" is not allowed under the U.S. Constitution. Therefore, the Supreme Court of the United States has ruled that mere membership in a subversive organization is not enough to justify dismissal or other non-criminal sanctions. The teacher must be shown to have intent to bring about the illegal objectives of the organization before he or she may be punished. The Supreme Court stated that the reasoning behind such a ruling is that:

> **Those who join an organization but do not share its unlawful purposes and who do not participate in its unlawful activities surely pose no threat, either as citizens or as public employees. Laws . . . which are not restricted in scope to those who join with the "specific intent" to further illegal action impose, in effect, a conclusive presumption that the member shares the unlawful aims of the organization.**[29]

Where there exists a compelling state interest, teachers can be required to disclose membership in various organizations, but absent such an interest, the teacher has a protected right of PRIVACY.

See also ANTI-SUBVERSIVE LAWS; FLAG SALUTE; LOYALTY OATHS; PLEDGE OF ALLEGIANCE.

FREEDOM OF RELIGION

DISCRIMINATION based on RELIGION touched members of every faith in the early 1900's. Jewish teachers had difficulty finding a teaching position nearly everywhere. Gentiles had difficulty finding employment in

---

[29] *Elfbrandt v. Russel*, 384 U.S. 11, 17 (1965).

Utah, while Mormons had trouble obtaining positions outside of large cities, Utah, and the Northeast. Catholics could find positions in large Northern cities, but had difficulties elsewhere. Agnostics and atheists were forced to remain in large cities.[30]

The Constitution forbids discrimination based on religion. As a result, it is unlawful to refuse to employ, to dismiss, or to fail to renew a teacher's contract based on his or her religion—or lack thereof. The Supreme Court also has declared non-sectarian exercises in the schools to be unconstitutional. It follows that a teacher would have the right to refuse to participate in non-sectarian exercises.

See also: ANTI-EVOLUTION STATUTES; BIBLE READING; PRAYERS; SEX EDUCATION.

PROTECTION FROM ARBITRARY, CAPRICIOUS OR DISCRIMINATORY ACTION

Teachers not only have a constitutionally-protected right of freedom from dismissals, NONRENEWALS, or other forms of punishment for exercising their substantive constitutional rights; they also are protected from state action which:

1. Is patently arbitrary or capricious; or
2. Is discriminatory.

To assure teachers that the state action is not in violation of substantive constitutional rights, is not patently arbitrary or capricious, or is not discriminatory, necessitates DUE PROCESS procedures. (See DUE PROCESS.)

See also: CIVIL RIGHTS ACT OF 1871; CIVIL RIGHTS ACT OF 1964; DISCRIMINATION; EQUAL PROTECTION; RENEWAL.

Construction. A school board's authority to contract for construction of of school BUILDINGS is governed by state STATUTES. Where such authority is either expressly or impliedly granted, school board officials may construct buildings which are suitable for educational purposes. Wide discretion is allowed.

---

[30] Beale, H. K. *Are American Teachers Free?* Charles Scribner's Sons, pp. 497-516 (1936).

In planning construction of school buildings, the board may employ an architect. The architect will be entitled to reasonable compensation for his or her work, even if the buildings he or she designs are not constructed. Bidding requirement statutes do not apply to employment of architects because of the professional and aesthetic nature of the employment.

Boards of education can require performance BONDS of the contractor with or without statutory authority. Bonds for payment insurance to laborers and material-men are sometimes required to be obtained by statute, and failure to acquire such bonds may subject the board members to personal liability. The Contractor will be entitled to recover the contract price, less deductions for omissions or delays, when the construction has been made in good faith and in substantial performance.

See also: MECHANIC'S LIEN; PROPERTY.

Contempt of Court. Contempt of court is any act which is calculated to embarrass, hinder, or obstruct a court in the administration of justice, or calculated to lessen its authority or dignity. "Direct" contempt of court is an act committed in the immediate presence of the court. "Indirect" contempt of court occurs when a person fails or refuses to obey a lawful order.

See also: INJUNCTIONS; STRIKES.

Continuing Contract Laws. Continuing contract laws generally provide for what is known as "spring notification." Continuing contract law of the spring notification type requires that the teacher be given advance notice of NONRENEWAL of his or her contract. Generally, these laws do not require that the teacher be given a statement of the reasons for the non-renewal.

Under a continuing contract law, unless the school board *properly notifies* the teacher to the contrary *by the date specified* in the statute, the teacher's contract is deemed to be automatically renewed for the succeeding school year. Where proper notice has not been given by the specified date, the teacher should communicate within a reasonably short period of time (ten-15 days) his or her acceptance of the "new" contract. If the school board refuses to issue the contract to the teacher, the teacher can bring an action in MANDAMUS which will compel the board to do so.

A basic difference between this type of law and a TENURE law is the absence of provisions requiring notice, a statement of the charges, proof of cause, and a right to a hearing before the teacher's employment can be terminated.

See also: DUE PROCESS; RENEWALS; TEACHERS, dismissals.

Contracts, construction. See BUILDINGS; CONSTRUCTION.

Contracts, teacher. A contract is a mutual agreement to definite terms that is supported by consideration. Both parties must have the capacity to sign and the contract must be lawful in its purpose or it is not binding.

The contract under which the teacher works is the single most important concern he or she should have. (In this section, the term teacher is meant to include administrators.) All of the express and implied rights, duties, and responsibilities could be outlined in the teacher's contract. Therefore, teachers should seek to obtain clear and comprehensive contracts.

Making up a contract is like making up a law. In other words, even though the law might not say a teacher has the right to an open hearing at any dismissal, that right can be granted by contract. If the law does not mention GRIEVANCE procedures, grievance procedures can be adopted pursuant to a binding AGREEMENT. If a teacher does not have TENURE rights, they can be granted through a contract. The teacher's contract is the most important thing under which he or she works. Unfortunately, it is often far too ambiguous and fails to be very inclusive.

In all contracts, there are terms. Generally, for example, the contract will say that the teacher is to teach in the school system at the elementary or secondary level. It is possible for teachers to negotiate that the contract will say at what school and at what grade level. Otherwise, a TRANSFER could be made without the teacher's approval. For example, teachers generally talk with their principal or superintendent and they agree at what school and at what grade the teacher will teach. However, the contract that is signed is generally silent as to that outside agreement. When the school year begins, it is therefore possible for the teacher to be assigned to a different school or a different level than actually agreed upon.

The terms under which the teacher works are not all in the signed agreement itself. There are outside terms that are often incorporated into the teacher's contract by reference. Somewhere in the contract one will almost always find a statement that says something like: "This agreement is subject to the laws of this state and the duly adopted rules and regulations of the State Board of Education and of the district, and by this reference, said laws, rules, and regulations are made a part of this agreement the same as if fully set forth herein." That sentence is very significant to the teaching agreement. By that sentence, the teacher is put under constructive notice of all RULES and regulations of the state and local board. Those rules and regulations are made to be terms of the contract. They bind the teacher, and if he or she violates the rules or regulations, he or she is breaching the contract. A breach of the contract is generally grounds for dismissal.

The contract also binds the school board. Therefore, if the local board adopts policies regarding board members' duties, administrators' duties, and various procedures for such things as EVALUATIONS, dismissals, grievances, and RENEWALS, the board is bound by these policies. If the board does not follow these policies, it would be in breach of contract. The teachers' negotiating committee should seek to have the board outline administrators' duties in relation to teachers, and the duties of the school board. The negotiating committee would be well-advised to seek a written policy providing that teachers will be afforded DUE PROCESS and fundamental fairness in cases of dismissal, NONRENEWAL of contracts, and in all matters relating to the teacher's duties of instruction, SUPERVISION, and safety toward students. Once the policies are adopted, the teachers are protected by their contracts. Sometimes that is a far better protection than the state STATUTES provide.

The Elements of a Contract

Up to this point we have been talking about contracts and their terms in general. In order to better understand the teaching contract and its importance, it is necessary to further develop what is required for a contract to come into existence and to be legally binding. First of all, a contract is an *agreement*. Two parties agree to bind themselves to certain terms. The contract, to be binding, does not always have to be signed. Oral contracts are just as binding as written contracts; they are just harder to prove. However, what is known as the statute of frauds does require that employment contracts lasting over a year, contracts for the sale of goods over $500, and contracts for the sale of real PROPERTY all have to be in writing. There are a few other types of contracts that have to be in writing, but in general, all other contracts are binding even though oral.

In addition to the agreement, there must be *consideration*. Consideration, for our purposes, is something of value given or promised for some act or promise by the other person. The teacher promises to teach. The board promises to pay for services rendered. This is valuable consideration and is therefore binding. Consideration given does not have to be of equal value. One can promise to give something or perform services which are of more value than what is promised in return, or vice versa, but the contract will be binding nevertheless.

In addition to agreement and consideration, all parties to a contract must have the *capacity* to enter into the contract or it is not binding. For example, a minor lacks the CAPACITY to enter into a binding contract, and his or her agreements are voidable. Teachers in order to effect a binding agreement must have proper legal capacity. In order for a teacher to have the capacity to enter into a contract, the teacher must have proper CERTIFICATION. In some states, the teacher must be certified prior to signing the contract. In other states, the teacher must only be certified prior to beginning the performance of his or her duties. Teachers who are not properly certified cannot force payment for their teaching services. This is important to note because many CERTIFI-CATES expire during the summer and are sometimes forgotten about until the school year begins.

The school board, as well as the teacher, must have the legal capacity to enter into a contract. (See SCHOOL BOARDS.) Only the board acting as a whole has the capacity to enter into contracts. The superintendent or individual board members all lack capacity in and of themselves to sign an agreement and bind the school district. Realistically, the superintendent makes the contract offer, but that offer is later ratified by the board and only then becomes binding.

In talking about contracts, it is necessary to mention the terms "offer" and "acceptance." A contract, though offered, becomes binding only upon acceptance. The offer must meet certain legal requirements. Generally, the offer must state: (1) the services the teacher is to render; (2) the compensation to be paid; (3) the time for the services to begin; and (4) the time for the services to end. Furthermore, the offer must be made with the present intent to enter into the contract and to bind oneself. Future intent does not constitute a binding offer.

Some difficulty arises in this area when districts do not come out with their contracts until after budgets and negotiations are settled. Therefore, in such cases, deadlines for renewal are passed and letters of intent are sent. These letters constitute binding offers even though they are not concrete proposals. The letters state that the board intends to hire the teacher, and asks if the teacher intends to accept. The board's offer is binding if the teacher accepts it. In the first place, if the board has passed the deadline for renewal notice, it is required to renew the teachers' contracts in most states. If the deadline for renewal notice has not passed, this is still a binding offer, subject to getting some of the terms finally settled. The teacher's acceptance is not necessarily binding even though the board's is. The board knows what the teacher has to offer, and the teacher's terms are not going to change. The teacher, on the other hand, does not know the essential ingredients of the board's terms, and so accepts "subject to" a final acceptance at a later date.

Once an offer is made, it must be accepted in order for a binding contract to come into existence. The acceptance must be clear and unequivocal and with the present intent to bind oneself. Furthermore, there are generally laws or procedures that have been adopted regarding proper acceptance. If the law says that the teacher must accept in writing, verbal acceptance would generally not be sufficient. If the law says that the teacher must accept within a certain period of time, then that time limit must be met. Time limits and procedures are extremely important, and the teacher is under constructive notice of those regulations.

In addition to offer and acceptance, there are things called counter-offers and rejections. These can be important. If an offer is made and it is not accepted, but the party makes a counter offer, the original offer dies and cannot be later accepted. For example, if the school board offered the teacher a position at $4000 and the teacher wrote back and said he or she would take the job if they offered $9500, the teacher has made a counter-offer. If the board rejects the counter-offer, the teacher cannot say, "Okay, I'll accept the job at $4000." Before the teacher can get that job, the board must reoffer the position or there is no contract.

A rejection does the same thing. If the board makes an offer and the teacher says he or she will not accept, the teacher cannot later change his or her mind and bind the board without another offer being made. It works both ways. An offer, once accepted, cannot be unilaterally rescinded. DAMAGES can be awarded according to the terms of the contract if one of the parties breaches the agreement.

Services Required Under Teaching Contracts

Problems frequently arise in the interpretation of teachers' contracts. All of the teacher's duties will not be listed in the contract or in the school

board policies. All teachers are bound by certain implied duties or responsibilities that come with the job of teaching. The school board has the right
to make reasonable RULES and regulations. The school board also has
the right to impose certain duties on teachers. This right, however, is
limited.

In the past, teachers were expected to wash the floors of their class, to
act as custodians after the children left, to participate in certain community activities, and to follow without question the instructions of the
local board. Today, it is clear that the teacher has no duty to do menial,
janitorial, or police services. However, the teacher, as a professional, has
the duty to do those things which are reasonable and which naturally
relate to instruction, supervision and safety. This means, for example,
that the teacher can be required to supervise a study hall or the cafeteria.
The teacher could be required to attend faculty meetings or open house,
or even go to a football game as a supervisor. Nevertheless, the extra
duties that are imposed on the teacher must be reasonable and they must
generally relate to the teacher's classroom position or to collateral activities
stemming from the classroom. The duties cannot violate the teacher's
constitutional rights, and in no way can the duty be punitive or discriminatory. All duties must be distributed impartially, they must be reasonable
in time and number, and all teachers should have to take their share of
the duty. (See also ASSIGNMENTS, non-classroom.)

Supplemental Contracts

"Collateral" or "supplemental" contracts cause many special questions
and problems to arise. Supplemental contracts are frequently entered into
where the teacher is hired to teach in the classroom and is also hired to
coach, direct plays, direct a musical band, or is otherwise required to
perform extra services that require a substantial amount of extra time.
In some districts, the classroom contract is agreed upon and signed, and a
separate supplemental contract covering the extra services is agreed upon
and signed. The problems are whether or not both contracts have to be
offered, and does breach of one constitute breach of the other. The answer
to these questions depends upon the facts and circumstances under which
one was hired. For example, if it was written or verbally agreed upon that
the teacher would teach English and also coach the baseball team, the
teacher would have to do both. In other words, if the two contracts are
really meant as one, and the coaching requirement was a major considera-

tion made in hiring the teacher, breach of one contract is a breach of the other. On the other hand, if the teacher were teaching English and the board asked him to coach baseball and he did so, he would not have to continue coaching in subsequent years because the coaching position was not contingent or dependent upon the teaching position. Therefore, the question is whether or not the coaching duties go to the essence of the teaching position. If they do, the two positions and the two contracts would legally be treated as one.

The reverse of the above is also true. The school board could not take the coaching position away from the teacher without complying with the state's dismissal law or other due process procedures if the teacher were hired for the purpose of teaching *and* coaching. This can be a very tricky area. In most instances, the supplemental contract is not a tenured type of right. Although the teacher may be tenured, it is seldom that he or she would have tenure as a coach unless hired that way in the original contract. Nonrenewal of the supplemental contract without reason is generally allowed unless the teacher can show that it goes to the very essence of the main teaching agreement. Nevertheless, if the teacher can show that the supplemental contract, though not part of the main agreement, was not renewed for reasons that are in violation of the Constitution, he or she would be entitled to have the contract renewed and the COURTS would do so. Many potential problems could be solved by including the duty of coaching in the main contract, or by establishing written procedures for termination of supplemental contracts.

Termination of Contracts

There are times when, after a contract has been signed, the teacher wants to be released from the obligation. Performance can be excused without liability in certain instances. An *"act of GOD," death, fraud, duress, impossibility of performance,* and *prolonged illness* are examples where one can be excused without liability. However, transfer of a teacher's spouse will not excuse performance.

One may also be excused for performance without liability where there is a mutual rescission. This means that where both parties agree to rescind their mutual obligations, they may do so without liability. Of course, this is true only where fraud or undue influence is not exerted. The rescission must come voluntarily, or there is no mutual agreement.

In addition to the aforementioned possibilities for excuse of performance, there are many state statutes which give reasons or excuses to rescind without liability. In many states, the teacher can rescind without liability 60-90 days prior to school beginning. If the teacher does so, there can be no liability even though the school board does not have the same right of rescission.

Performance is also not required under certain conditions where the contract is "void" or "voidable." A void contract is one that is unenforceable at its inception and forever. It simply does not exist. A voidable contract has the possibility of becoming permanently valid. In fact, a voidable contract is valid in its inception. It has all of the elements, but there is something wrong with it that makes it possible for one of the parties to set it aside. Examples would be where the contract is signed by the superintendent under his apparent authority (not actual authority) or a contract that is signed at an improperly called board meeting. These contracts could be set aside and declared void by the school board. If they were, they would not become binding. However, once the voidable ingredient of the contract is eliminated (such as later adopting the contract at a proper meeting), the contract becomes enforceable for both parties.

Breach of Contract

As one can see, there are times when contracts can be terminated without liability. However, without a lawful excuse, if one party wrongfully fails or refuses to perform his or her duties under a contract, he or she is said to have "breached" the contract. For wrongful breach of contract, DAMAGES may be assessed against the breaching party. However, if no injury results, there will be no grounds for assessment of damages unless the state sets up certain penalties. For example, if a teacher walked out of the school building improperly, and refused to return to his or her teaching duties, that teacher would be in breach of contract. If the school district were able to find a substitute teacher of the same general caliber and for the same amount of money, there would be little financial loss, if any, to the district, and therefore the amount of damages to be assessed would be negligible. Because of this, some states have enacted laws providing for financial penalties for wrongful breach of contract (e.g. unlawful STRIKES), and many state laws provide that if a teacher improperly resigns, his or her teaching certificate can be revoked for a certain period of time. Also, some statutes have declared that where a teacher has a contract with one district, any contract made with another district covering that same period of time is automatically void. This type of statute acts as a deterrent against improper breaches of contract on the part of teachers. It works to a certain extent. However, one should note that the local school district does not have the power to revoke the teaching certificate. That power lies only with the state board of education which granted the certificate. The local board may only initiate the action and recommend that the certificate be revoked. Without the recommendation, no revocation will be made, and even with a recommendation, the ultimate decision rests with the state board.

If, instead of the teacher breaching the contract, the board improperly breaches, the teacher's damages are not automatic. In other words, there is a duty on the part of the teacher to mitigate or lessen the damages as much as possible. For example, assume that a teacher is hired for one year at $9000. After three months, the local board improperly dismisses him or her. The teacher has been paid $3000, and therefore has $6000 coming on the contract. In addition to other possible damages, one would ordinarily expect to get $6000-plus. This, however, is not necessarily true. It is the teacher's duty, even though he or she is not the wrongdoer, to go out and try to find another teaching job. The teacher must try to lessen the school board's damages. If another teaching job is: (1) available; (2) within reasonable distance of the old position; and (3) is of the same general status and pay, the teacher is generally obligated to try to obtain the position. On the other hand, if the position is inferior, an unreasonable distance away, or is not available, *the teacher does not have to go to work.*

Mitigation of damages has some other implications one should know. If the teacher does take another position, even though it is inferior, the money earned will be subtracted from the original damages. The point made before was that if an equal position was available, the teacher *had* to take it or the money he or she "would have" earned would be deducted. Where there is an inferior position available, the teacher is not obligated to accept, but if he or she does, the money may be subtracted.

The money the teacher earns is not subtracted automatically. If the position the teacher accepted could have been performed while teaching at the old position, that money will not be subtracted. For example, if the teacher secured an evening sales position, that money would not be subtracted from the $6000 because the teacher could have held down the sales position while teaching at the same time.

"Substitute teaching" is considered not to be of an equal status to a regular teaching position. If the school board wrongfully dismisses a teacher, that teacher should try to mitigate damages, but since substitute teaching is not of the same status, the teacher is not obligated to do this kind of work. However, if the teacher does accept substitute teaching employment, the amount of money earned may be used to mitigate damages because the teacher could not have earned this money had he or she been employed under the original contract.

For a further discussion of dismissal of teachers under contract, see DUE PROCESS; TEACHERS, dismissals.

Contributory Negligence. If a person is injured as a result of another person's NEGLIGENCE, but that person was also acting in a negligent manner and, therefore, contributed to his or her own injury, the person is said to have been contributorily negligent and, under many states' laws, he or she cannot hold the other person liable.

Contributory negligence is the oldest and most commonly used defense against negligence. Under this rule, even if a teacher or an administrator was negligent, he or she will not have to pay if the injured party was also negligent. This same rule applies in everyday life. If one is driving at an excessive rate of speed and someone negligently drives out in front of the first person's car, both are negligent and neither one can collect, unless there is "no fault" insurance or the state in which the accident occurred has abolished contributory negligence and has adopted a system of COMPARATIVE NEGLIGENCE.

It is ordinarily difficult to prove that a child is contributorily negligent. At COMMON LAW, there was a conclusive PRESUMPTION that a child under the age of seven could not be contributorily negligent. From age seven to fourteen, there was a rebuttable presumption that a child was not capable of contributory negligence; and beyond the age of fourteen, it was assumed that a child of that age could contribute to his own injury. Although these age limits are not hard and fast rules today, they still work as measuring sticks to determine contributory negligence. The jury will also consider the maturity and intelligence of the child involved. The ultimate question is: Did the student act as a reasonable and prudent person of like age, intelligence, and experience would have acted under the same or similar circumstances? If not, under contributory negligence laws, there will be no liability even though there was negligence on the part of the teacher or administrator.

Controversial Matters, right to teach. Generally, see ACADEMIC FREEDOM; CONSTITUTIONAL RIGHTS OF TEACHERS AND ADMINISTRATORS; CURRICULUM.

Evolution — see ANTI-EVOLUTION STATUTES.

Obscene literature—see CONSTITUTIONAL RIGHTS OF TEACHERS AND ADMINISTRATORS; OBSCENITY.

Religious matters — see BIBLE READING; PRAYERS; RELIGION.

Sex — see SEX EDUCATION.

Social issues — see CONSTITUTIONAL RIGHTS OF TEACHERS AND ADMINISTRATORS.

Corporal Punishment. Corporal punishment is disciplinary action through the use of physical force.

School officials have to exercise reasonable control over the students who are for the school period within their charge. The oldest method of control is the use of physical force. Physical force as a method of disciplining students is not uncommon within the school systems in the United States, and there are many arguments for and against such discipline.

Many people are under the belief that the concept of IN LOCO PARENTIS is diminishing within the schools. Nevertheless, the COURTS are willing to uphold the teacher's right to use reasonable force to correct student conduct, and in stating the reasons for upholding this right, many courts say that the teacher stands in the shoes of a parent.

However, what the courts feel and what educators feel may be two different things. The courts may hold that a teacher has the right to use corporal punishment, but at the same time, there seems to be a trend in education to limit its use by very restrictive standards and to very limited circumstances. Furthermore, even though the courts generally hold that a teacher has the right to use corporal punishment, local school board policies or administrative rules can seriously limit its use, and these policies and rules must be followed.

As of September, 1973, only two states (Georgia and New Jersey) have laws which state that corporal punishment is not to be used. Even so, exceptions are carved out by the cases and by statute. All other states allow corporal punishment to some extent. Many states provide that corporal punishment shall only be administered by the chief school officer or the principal, and in the presence of another adult. Other states make it necessary to notify the parent first except in cases of open and flagrant violations of the school's authority. Furthermore, there is some authority to the effect that, if a parent refuses to grant permission to use corporal punishment, that refusal must be given consideration. Generally, however, a parent has no right to stop the punishment unless it is unreasonable or in violation of state law.

Over the years, guidelines have been developed that need to be followed. These must be followed very carefully if one wishes to escape liability. First of all, the teacher is still a substitute for the parent to a certain extent, and may administer moderate correction. However, one must be certain that the action is reasonable, prudent and necessary under the circumstances. Generally, it is reasonable and prudent if:

1. State law allows corporal punishment.
2. It is administered for correction purposes and without malice.
3. The student knows why he or she is being punished.
4. It is not excessive and is in consideration of the student's age and sex.
5. It is administered in the teacher-student relationship.

Remember, one should never hit a student in the face, unless it cannot be helped. Also, a teacher should never use force likely to cause permanent physical injury. If the teacher does use excessive force, or causes extreme or serious injury, there are times when he or she may be held liable for BATTERY. On the other hand, if the physical contact is reasonable under the circumstances, and if the teacher follows the aforementioned five guidelines, liability will not be imposed. This is true even if there are other alternatives for reprimanding a student and controlling his or her conduct.

See also: GOVERNMENTAL IMMUNITY.

Courts, organization of the federal system. Article III, Section I of the Constitution of the United States provides that, "The judicial Power of the United States shall be vested in one supreme Court, and in such inferior Courts as the Congress may from time to time ordain and establish." The Supreme Court of the United States is, therefore, the highest court in the land, and its decisions are the law of the land.

Below the Supreme Court, the Congress has established the United States

Courts of Appeals. These are federal circuit courts, and the United States has been divided into ten circuits plus the District of Columbia circuit. There is one Court of Appeals in each circuit. These courts review decisions of the district courts.

Below the U.S. Courts of Appeals are the U.S. District Courts. These are trial courts for cases under federal jurisdiction. Except for a few special kinds of cases, decisions of the district courts may be appealed to the Court of Appeals.

The Supreme Court *can* review all lower federal court decisions, and any cases in state courts which involve questions concerning federal statutes or the U.S. Constitution. There are two methods of bringing cases before the Supreme Court: (1) by writ of CERTIORARI; and (2) by appeal. The Supreme Court does not have to review a case, but it will review a case if it qualifies for Supreme Court review and has sufficient merit to warrant additional hearings.

The chart on page 91 describes the federal court system. However, the Court of Customs and Patent Appeals have not been included, as they seldom are involved with school cases.

Courts, organization of the state system. As a check upon the legislative and executive branches of government, the judicial branch was established to ensure impartial justice. The state judicial power is frequently vested in one state supreme court, along with an intermediate court of appeals in some states, circuit courts, and inferior courts which the state legislature establishes.

In addition to the regular court system, and in order to ease the burden on the courts and alleviate excessive costs and time, several states have vested certain ADMINISTRATIVE AGENCIES with the power to settle GRIEVANCES in the educational system. (See COMMISSIONER OF EDUCATION.)

The courts to a large extent exercise a policy of non-interference with school administration. Since the legislature has the responsibility for determining educational policy, the courts will rule on the legality of school RULES and action, but will not question the propriety.

The courts usually follow precedent in making rulings, but they are not forced to do so, and will not do so where the facts and circumstances are different and where the important factors are different due to changing times. However, as Justice Holmes once stated, "The life of law has not been logic; it has been experience." (See also STARE DECISIS.)

FEDERAL JUDICIAL SYSTEM

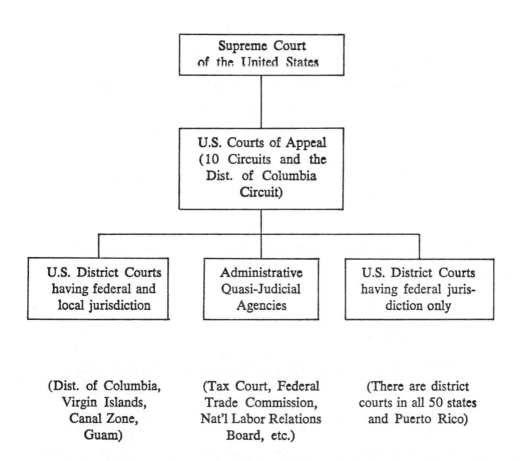

STATE JUDICIAL SYSTEM

```
┌──────────────────────────────┐
│       State Supreme Court     │
└──────────────────────────────┘
```

(The title of this court varies, but it is generally called by one of the following names: Supreme Court, Supreme Court of Errors, Court of Appeals, Supreme Judicial Court or Supreme Court of Appeals.)

```
┌──────────────────────────────┐
│          Trial Courts         │
└──────────────────────────────┘
```

(Less than half of the states have intermediate appellate courts; but where they do, a majority of cases are finally decided by them, and the cases are not heard by the State Supreme Court.)

```
┌──────────────────────────────┐
│    Circuit or Superior Courts │
└──────────────────────────────┘
```

(These are trial courts having general jurisdiction. The title of this court varies, but it is often called a Circuit Court, District Court, Court of Common Pleas, Superior Court, Chancery Court, and in New York, Supreme Court.)

```
┌──────────────┐   ┌──────────────┐   ┌──────────────┐
│ Probate Court│   │ County Court │   │Municipal Court│
└──────────────┘   └──────────────┘   └──────────────┘
```

(Also called a Surrogate Court or Orphans' Court. This court handles wills, administration of estates, guardianship of minors and incompetents.)

(This is also called a district court in some states. It has limited jurisdiction in both civil and criminal cases.)

(This is a city court which generally handles traffic cases and other less important matters.)

```
┌──────────────────────────┐
│   Justice of the Peace    │
│           and             │
│     Police Magistrate     │
└──────────────────────────┘
```

(These courts have very limited jurisdiction
in both civil and criminal cases.)

Cross-Examination. Cross-examination is the questioning of a witness in a trial or a hearing, or the taking of a deposition, by the party opposed to the one who produced the witness.

See also: DUE PROCESS; EXPULSION OF STUDENTS.

Curriculum. The legislature of each individual state has the power to prescribe the kind of curricula the schools shall or shall not offer, and the manner in which it shall be offered. This is true so long as the curricula does not conflict with the state's constitution or the Constitution of the United States.

Most of the state legislation prescribing certain subjects to be included in the school's curriculum involves requirements that instruction be given on the U.S. and state constitutions, in civics, American history, citizenship, and a few others. In addition, some state constitutions and statutes specify that instruction is to be given in the English language. Nevertheless, in states or districts where there are many students who speak a foreign language and do not speak English very well, instruction by teachers trained in the additional language may be required.

However, for the most part, state legislatures only prescribe broad general guidelines and delegate the authority to prescribe the specifics of the curriculum to the state board of education and local SCHOOL BOARDS. As a general rule, with the notable exception of curriculum of a sectarian nature, the COURTS have been reluctant to interfere with school board authority in prescribing curriculum. There are some cases providing certain legal principles which are to be noted though.

The COURTS have upheld the right of the school board to include language, arts, music, math, science, dance and physical education in its curriculum. However, the board cannot require students to engage in BIBLE READING, FLAG SALUTES, the PLEDGE OF ALLEGIANCE, or PRAYERS.

If the school has RULES requiring students to take certain prescribed courses, the question often arises as to what action should be taken if a parent refuses to allow a child, or the child himself refuses, to take a certain course. One early case established the rule that if a student refuses to take a required course, the proper administrative action is expulsion, not physical punishment of the child. In this case, *State v. Mizner*, 50 Iowa 145 (1878), the child had refused to take an algebra class because her father had instructed her not to do so because of her rather frail physical condition. School officials had decided to punish the child by whipping her.

Where the student's objection is based on religious or constitutional reasons, the school may have no power to force the student to take the objectionable course. The school would have to make reasonable allowances for the child, and would have no right to punish the student for refusing to take the course. For example, in a 1962 Alabama case, a high school girl contended that she could not be required to participate in a physical education class because the costume was immodest and sinful, and even if she were allowed to dress in a costume which she personally did not find immodest, she could not be forced to remain in the presence of other girls who were dressed in an immodest and sinful manner. She also objected to some of the kinds of required exercises. School officials, when confronted with the girl's religious objections to the course, reacted very responsibly. They proposed that the girl could wear clothing that she herself considered to be suitable, and that the girl would not be required to perform exercises which she considered immodest. The girl and her parents still objected, and sued the school. The court held that the school's concessions were sufficient to overcome the girl's religious objections to the manner of dress, and that there was no violation of her constitutional rights by requiring her to be in the same class with girls who were dressed in a manner which she considered immodest and performed exercises to which she objected. *Mitchell v. McCall,* 143 So.2d 629 (Ala. 1962).

The school has the authority to prescribe that certain courses shall be offered, but cannot require students having religious objections to participate. This rule frequently arises in cases involving such courses as dancing and SEX EDUCATION.

School boards have the authority to require members of a school supported athletic team, of which participation in is voluntary, to wear prescribed special uniforms. Authority of the school to purchase such uniforms is dependent upon state statutes. (See FUNDS.)

D

Damages, contract. Damages is the pecuniary compensation which may be recovered in the courts by any person who has suffered loss, detriment or injury to his person, property, or rights through the wrongful act or NEGLIGENCE of another.

Damages may be recovered where the school board has breached its contract with a teacher or administrator, or where the board has dismissed or failed to renew a teacher's or administrator's contract for reasons which are in violation of the Constitution. Where appropriate, such damages may include the following items:

1. Back pay. Loss of salary is recoverable. However, if the person accepts or is offered employment of a same general status, pay, and location, part of the salary received or available from the offered employment may be used to mitigate damages. (See CONTRACTS.)

2. Difference between new salary and salary from former position. Consideration will be made of the increments the person would have received.

3. Losses or costs incurred in attempting to find new employ-

ment. These costs include such items as resume or printing
costs, placement services costs, postage, telephone, travel
expenses, costs incurred in obtaining additional training,
etc.

4. Cost involved in selling old residence and moving to a new
place of residence. These costs include real estate broker
fees, travel costs, costs of motels and meals while seeking
or waiting for a new home, closing fees involved in purchase of new home, etc.

5. Losses from withdrawal from a state or local retirement
system, if the new position does not provide the same or
an equivalent system.

6. Medical or dental expenses incurred which would have
been covered under the school district coverage and fringe
benefits.

7. Medical or dental insurance costs incurred to obtain coverage equivalent to the employer's policies.

8. Loss of compensation from a part-time position the person
or his spouse had, but lost.

9. Costs of transportation to a school which is further from
the old school.

10. Damages for emotional pain and suffering.

11. Attorney's fees in some cases.

See also: CIVIL RIGHTS ACT OF 1871.

Damages, torts. In torts, damages means the money which is awarded an
injured party and which is paid by the wrongdoer.

In torts, whether intentional or negligent, there are basically three types
of damages that are awarded. First of all, there is what is called "compensatory damages." Compensatory damages are awarded in order to make an
injured party "whole." If a student breaks a leg as the result of someone
else's NEGLIGENCE, he or she has to be made whole again. One cannot
give back an unbroken leg, so a price tag is put on the suffering. That is,
the jury decides how much the broken leg is worth, and grants the injured
party a judgment for that amount. Included in compensatory damages is
anything the injured party lost. Doctor bills, lost wages, property damages,
and the like are all included. The court attempts to put the injured party

back into the position he or she was in prior to the injury, or would have been in had the injury not occurred.

In addition to compensatory damages, there is something called "punitive damages." Rather than making one whole, punitive damages are awarded for the purpose of deterring further acts of the kind which caused the injury. These damages are meant to punish the wrongdoer. For ordinary negligence or contract breaches, punitive damages are not allowed. They are generally only allowed for gross acts which shock the public conscience. If the jury finds that the defendant acted with willful, wanton disregard, there is a possibility that punitive damages will be allowed. Also, these damages may be awarded when "intentional" torts or injuries are committed.

The third type of damages awarded are called "nominal damages." These damages are awarded when there is really no injury or the injury is only slight. The amount of money awarded is nominal, but in some cases, punitive damages of a more significant sum may accompany the award. These damages are awarded to prove a point.

Debts, authority of school to incur. See BONDS.

Decertification. In cases of decertification of teachers or administrators, the requirements of DUE PROCESS must be complied with. Along with the necessity for compliance with procedural due process (e.g. a fair hearing), the act complained of as grounds for decertification must relate to the person's fitness as a teacher or as an administrator. For example, the mere fact that a teacher had engaged in a limited non-criminal HOMOSEXUAL relationship was held to be not valid as a grounds for revocation of the person's teaching CERTIFICATE. The court explained that there must exist a nexus between the conduct complained of (i.e. being a homosexual), and being able to perform the duties of a teacher (i.e. fitness as a teacher). *Morrison v. State Board of Education,* 461 P.2d 375, 386 (Cal. 1969).

The grounds for decertification are specified in state STATUTES. The grounds differ somewhat among the states, but the laws frequently specify that grounds for decertification may exist where the person:

1. Has been convicted of a crime involving MORAL TURPITUDE;
2. Has been convicted of a crime involving various sexual offenses;

3. Knowingly made any false statement in applying for a certificate; or

4. Has been guilty of gross neglect of duty or any gross unfitness.

Additional grounds are commonly added to the above. Grounds for the decertification, and the procedures required, frequently are more stringent than the grounds required for dismissal.

See also CERTIFICATION, teachers.

Defamation. As a noted legal writer once stated:

> **A defamatory communication usually has been defined as one which tends to hold the plaintiff up to hatred, contempt, or ridicule, or to cause him to be shunned or avoided. This definition is certainly too narrow, since an imputation of insanity, or poverty, or an assertion that a woman has been raped, which would be likely to arouse only pity or sympathy in the minds of all decent people, have been held to be defamatory. [Rather:] Defamation is . . . that which tends to injure "reputation" in the popular sense: to diminish the esteem, respect, good will, or confidence in which the plaintiff is held, or to excite adverse, derogatory, or unpleasant feelings or opinions against him . . . [It] is defamatory upon its face to say that the plaintiff has attempted suicide, that he refuses to pay his just debts, that he is immoral or unchaste, or "queer," or has made improper advances to women, or is having "wife trouble" and is about to be divorced; that he is . . . an anarchist . . . a bastard [or] a eunuch . . . because all of these things obviously tend to affect the esteem in which he is held by his neighbors. Prosser, William L., *Law of Torts* (3rd Ed. 1964), West Publishing Co., St. Paul, Minn., pp. 756-758.**

Civil defamation resulted from the belief that except where certain necessary privileges are granted for special statements, people have a right to enjoy their reputations free from false or defamatory remarks. The most important element of this tort is that the PLAINTIFF'S reputation must have been injured by statements, written or oral, which were made by the DEFENDANT. The above quoted definition points out that in order to injure a person's reputation, that person must have been lowered in the esteem or opinion of persons whose standard of opinion can be determined by the court. The remark does not have to lower the plaintiff in the esteem of everyone in the community or even the majority, but it must lower him or her in the opinion of a respectable majority. Note that for defamation to occur, it necessarily requires communication with a third person. As a result, if a person were to write a letter in which false and malicious statements were made regarding person B, there would be no possible action for defamation unless the letter was read by someone other than A or B.

Much has been written about defamation, and teachers and administrators must be aware of the liability that can be imposed for committing this intentional tort. By "intent," we do not mean to say that the teacher or administrator "intends" the injury. In torts, the law provides that where a person intends to do an act, he or she is deemed to have intended all of the consequences which reasonably result from that act.

Unfortunately, faculty rooms seem to be a "hot spot" for rumors about students, teachers, and administrators. People do not have the right to cast untrue aspersions on others, but there are times when it is necessary to make disparaging comments simply because they are required for reports and files. This raises the question of when can a teacher or administrator make such comments without being subject to liability.

The law provides protection for certain "privileged" statements, and when such protection is granted, liability will not be imposed even though the statements made are defamatory. What is termed an "absolute privilege" exists in court proceedings. Under this privilege, a witness may make a statement which, even though not true, can be made without liability being imposed. This protects a witness who might not otherwise speak. The liability for deliberate lying under oath is perjury, not slander.

Another privilege is called the "qualified privilege." This means that although certain statements are privileged, the privilege is qualified by the requirements of "good faith" and "statements made within the scope of one's duty." In other words, the person making the statement can have no malice, and the statement must be based upon reasonable grounds. Furthermore, even if there is good faith, the statement must be made within the scope of the teacher's or administrator's duty.

There are some additional defenses available in defamation suits. It has been said that "truth" is always a defense. That is not exactly true. Truth is a defense, but only so long as there is no malice involved. If one person knows of something another person did in the past, he or she cannot go spreading it around with the intent to maliciously injure that person. On the other hand, if the person merely comments on the defamatory fact without any malice intended, then truth will be a defense.

Many times an educator is asked to evaluate students and to make comments about their progress or personality. Psychological evaluations should be totally left out of the opinions, unless the person making the statements is a qualified counselor. Such comments can be not only erroneous, but also defamatory. Even though one acts in good faith, that person must be competent to make the judgments. However, where the educator, acting in good faith and with reasonable grounds, makes a statement regarding a student's conduct, personality, etc., that statement will enjoy the protections of a "qualified privilege," and that educator will not be liable for defamation. (See also STUDENT RECORDS.)

Defendant. The defendant is the party in a lawsuit who is being sued.

Demotions. Where a teacher is reassigned, the new position must be one of equal pay and status or the reassignment may be considered tantamount to a demotion. If it is in fact a demotion, the teacher would be entitled to his or her DUE PROCESS rights and cause is generally required in order for a demotion to be allowed without liability for DAMAGES.

Sometimes it is difficult to determine which positions have equal status. Reassignment of an assistant principal to a classroom teaching position would be considered a demotion. However, it has been held that it is not a demotion to reassign a ninth grade teacher to teach the sixth grade, where the sixth grade teaching assignment is at an equal salary. The court reasoned that:

> There is no less importance, dignity, responsibility, authority, prestige, or compensation in the elementary grades than in the secondary. Here the young student still pliant, still susceptible, still in the formative stage, receives his earlier impression, his inspiration, his direction. To be charged with the responsibility for children in this critical time of their lives is no demotion. *In re Santee's Appeal*, 156 A.2d 830, 832 (1959).

The reassignment must be to a position in which the teacher is certified. If the teacher is forced to incur new training at his or her own expense, to remain certified in the new position, the reassignment would be tantamount to a demotion.

Desegregation. In the 1950's and 1960's, the courts took affirmative action to force the desegregation of public schools. The separation, seclusion, or isolation of a group of persons from the general mass is impermissible even though it results from either intentional segregation or what is termed "de facto" segregation. De facto segregation exists where individual schools have large portions of minority students, even though no affirmative action to segregate is made by the school board. Housing patterns and belief in the "neighborhood school" has been the chief cause of de facto segregation, but many times attendance zones, transfer policies, etc. contribute. Today, court rulings as well as some state statutes and local board policies prescribe that the school board has the duty to take affirmative action to achieve racial balances and correct segregation of all forms, including de facto segregation. Exactly how desegregation is to be achieved will depend on the facts and circumstances existing in the individual district; but a look at the history of the court decisions will provide an insight into the kind of action which is required under the law.

In 1890, Louisiana enacted a statute which provided for "equal but separate accommodations for the white and colored races, by providing two or more passenger coaches for each passenger train. . . ." A black man refused to abide by the law, entered a coach designated for whites, and refused to leave. In challenging the constitutionality of his arrest, he contended that DISCRIMINATION on the basis of color violated the Fourteenth Amendment of the U.S. Constitution. The Supreme Court said that the state law was not discriminatory, and thereby gave legal sanction to the concept of separate but equal.[31]

The separate but equal principle prevailed until 1954. At this time, the Supreme Court in the famous *Brown v. Board of Education* [32] case, reversed the earlier decision and ruled that segregation in the public schools solely on the basis of race deprives the children of the minority group of equal educational opportunities, even though the physical facilities, faculty, and other tangible assets may be equal. Under this Supreme Court ruling, the law provides that segregation solely on the basis of race denies EQUAL PROTECTION as guaranteed under the Fourteenth Amendment of the U.S. Constitution. Where the state undertakes to provide education, it must make it available to all persons on an equal basis.

In 1955, the Supreme Court said that it was up to the courts to decide whether or not school officials implement desegregation, and provided that the local courts must supervise compliance with the Supreme Court's

---

[31] *Plessy v. Ferguson*, 163 U.S. 537 (1896).
[32] *Brown v. Board of Education of Topeka*, 347 U.S. 483 (1954).

decision in the 1954 *Brown* case.[33] School officials were required to implement desegregation in *good faith and with all deliberate speed*. However, local courts were allowed to consider problems in administration, transportion, personnel, etc., as well as the adequacy of plans to effectuate transition to a non-discriminatory school system.

By the mid-1960's, the Supreme Court realized that the test of "good faith and all deliberate speed" was not moving at a rapid enough pace. In 1965, the Supreme Court ordered immediate desegregation in one case,[34] and it also ruled that desegregation of faculties was mandatory.[35] In 1968, the Supreme Court stated that the school board had a "responsibility to achieve a system of determining admission to the public schools on a non-racial basis." The Court added that: "The burden on a school board today is to come forward with a plan that promises realistically to work, and promises realistically to work *now*." [36] "Freedom of choice" plans allowing students to choose their own public school were found unacceptable because they were ineffective in causing desegregation. However, such plans were allowed if a clear showing could be made that a proper *result* occurred and that there were no more effective, speedy systems.

These cases forecast the Supreme Court's decision of 1969, which resulted in a ruling that: ". . . continued operation of segregated schools under a standard of allowing 'all deliberate speed' for desegregation is no longer constitutionally permissible. . . . The obligation of every school district is to terminate dual school systems at once and to operate now and hereafter only unitary schools." [37] As a result, desegregation is now required to be implemented immediately in all school districts. School officials must desegregate and tokenism will not be tolerated by the courts.

In deciding how to desegregate and whether or not the board is taking affirmative action, the following areas of consideration are often mentioned by the courts:

1. Racial quotas. As a starting point, some courts suggest that the district-wide black-white ratio may be used as a guideline for desegregating the schools.

---

33 *Brown v. Board of Education of Topeka,* 349 U.S. 294 (1955).
34 *Rogers v. Paul,* 382 U.S. 198 (1965).
35 *Bradley v. School Board of Richmond,* 382 U.S. 103 (1965).
36 *Green v. County School Board of New Kent County,* 391 U.S. 430 (1968).
37 *Alexander v. Holmes County Board of Education,* 90 S.Ct. 14 (1969).

2. Zoning. Zoning, pairing or grouping is allowable as a means of desegregation *if it works*. Cost, convenience, and travel time should also be considered in determining if this is an equitable solution.
3. Transportation (busing). Although no one wishes to see the demise of the neighborhood school, in some cases, busing of students may be the only way in which the board can affirmatively desegregate "now."
4. Desegregation plans. These are most important. Schools may have the duty to establish plans to provide space and free transportation to "segregated" schools. If supported by valid reasons and equitable considerations, it may be possible to maintain a one-race school if it does not indicate de jure segregation.

The important thing to recognize is that the COURTS are saying that the schools must do everything within their power to desegregate. They must use all of their available resources when necessary, and this includes staff assignments, pupil transfers, selection of school sites, and transportation. In the past, busing was used to maintain segregated schools; it is also possible to use busing as a means of establishing unitary school systems.

In considering racial quotas, many school districts and some courts differ in their philosophy regarding the requirements of desegregation. The main question advanced is, "Is a majority white racial ratio in each school constitutionally required?" In Richmond, Virginia, the city's school district plans for desegregation were required to be designed to create a white majority of students in each school.[38] The theory behind this controversial 1972 court decision was that advantaged children will teach their less advantaged peers (i.e. the "peer group learning" theory). Also advanced in support of this plan was the "disparity theory," suggesting that schools having predominantly white students have superior resources. Under this rationale, it is believed that a white majority in every school is the key to equal educational opportunity.

Some courts have rejected the "white majority" theory. One court said:

> **[The white majority theory] . . . is no more than a resurrection of the axiom of black inferiority as justification for separation of the**

---

[38] *Bradley v. School Board of City of Richmond, Va.,* 462 F.2d 1058 (4th Cir. 1972).

races, and no less than a return to the spirit of *Dred Scott*. The inventors and proponents of this theory grossly misapprehend the philosophical basis for desegregation. It is not founded upon the concept that white children are a precious resource which should be fairly apportioned. It is not . . . because black children will be improved by association with their betters. Certainly it is hoped that under integration, members of each race will benefit from unfettered contact with their peers. But school segregation is forbidden simply because its perpetuation is a living insult to the black children and immeasurably taints the education they receive.[39]

As these cases demonstrate, the desegregation issues are not settled now, nor can they be in a few definitive court decisions. The legal arguments for both sides also are not well settled. Much of the responsibility must be shouldered by Congress, state legislatures, and state and local school boards. By attacking what may at first seem the outer edges, (e.g. discrimination in housing and employment), the desegregation problems are at the same time being attacked.

Fiscal disparity reform, although given life-strengthening blood by the *"Serrano"* [40] and *"Rodriguez"* [41] decisions, suffered a setback by the Supreme Court in 1973.[42] *But,* their effect was not transitory. As a result of these two cases, many legislatures and school boards will in the future be confronting school finance with attention being given to financial distribution on a power-equalizing formula. By confronting the causes as well as the immediate effect of social disparity, desegregation is also being attacked, but with a much more long-lasting effect.

See also: CONSTITUTIONAL LAW.

Detention. See FALSE IMPRISONMENT.

Diplomas. Legal questions occasionally arise as to when and for what reasons may the school district withhold a diploma. School officials have the authority to make the determination as to whether or not a student has completed the required courses necessary for his or her degree. If the student has not done so, the diploma may be withheld.

---

[39] *Brunson v. Board of Trustees*, 429 F.2d 820, 826 (4th Cir. 1970).
[40] *Serrano v. Priest*, 487 P.2d 1241 (Cal., 1971).
[41] *Rodriguez v. San Antonio Independent School District*, 337 F.Supp. 280 (U.S. Dist. Ct. Texas, 1971).
[42] *San Antonio Independent School District v. Rodriguez*, 93 S.Ct. 1278 (1973).

A diploma may not be withheld where a student refuses or fails to participate in a COMMENCEMENT EXERCISE. The reason for this is that the actual granting of the diploma is merely a ministerial act. Therefore, where the student has successfully completed the necessary courses, school officials are obligated to grant the student his or her diploma.

See also: CURRICULUM.

Discharge of Teachers. See DUE PROCESS; TEACHERS, dismissals.

Discretion, school board. See SCHOOL BOARDS.

Discrimination. Discrimination on the basis of race, sex, or RELIGION is prohibited by the Constitution of the United States and by various federal and state laws. What this means to each particular school district, student, or teacher cannot be simplified into set tests or categories. Each case must be considered separately, giving due weight to all of the varying facts and circumstances. However, there are certain questions which frequently arise and the COURTS have provided answers to these questions as well as to problems which are similar in nature.

Race or sex may be considered in making certain determinations where there is strong public policy supporting such considerations. For example, it is permissible to take race into account in order to remedy the effects of past racial discrimination. Granting blacks the first opportunity to apply for positions, or hiring a certain quota of minority persons before considering white applicants has been found to be valid and lawful.

Discrimination on the basis of sex is not allowed unless a showing can be made of a compelling governmental interest sufficient to uphold the reasonableness of the discrimination. Under this rule, it is allowable to select males to teach wrestling for boys, etc., but it is not permissible to pay women less for performing the same tasks male teachers perform, and promotions to administrative positions cannot be prevented. The CIVIL RIGHTS ACT OF 1964 also forbids discrimination in employment practices without a showing of bona fide occupational reasons. (See also MATERNITY LEAVE.)

It is discriminatory to single out one particular group of teachers for special treatment unless there is a reasonable basis for such classification. Therefore, it is illegal to discipline a group of teachers merely for belonging to a particular civil rights organization or to a certain political party.

In addition, although a particular school rule or policy may be valid, if it is applied in a discriminatory manner, it will be held to violate the requirements of EQUAL PROTECTION.

See also: ATHLETICS; CONSTITUTIONAL LAW; CONSTITUTIONAL RIGHTS OF TEACHERS AND ADMINISTRATORS; DESEGREGATION; RELIGION.

Dismissal, teacher. See DUE PROCESS; TEACHERS, dismissals.

Disposition of School Property. See REORGANIZATION. ·

Dissolution of School Districts. See REORGANIZATION.

District Reorganization. See REORGANIZATION.

Donations, acceptance of. School districts may accept donations of PROPERTY to be used for school purposes. However, if there is a personal interest involved on the part of a school official, the COURTS will invalidate the gift. The same is also true if the donated property will create an undue influence on the school board members.

Where there is no undue influence created, and the site is not improper or unsuitable for a proposed school, the school board may accept a donation of land. It has been held that no undue influence is created where a board member grants land to the school district, even though the member may indirectly benefit. For example, in one case, a board member gave some property to the school district. This was challenged on the grounds that the member owned adjoining property, and this gift would therefore increase the value of his remaining property. The court held that this was an insufficient reason to void the gift because there was no undue influence created and the site was suitable for a proposed school. *Territory v. McGuire,* 76 P.165 (Okla. 1904).

Dress, manner of. See APPEARANCE; CONSTITUTIONAL RIGHTS OF TEACHERS AND ADMINISTRATORS; STUDENT RIGHTS.

Dual Enrollment. See SHARED-TIME.

Due Process. (For a preliminary introduction, see CONSTITUTIONAL LAW and CONSTITUTIONAL RIGHTS OF TEACHERS AND AD-

MINISTRATORS.) Due process of law is a fundamental right guaranteed to citizens of the United States under the Fourteenth Amendment of the Constitution. This amendment provides in part that: "No State shall . . . deprive any person of life, liberty or property, without due process of law; . . ." Basically, due process is a course of proceedings following established rules which assure enforcement and protection of individual rights. The guarantees of due process require that every person is entitled to the protection of a fair trial.

The main essential element of due process is *fundamental fairness*. Generally, this means a fair hearing, a fair trial, and a fair judgment. State ADMINISTRATIVE AGENCIES, like SCHOOL BOARDS, are prohibited from taking arbitrary or capricious action, and this means that every citizen must be given a fair opportunity to present his side of a dispute where the dispute implicates interests of life, liberty, or property.

The formality and extent of the due process requirements depends on the seriousness of the threatened harm to the interests of life, liberty, or property. Teachers, administrators, and students all have a right to due process of law. The due process rights of non-tenured teachers and administrators are at times different from those of tenured teachers and administrators. The requirements of due process where teachers and administrators are concerned is explained in the following section. Students' rights to due process are examined in the section of this book entitled "EXPULSION OF STUDENTS."

Teachers' and Administrators' Due Process Rights

Substantive protections guaranteed under the Constitution are of little benefit if procedural protections do not exist. Without requiring certain procedures to be complied with in order to remove or punish a teacher for an alleged wrongdoing, the teacher is left with only an administrator's honesty and good faith. Administrators also need procedural protections to safeguard them from the arbitrary or unconstitutional actions of their superiors. Both teachers and administrators are entitled to due process. However, in the remainder of this section, for reasons of simplification, only the term teachers will be used to explain the protections of due process.

Due process procedures are necessary to assure teachers that the reasons for their dismissal, NONRENEWAL, or DEMOTION do in fact exist, and that they are not based on rumors, false facts, or reasons which are in violation of their constitutional rights. The chilling effect on substantive rights without such procedures is clear.

In cases involving the demotion, nonrenewal, or dismissal of a teacher, three questions must be asked in order to determine whether or not minimum due process has been granted:

1. Does the teacher have a right to a statement of the reasons for the proposed action?
2. Does the teacher have a right to a hearing?
3. Where a hearing is required, what kind of hearing is necessary? i.e., What procedures are demanded in order to satisfy the requirements of due process?

The answer to these questions depends to some extent on the status of the teacher; i.e., whether the teacher is tenured or nontenured.

Tenured Teachers

Tenured teachers have a right to a statement of the reasons for the proposed action and a fair hearing. A tenured teacher cannot be lawfully dismissed unless both of these requirements are complied with. Where they are not, the teacher will be entitled to DAMAGES and RE-INSTATEMENT.

TENURE is granted by state STATUTES and, in some cases by local school board policies. In the states which provide for tenure by statute, the law also prescribes certain procedures which must be complied with in order to lawfully dismiss a tenured teacher. In the nearly 40 states which have provided these procedures, *strict* compliance with the procedures is mandatory.

The dismissal procedure required is fairly formal. In a few states, the school board has the power to set up its own dismissal procedures, while in other states, the statutes prescribe the procedure. Nevertheless, the school board must comply with the rudiments of due process. As a result, there is a great deal of uniformity in this area, and the following dismissal procedure is either identical or substantially similar to the procedure required in nearly all states. (*Note—the following dismissal procedure uses the words "you" and "your" to mean teachers.* This procedure is quoted from: Gatti and Gatti, *The Teacher and the Law,* Parker Publishing Co., West Nyack, N.Y., 1972, pp. 118-121.)

Dismissal Procedure

Suspension:

If your school principal has reason to believe it is necessary for the best interests and proper functioning of the school, you may be temporarily suspended without a hearing. The allowable period is usually five days, and most states provide that you are entitled to your salary during this period. If desired, dismissal proceedings must be initiated during this period or you must be reinstated. *For a tenured teacher, the dismissal procedures required for termination of a contract during the term are the same as the procedures required if the school board intends to consider non-renewal of your contract.* (This procedure is also required in most states for the dismissal *during the contract term* of a non-tenured teacher, but not where merely non-renewal of his contract is in issue.)

Recommendation to Terminate:

If it is believed that *cause* exists which would justify your dismissal, written notice is filed by the superintendent, or sometimes the school principal, with the school board. This notice recommends termination and states the evidence on which the recommendation is based.

Investigation:

A great majority of the states provide that the school board handles the hearing and all of the procedures involved. (Many people feel that the board cannot be impartial in deciding the issues, and as a result, several states have provided for the hearing to be handled by others, who in turn make a recommendation to the board. . . .) An investigation of the complaint is often made by the school board. Usually, the board has the school superintendent or principal interview teachers and students, and in general do the investigating.

Notice to You:

If the board determines that good cause probably exists which makes it desirable to consider termination or non-renewal of your contract, it must furnish you with written notice of intent to dismiss. This notice must be informative, and must clearly tell you that your proposed discharge is to be considered at a designated time and place, at which you will be given an opportunity to answer the charges. This notice must state the reasons for the proposed dismissal. Merely stating the statutory cause is insufficient; the testimony and evidence giving rise to such cause must be summarized.

In other words, the notice must be sufficiently specific to allow you to prepare to meet the allegations.

A few states (e.g. California) and individual school districts provide that you must receive advance notice (90 days) of any teaching deficiencies. This is intended to provide you with an opportunity to correct any remedial deficiencies.

Right to a Hearing:

Tenured teachers have a right to a hearing on dismissal or non-renewal for cause. You must request a hearing within a set time limit or you are deemed to have waived the right. This time limit normally is stated in the notice you receive, and is generally between 15 and 20 days. If you feel that the notice you received was inadequate, demand proper notice before you participate in the hearing; otherwise, you are deemed to have waived any defects in notice. The school board will set a date for a hearing if such a date was not specified in the notice you received.

Preliminary Evidence:

Any evidence which the school board has is generally put on file for you or your attorney's inspection. All of this evidence may be used at the hearing. This means, however, that you may cross-examine opposing witnesses on statements they made in the preliminary evidence, as well as on any testimony they give at the hearing.

Witnesses:

You may subpoena any witnesses or evidence you will need or desire to have at the hearing.

General Nature of the Hearing:

The hearing is basically a formal process. Its main purpose is to allow you to offer evidence and reasons as to why you should not be terminated. The school board must act in good faith in attempting to provide a fair and impartial hearing. The hearing must not be provided merely to announce a prior decision that you have been dismissed; it must be to help the board make a fair and impartial decision.

The Hearing:

The hearing consists of a formal presentation of evidence, and you are given a chance to fully reply to the charges made against you. There is some variation on the formal elements, but most hearings will provide the following safeguards:

THE HEARING'S PROCEDURAL SAFEGUARDS

Right to Counsel—You have a right to be represented by an attorney or your educational union or association. The school board almost always is represented by their attorney.

Testimony of Witnesses Is Given Under Oath—All witnesses are sworn and administered an oath.

Right to Cross-Examine Opposing Witnesses—You have a right to cross-examine witnesses on any testimony they give at the hearing, and on any statements they made in the preliminary evidence. You may impeach the testimony of the opposing witnesses by showing an unworthy reputation for truth and veracity, or by showing bias or prejudice.

You May Introduce Evidence on Your Behalf—You have a right to introduce witnesses or evidence on your own behalf.

You have a right to present any evidence which tends to show that the charges against you are not bona fide, but are really a cover up for bias or violation of your constitutional rights.

Restriction of Evidence—You and the superintendent are generally allowed to present only that evidence which pertains to the charge of misconduct of which you were given notice. Only evidence which is trustworthy should be admitted, but there are few formal rules of evidence. Hearsay is allowed in many circumstances.

Burden of Proof—The burden of proof is on those who are trying to dismiss you. They do not have to prove beyond a reasonable doubt, but only by a "fair preponderance of the evidence." The evidence is sufficient where the alleged facts are established and reasonable inferences may be drawn.

A great deal of discretion is given to the board. The main limitation is that the board's decision must rest on evidence presented at the hearing, not on the board members' personal knowledge of the case, suspicion or speculation.

Stenographic Transcript of the Proceedings—A written record of the hearing is required, in order to facilitate appeal and review.

Written Decision—The school board must make a written decision. This decision must state the cause for the dismissal, if that is the result, and the evidence on which the board relied to support it. Decision of dismissal must be supported by a vote of at least a majority of the entire board.

Resignation—If you intentionally, deliberately, and voluntarily resign before, during, or after the hearing, and your resignation is accepted by the board, it is final. However, if your resignation was due to duress or threats by the school board, it is voidable.

Review of Dismissal Proceedings:

All states provide for some form of review, but the appeal procedures vary greatly among the states. Some states provide for direct appeal to the courts, while some provide for appeal to a state public employee relations board. Still others provide for combinations of these. On appeal, the reviewer will check to see if the proper procedure was followed, if it was fair, and if the decision was supported by the evidence.

Due process also requires an impartial decision. In many instances, it is difficult to expect the school board to render an impartial decision, particularly when the dismissal concerns a controversial teacher who has caught the public's attention. The problem arises from the board's dual role of being the prosecutor and the judge. In addition, the board has employed the administrators who may be recommending the dismissal, and frequently the board must feel compelled to demonstrate confidence in the judgment of such administrators. This is laudable, but it does not make for an impartial decision.

In order to insulate the board from public pressure, the role of both prosecutor and judge, and other potential prejudicial influences, several states have enacted laws which transfer the hearing on dismissal of a tenured teacher: (1) to the courts (as in California[43]); (2) to a state official (as in New Jersey[44]; (3) to a panel composed of one member selected by the teacher, one by the board, and one by the other two (as in Colorado[45]); and (4) to a board composed of educators, teachers, school board members, administrators, and members of the general public (as in Oregon[46]). These are relatively new and progressive laws. They should prove to be beneficial in providing tenured teachers with a fair and impartial hearing. See also ADMINISTRATIVE AGENCIES.

---

[43] Cal. Educ. Code § 13412-13 (1960).
[44] New Jersey Teacher Employees Hearing Act; New Jersey Stat. Ann. § 18 A: 6-10 (1960).
[45] Colo. Rev. Stat. Ann. § 123-18-17 (1968).
[46] O.R.S. §§ 342.085 to 342.955 (1971).

Nontenured Teachers

In January of 1969, David Roth, a nontenured assistant professor at a Wisconsin University, was notified that he would not be rehired at the end of his one-year contract. No reasons were given, and no hearing was offered. Mr. Roth sued the Board of Regents claiming, among other things, that failure to advise him of the reasons for nonretention and failure to grant him a hearing violated his right to procedural due process.

In 1969, Robert Sinderman, a member of the faculty at Odessa Junior College in Texas, was notified that his one-year teaching contract was not being renewed. No explanation for the action was given, and Sinderman was not granted a prior hearing. In his suit seeking reinstatement and damages, Sinderman contended, among other things, that the Regents' failure to provide him with a hearing violated his right to due process.

The *Roth* and *Sinderman* cases were quite similar in the legal issues which they presented. Both cases were appealed through the COURTS and eventually wound up in the hands of the Supreme Court of the United States. The Supreme Court heard the arguments presented in these cases on the same day, and rendered its decisions in the middle of 1972.[47] The Supreme Court held that the requirements of procedural due process apply only where an individual is being deprived of his or her protected interests of "liberty" or "property." When the individual is being deprived of one of these interests, he or she must be granted "some kind of prior hearing." Under this test, Roth lost his case, but Sinderman won his.

The Supreme Court pointed out the fact that mere nonrenewal of a non-tenured teacher's contract is insufficient to require that a hearing be granted. A nontenured teacher's right to a hearing on nonrenewal of his or her contract depends upon whether or not the nonrenewal will deprive him or her of "liberty" or "property." Where either of these interests are implicated, the teacher has a right to a hearing *prior* to the board making a decision regarding nonrenewal. Where the hearing is denied, the teacher is entitled to damages and reinstatement.

The question is therefore, "What is an interest in liberty or property?" The Supreme Court did not attempt to define exactly what the interests are, but it did suggest some definite guidelines. With regard to "liberty," the Supreme Court says that in a free society "the meaning of 'liberty'

---

[47] *Board of Regents v. Roth,* 408 U.S. 564 (1972); *Perry v. Sinderman,* 408 U.S. 593 1972).

must be broad, indeed." Several examples the Court gave were that "liberty" is implicated where nonrenewal:

1. Is based on a charge which might seriously damage a teacher's standing and associations in the community; or
2. Would impose a stigma or other disability on the teacher, such as to foreclose a range of opportunities.[48]

A teacher's standing and associations are seriously damaged where he or she is charged with dishonesty or immorality. In addition, the court said that if a teacher's "good name, reputation, honor, or integrity is at stake" the board must grant notice and a hearing. Remember, "liberty" is to be interpreted broadly, and arguably, charges of disloyalty, incompetence, and insubordination may seriously damage a teacher's standing and associations, particularly in smaller communities. Where no charges have been made, the teacher can attempt to show that a range of opportunities have been foreclosed by the nonrenewal and that this imposes a stigma.

With regard to "property" interests, the Supreme Court said that these take many forms, and that teachers clearly have a property interest safeguarded by procedural due process where:

1. They are "dismissed from an office held under tenure provisions, . . ." [49]
2. They are "dismissed during the terms of their contracts, . . ." [50]
3. They were "hired without tenure or a formal contract, but nonetheless with a clearly implied promise of continued employment." [51]

Property interests protected under the Fourteenth Amendment have certain attributes:

> To have a property interest in a benefit, a person clearly must have more than an abstract need or desire for it. He must have more than a unilateral expectation of it. He must instead, have a legitimate clim of entitlement to it.[52]

---

48 *Board of Regents v. Roth,* 408 U.S. 564, 572 (1972).
49 *Id.* at 576.
50 *Ibid.* at 573.
51 *Ibid.* at 573.
52 *Ibid.*

This legitimate claim can arise out of state law or the rules or under-standings of the parties with regard to the rights and benefits the teacher has secured.

Under the Supreme Court's "property interest" test, a teacher, for example, would have a legitimate claim or entitlement to his position where the district has established a "de facto" tenure policy. This could be done either by written policies, or by statements in the district indicating a clear course of conduct giving rise to the conclusion that teachers in the district shall continue in their positions and shall be removed only for *cause*. Also, some continuing contract laws are written in such a manner as to arguably amount to a sufficient property interest. In their contract negotiations, teachers can seek to have such a de facto tenure policy established.

As a result, where the teacher can show that he or she has a property or liberty interest which is protected by procedural due process, he or she would have a right to a hearing upon request. Proof of the property or liberty interest does not, however, entitle the teacher to reinstatement. At the hearing, he or she must be informed of the grounds for nonretention and must be given an opportunity to challenge their sufficiency. In the absence of statutes or school board policies or understandings to the con-trary, nontenured teachers' contracts may be nonrenewed with or without establishment of *cause*. As a result, unless the teacher can show that the reasons for nonretention are arbitrary, capricious, wholly unsupported in fact, or in violation of his or her constitutional rights, the school board would not be compelled to renew the teacher's contract.

Type of Hearing Required

The final question which must be answered is: "What are the procedural requirements sufficient to safeguard due process?" As previously stated, these requirements vary accordingly to the kind of interest at stake and the seriousness of the threatened harm to an interest.

When a teacher has tenure, due process requires that a procedure identical or substantially equivalent to the dismissal procedure provided on page 109 be followed. This is a formal, strict procedure, but a tenured teacher has an extremely strong property interest and the threatened harm is great.

When a nontenured teacher has a contract and is being threatened with *dismissal during the term of the contract,* due process would require com-pliance with a formal procedure identical or substantially equivalent to the dismissal procedure required to be followed with regard to dismissal of a tenured teacher. This is specifically required by statute in many states, including California and New York. In addition, this is required by a long line of cases, and it was also suggested to be the rule by the Supreme Court in the *Roth* case.

When a nontenured teacher is being subjected to a nonrenewal which implicates interests of liberty and property, the procedural requirements are totally dependent on the interest at stake. Where the district has a "de facto" tenure policy, it will, of course, be required to comply with the established procedure necessary to dismiss tenured teachers. However, in the absence of a "de facto" tenure policy, a nontenured teacher may be nonrenewed for little or no reasons at all. As a result, due process would only require an informal type of hearing. The teacher must be granted the opportunity to submit evidence on his or her behalf. Also, the BURDEN OF PROOF rests with the teacher and not with the board. Only where the teacher can make a reasonable showing that the reasons for the nonrenewal are arbitrary, capricious, wholly unsupported in fact, or in violation of his or her constitutional rights would the school administration be obligated to show that the reasons are valid.

In summary, no teacher may be dismissed, suspended or in any manner substantially punished without a hearing where:

1. The teacher is tenured;
2. The teacher is under contract; or
3. The reasons for the action would deprive the teacher of "liberty" or "property."

Most of the hearings required are formal in nature, but in some cases involving nonrenewal or nontenured teachers, due process may be satisfied by an informal hearing. In the absence of deprivation of interests of liberty or property, a nontenured teacher whose contract is not being renewed is not entitled to a hearing or even a statement of the reasons.

Dues Checkoff. When authorized by statute, dues checkoff permits public employers, on the voluntary written authorization of the public employee, to regularly withhold organizational dues from the employee's wages and to transmit such funds to the designated employee organization. Only recognized employee organizations representing a majority of the employees in an appropriate unit are eligible for dues checkoff privileges.

Duties of Teachers. See CONTRACTS; NEGLIGENCE.

E

Elementary and Secondary Education Act of 1965. This act was aimed at "poverty." Title I of the act granted federal aid in excess of one-and-one-half billion dollars for expenditures made on children of low income families. Title II made millions of dollars available to the states for acquisition of library resources, texts, and audio visual materials. Title III granted money to local school districts to establish supplementary education programs. Preschool education and replacement of inadequate facilities was also encouraged under the provisions of Title III. Title IV made money available for education research and training facilities. Title V made $25,-000,000 available to state departments of education for improvement of services to local districts. Title VI provided for the establishment of a bureau within the office of education to handle the education and training of handicapped children; while Title VII set up general provisions.

Parts of this act have been continued. It is important to note that the administration of federal financial programs, such as the ones established under this 1965 act, are subject to the CIVIL RIGHTS ACT OF 1964.

Eminent Domain. See BUILDINGS; PROPERTY.

Employee Organizations, right to join. See ASSEMBLY; COLLECTIVE BARGAINING; CONSTITUTIONAL RIGHTS OF TEACHERS AND ADMINISTRATORS.

Enjoin. To enjoin means to require a person, by writ of INJUNCTION from a court of equity, to perform, or to abstain or desist from, some act.
See also: STRIKES.

Equal Employment Opportunity Commission. See CIVIL RIGHTS ACT OF 1964; DISCRIMINATION; EQUAL PROTECTION.

Equal Protection. The Fourteenth Amendment to the U.S. Constitution provides in part that: "[N]o state shall . . . deny to any person within its jurisdiction the equal protection of the law." Through this provision of the Constitution, the COURTS are able to protect people against DIS-CRIMINATION. The schools have been involved in many suits involving the equal protection clause, many of which have involved DESEGREGA-TION, MARRIED STUDENTS, PREGNANT STUDENTS, and preg-nant teachers.

The equal protection clause does not necessarily require that every person must be treated in exactly the same manner. People may be classi-fied in a manner which is relevant to a rule or program where that rule or program is constitutionally permissible. As a result, when a question of equal protection arises, two things will come under close scrutiny by the courts: (1) the *purpose* of the rule, and (2) the *classification*. The classi-fication will be strictly reviewed by the courts, when fundamental interests of individual liberties are implicated. Classifications based on race, RE-LIGION, or national origin are *presumed invalid* because they are almost always *irrelevant* to a valid purpose of a permissible rule or program.

In the past, classifications *based on sex* were almost always upheld. The courts of the past could rightfully be termed "chauvinistic," as their opinions reflected the view that women were meant to be homemakers. For example, in 1908, the Supreme Court upheld maximum working hours for women;[53] and in 1948 a Michigan law prohibiting women from tending bar was upheld.[54] In 1956, an Oregon court ruled that a law which prohibited women from wrestling was valid.[55] But women's status in the eyes of the law began to change, and by the late 1960's and early 1970's, the courts were willing to scrutinize classifications based on sex. Many laws and rules which singled out women for special treatment were found to be un-

---

[53] *Muller v. Oregon*, 208 U.S. 412 (1908).
[54] *Goesaert v. Cleary*, 335 U.S. 464 (1948).
[55] *State v. Hunter*, 300 P.2d 455 (Ore. 1956).

constitutional, including those which: required unmarried women under the age of 21 to live in the dormitory when attending a state college;[56] excluded women from an all male college in the state university system;[57] and required pregnant women to take mandatory MATERNITY LEAVES.[58]

In an important landmark decision, the California court invalidated a prohibition against women tending bar. In doing so, the court said:

> **Sex, like race and lineage, is an immutable trait, a status into which the class members are locked by accident of birth. . . . [As such it] frequently bears no relation to ability to perform or contribute to society.[59]**

The court went on to say that a suspect classification like sex tends to impose a "stigma of inferiority and second class citizenship on those persons who are so wrongfully classified."

The Supreme Court of the United States also was faced with an equal protection case involving discrimination on the basis of sex. An Idaho statute provided that when both a male and female were equally entitled to administer a decedent's estate, the male was to be preferred. In 1971, the Supreme Court said that such a classification based merely on sex was subject to scrutiny under the equal protection clause. The Court enunciated the test to be applied in determining the validity of classifications based on sex:

> **A classification "must be reasonable, not arbitrary, and must rest upon some ground of difference having a fair and substantial relation to the object of the legislation, so that all persons similarly circumstanced shall be treated alike."** [60]

One main question is frequently asked regarding special classifications for women: "Aren't women more delicate than men?" In a 1972 case, a court answered this question in the following way:

---

56 *Mollere v. Southeastern Louisiana College*, 304 F.Supp. 826 (U.S. Dist. Ct. La., 1970).

57 *Kirstein v. Rector and Visitors of University of Virginia*, 309 F.Supp. 184 (U.S. Dist. Ct. Va., 1970).

58 *Williams v. San Francisco Unified School District*, 340 F.Supp. 438 (U.S. Dist. Ct. Cal., 1972).

59 *Sail'er Inn, Inc. v. Kirby*, 485 P.2d 529, 540 (Cal. 1971).

60 *Reed v. Reed*, 404 U.S. 71, 76 (1971); (footnote omitted).

> To anyone who even once has viewed women participating in a roller derby, the argument that all women are the weaker sex, desirous of only the more genteel work, carries little weight. The success of women jockeys is further evidence of which we take notice. It is no longer possible to state that all women desire or have an "interest" in any one type or classification of work. Some women have the desire, ability, and stamina to do any work that men can do." [61]

Through this line of cases, it is apparent that the equal protection clause prevents discrimination on the basis of sex, as well as on the basis of race, religion or national origin. School districts' hiring and promotional practices and distribution of benefits are all subject to this provision of the Constitution.

See also: ATHLETICS; CIVIL RIGHTS ACT OF 1964; CONSTITUTIONAL LAW; CONSTITUTIONAL RIGHTS OF TEACHERS AND ADMINISTRATORS; STUDENT RIGHTS.

Establishment of Religion. See RELIGION.

Evaluations. Evaluations are used to judge a teacher's effectiveness within the classroom. Generally, the purpose of an evaluation is to aid the teacher in improving his or her teaching methods.

Many state statutes require that teachers be evaluated a certain number of times during each school year. Evaluation forms are recommended and certain procedures are given. In some states, local school districts are allowed to prescribe their own evaluation procedures. Once these procedures are enacted, they must be followed, or else the evaluation is without legal effect.

In order to promote cooperation, the teacher should be notified of the time proposed for an evaluation. Time should be set aside after the evaluation to discuss any possible problems. The teacher also should have an opportunity to rebut any evaluation he or she thinks is unfair. Furthermore, the teacher should have the right to have others evaluate his or her performance, if he or she thinks the first evaluation is too subjective or inaccurate.

---

[61] *Pittsburgh Press Co. v. Pittsburgh Commission on Human Relations,* 287 A.2d 161, 168-169 (Pa., 1972).

Evaluations are more of an administrative function than a legal one. However, many statutes provide that the teacher has a right to a copy of the evaluation, must sign that it has been read, and that there must be provided a space on the evaluation form to rebut anything which has been said. Since the purpose of evaluations is generally improvement, if the evaluation is for any other purpose, the teacher must be told in advance. Otherwise, the evaluation is invalid.

Proper procedures must be followed. This means that if the statute says a teacher is to be "observed," a reasonable observation—long enough to determine areas needing improvement—should take place. An actual evaluation must take place, and as earlier stated, the teacher must be given an opportunity to see and rebut the remarks.

In every teacher dismissal proceeding, evaluations are used wherever possible. Embarrassment at times may result because proper procedures have not been followed, or because the evaluations have not been truly objective. For example, if a teacher is being dismissed for "incompetency," an administrator might, in such case, be confronted by past evaluations directly to the contrary. Another example of a singularly strange occurrence might be where a teacher who has been evaluated only once each year suddenly finds that he or she is evaluated several times after becoming president of the local teachers' association. In some of these instances, it may be possible to show that the real purpose of the evaluation was not for improvement purposes but was really intended as a means for obtaining a possible grounds for dismissal. The teacher would have a right to advance notice of the purpose. The potential for possible prejudice is obvious. It is legally proper to evaluate a teacher more often than is required by statute, but it is not proper to evaluate for wrongful purposes.

Evolution. See ANTI-EVOLUTION STATUTES; RELIGION.

Executive Sessions, school board. See SCHOOL BOARDS, meetings.

Exhibits. An exhibit is a paper, document or other article which is produced and exhibited to a court or an ADMINISTRATIVE AGENCY during a trial or a hearing.

Express Authority. Where a power or right to act is granted in express direct terms, the person to whom this power is granted is said to have the express authority to act on another's behalf without incurring liability. Express authority generally involves some IMPLIED AUTHORITY.

Expulsion of Students. In the past, school officials were practically free to prescribe any and all rules governing student conduct, to enforce such rules, and to discipline or expel students in any manner they deemed desirable. However, in the late 1960's, the COURTS began to give recognition and protection to the idea that education is a right which cannot be denied without a proper reason and without compliance with procedures designed to assure a student that a proper reason does in fact exist. Subsequent to the 1969 Supreme Court ruling that students do not shed their constitutional rights at the schoolhouse gate, the rule of law was clearly established that a student must be granted DUE PROCESS of law in any action by school officials which may result in "serious disciplinary punishment."

The Fourteenth Amendment of the U.S. Constitution provides in part that neither the state nor any of its employees can deprive ". . . any person of life, liberty, or property without Due Process of law." Exactly what this means in relation to student discipline has not been precisely defined. However, as a basic starting point, it is clear that due process requires fairness. The minimum standards of fairness in student disciplinary actions generally require that:

1. School rules must be fair, not ambiguous, and must reasonably relate to the educational purposes of the school.
2. Students and parents must be informed of rules affecting them and for which they may be disciplined.
3. Rules must be specific enough so students can understand what they may or may not do.
4. Where "serious disciplinary punishment" is involved, certain required minimum procedures must be complied with.

School Rules

Three of the above mentioned minimum standards of fairness relate to school rules. Although most of the pertinent aspects of these requirements of due process are covered in the sections of this book entitled "RULES" and "STUDENT RIGHTS," several additional points should be made. Most notably, it must be recognized that a court determination of whether or not a school rule infringing to some degree on an individual's liberty violates the substantive requirements of due process, will be determined in a narrow way. The courts will not rule on the wisdom or expediency of the rule, but instead the courts will question only two things:

1. Whether or not the rule deals with a matter of legitimate state interest; and
2. Whether or not it is a reasonable rule.

Rules deal with a matter of legitimate state interest where they are necessary to protect:

1. The *health* of the students;
2. The *safety* of the students;
3. The *welfare* of the students; or
4. The school from a material and substantial disruption with the order and efficiency in the operation of the school.

Rules are reasonable where they meet the test of dealing with a legitimate state interest, and where the rule has a rational basis and reasonable connection in fulfilling the legitimate state interest. Even though the rule may be harsh or inequitable does not necessarily make it invalid. However, if the rule is in violation of the students' constitutional rights, the school will have to meet a substantial burden of justifying that the rule is necessary to promote the efficient operation of the school. In addition, reasonableness of a rule must be considered in light of:

1. Possible alternatives (e.g. to promote safety around shop class equipment, a hair net may work as well as a hair cut);
2. Seriousness of the punishment (e.g. a rule denying an unmarried PREGNANT STUDENT the right to attend school could only be upheld where a very compelling state interest can be shown);
3. Consistency of application (e.g. if the rule is only haphazardly enforced, it will be seen as arbitrary and unreasonable); and
4. EQUAL PROTECTION (i.e. if the rule applies only to certain classes of individuals, the distinction must reasonably relate to the purpose for which the classification was made).

The question frequently is asked: "Does the student have a right to *notice* of existence of the rule and must the rule be in *writing?*" Generally, the law is that a student must be put on notice that certain conduct is prohibited, at least where the rule infringes on the student's constitutional rights. However, although it might seem appropriate, the courts do not choose to bind school officials to take disciplinary action based only on written rules, because the courts recognize that school officials cannot possibly anticipate all of the possible kinds of student action. As one court stated:

> . . . [W]e would not wish to see school officials unable to take appropriate action in facing a problem of discipline or distraction simply because there was no preexisting rule on the books. *Richards v. Thurston,* 424 F.2d 1281, 1282 (1st Cir. 1970).

Required Expulsion or Suspension Procedures

As previously mentioned, it is not only required that a valid school rule exist before a student can be legally disciplined, it is also imperative that where a "serious disciplinary punishment" is involved, certain minimum procedures must be complied with or the discipline will be in violation of the student's right to due process.

A serious disciplinary punishment is one which involves:

1. A long-term suspension or expulsion (e.g. a suspension from school for more than *5 days* has been held to require a due process hearing);
2. Withholding of a diploma; or
3. A punishment which seriously jeopardizes a student's education or future (e.g. certain kinds of entries made on a student's permanent record will seriously jeopardize his or her future).

Minor misconduct which does not call for serious discipline is not serious enough to require a set procedure, and therefore, summary discipline is allowed (e.g. detention, spanking). However, in the above mentioned cases of possible serious disciplinary punishment, the student is entitled to:

1. Notice of the charges, nature of the evidence supporting the charges, and the consequences if the charges are proven to be true;

2. Notice of a right to a hearing at which he or she may respond to the charges;

3. A fair hearing, including the right to present witnesses and evidence; and

4. A fair and impartial decision.

These four items constitute the minimum requirements of due process. If the student is not granted a right to these protections, any disciplinary action taken will be invalid, will be reversed by the courts, and the student may be entitled to DAMAGES in some cases.

No exact hearing procedure is mandated by the laws of most states. The procedures must therefore be established by the state board of education or by the local school boards. The procedures must be fair and must be reasonable. The following safeguards specify the requirements of a fair and reasonable hearing procedure.

HEARING PROCEDURE FOR SUSPENSION OR EXPULSION OF STUDENTS

1. Rules of procedure for hearings on suspension or expulsion of students should be prepared by all persons concerned: students, teachers, administrators and parents. However, only the school board has the authority to adopt and promulgate the rules.

2. The hearing procedure should be written and circulated to students, teachers, administrators and the students' parents.

3. The hearing procedure rules should specify that in cases of minor infractions, "summary discipline" may be imposed, and no formal due process procedure is required.

4. Written rules specifying "most" of the kinds of conduct for which serious disciplinary punishment may be imposed should be circulated to the students and parents.

5. In a case of serious misconduct for which a serious disciplinary punishment may be imposed, the student is entitled to written notice of the charges and that he or she has a right to a hearing on the charges. The written notice of the charges must be given to the student and his or her

parents. Such notice should include a statement of the evidence against the student as well as what the possible punishment is. This notice should be given at least five days prior to the hearing, in order to give the student time to adequately prepare a response to the charges.

6. An informal procedure for expelling or suspending the student is legally permissible, where the student has been informed of his or her right to a hearing pursuant to section 5 as stated above, but voluntarily chooses the informal procedure.

7. If, pursuant to section 5 as stated above, the student requests a hearing on the charges, the following procedures are required:

   a. *Right to inspect evidence.* The student has a right to inspect the evidence against him or her prior to the hearing. Such evidence generally includes a list of the school's witnesses and copies of their statements.

   b. *Right to present evidence.* The student has a right to present evidence on his or her own behalf and to refute evidence presented against him or her.

   c. *Right to counsel.* There exists a split of authority on this point. The better rule is that a student is too immature and inexperienced to present his or her own side of the issue. Expulsion of a student can seriously impair his or her future opportunities. As a result, in the future, a majority of courts will most likely rule that a student has a right to *retained* but not appointed counsel.

   d. *Witnesses.* The student has a right to call his or her own witnesses.

   e. *Cross-examination and confrontation.* This is another area in which the courts are divided. An opportunity to confront his or her accusers and to cross-examine them will at times be a necessity if the student is to have a fair hearing. This is particularly true where the credibility of the opposing witnesses is at issue. Although it would be a good policy to provide for this, the majority of courts have not as yet made it mandatory.

f. *Self-incrimination.* A good policy would be to provide that a student has a right to refuse to testify against himself or herself. However, some authority exists which suggests that school disciplinary proceedings are administrative in nature and are not sufficiently criminal to require the Fifth Amendment's protection against SELF-INCRIMINATION. The question of self-incrimination arises when the student's conduct may result in his or her being charged with breaking a school rule and violating a criminal law. If compelled to testify about the conduct, such testimony may be used to incriminate the student in a later criminal proceeding. As a result, some cases have held that this right should be granted in school disciplinary proceedings.

g. *Sufficiency of the evidence.* Any disciplinary action taken must be supported by the evidence presented in the hearing. As a general rule, the proof against the student must be clear and convincing.

h. *Mass hearings.* These have been used in cases involving large numbers of disruptive demonstrators. Such hearings have been found to be permissible.

i. *Public hearing.* A public hearing is not required.

j. *Transcripts.* The courts have divided in ruling as to whether or not a right to a transcript exists. If it is known that an appeal is probable, a transcript would seem to be required unless a de novo review is provided.

k. *Appeal procedure.* In most states, the school board has the authority to expel students. Various appeals are possible once administrative channels have been exhausted. During the appeals, the penalty may be imposed unless an order is made to the contrary at the initial hearing or at subsequent levels.

8. Interim suspension, pending the hearing required under section 7 above, may be imposed where the student's continued presence poses a threat to the safety or well-being of other students or school personnel, or would interrupt or threaten the efficient operation or necessary discipline in

the school. However, an informal preliminary hearing should be held either before or shortly after the interim suspension unless such a hearing is impossible or unreasonably difficult.

9. The main test of the school's expulsion or suspension procedure is one of *fairness*. If the school board acts fairly and in good faith in expelling a student, its action will be upheld by the courts.

Several states, most notably Indiana, have by statute provided for procedural safeguards on student disciplinary treatment which extend beyond the minimum requirements of due process. When this is the case, the local school boards are required to strictly comply with the state's prescribed procedures.

It is also interesting to note that the Indiana statute provides a sort of student GRIEVANCE procedure. The student is allowed to invoke this procedure whenever he or she feels that he or she has wrongfully been denied participation in an extracurricular activity or has been subjected to an illegal or unreasonable rule. This is an excellent idea. It provides a forum for student complaints without the necessity of court interference.

External Benefit Theory. Under the external benefit theory, aid granted to private or parochial schools is viewed as being for the external benefits which our society receives from these educational systems, and is not meant as aid to help foster RELIGION. The courts often find it difficult to use this test to uphold government aid to parochial schools because it is hard to establish a viable rationale for separating the secular benefits derived from parochial schools from their religious oriented instruction.

See also: PRIVATE AND PAROCHIAL SCHOOL AID.

Extracurricular Activities. See MARRIED STUDENTS; STUDENT RIGHTS.

Extracurricular Duties. See ASSIGNMENTS, non-classroom.

F

Factfinding. Factfinding is the investigation of a labor dispute by an individual, a panel, or a board. The factfinder issues a report which describes the issues involved and may make recommendations for settlement of the dispute. The report is frequently made public if the parties fail to resolve their dispute or accept the recommendations.

Factfinding is relatively formal. Factfinders hold hearings, gather evidence from parties interested in the dispute, and make public recommendations. Theoretically, public opinion on the labor dispute issues will be influenced by the factfinder's recommendations, and will pressure the parties into agreeing on a solution to their dispute along the lines of the recommendations. However, the parties are not forced to accept these recommendations.

See also: ARBITRATION; COLLECTIVE BARGAINING.

False Imprisonment. A student is falsely imprisoned when he or she is confined within boundaries stipulated by the teacher or administrator without authority. This is an intentional tort. False imprisonment exists where the teacher or administrator wrongfully detains a student for an unreasonable amount of time or in a wrongful manner.

Teachers and administrators have the authority to detain students from participating in such things as recess, play activities and field trips. They may also keep a student after school, provided the student has a way of getting home. (If the teacher or administrator takes the student home, he or she has the responsibility of exercising due care, or possible liability for NEGLIGENCE may result if the student is injured in an automobile accident.)

The detention must be reasonable. Assume, for example, that a teacher believes that a student has in his or her possession illegal or dangerous contraband. Also assume that one may easily dispose of this illegal or dangerous contraband. Under these circumstances, the teacher would have the right to detain the student. If the belief is based on probable cause or reasonable grounds, the teacher cannot be held liable for false imprisonment even if it is later found that the student did not in fact possess any illegal or dangerous contraband.

It should be noted that even if the detention would normally be considered reasonable, the detention cannot be based on ill will towards the student. Furthermore, detention cannot be used to enforce an unreasonable rule. Liability for false imprisonment will generally not amount to a great deal in the nature of compensatory DAMAGES. However, where it can be shown that the imprisonment was willful or grossly unreasonable, punitive damages may be assessed against the wrongdoer.

See also: MENTAL DISTRESS.

Federal Aid to Education. See CIVIL RIGHTS ACT OF 1964; CONSTITUTIONAL LAW; ELEMENTARY AND SECONDARY EDUCATION ACT OF 1965; PRIVATE AND PAROCHIAL SCHOOL AID.

Federal Constitution. See CONSTITUTIONAL LAW.

Federal Courts. See COURTS.

Fees. Most state constitutions require the state to establish free public schools. Questions frequently arise as to whether or not such constitutional provisions allow the schools to charge any fees.

Various forms of *registration fees* have been found to be in violation of constitutional provisions requiring free public schools. Although the school may charge for use of special athletic, literary, or library facilities, it may not condition entrance into school upon payment of such fees.

The school may not charge resident students a *tuition fee.* However, unless barred by statute, the school may charge a TUITION fee to students who are residents of other school districts.

Some *incidental fees* are allowable, even though the state is required to provide free schools. Nevertheless, the validity of such fees depends to a large degree upon the specific constitutional and statutory provisions. These must be carefully examined before a determination of the legality of the specific incidental fees can be made. Under most state laws, many of the following kinds of incidental fees and others not noted will be allowed:

1. Traffic safety education fees;
2. Damage deposits;
3. Fees for TRANSPORTATION for extracurricular activities;
4. Fees for student insurance premiums;
5. Class picture and yearbook fees;
6. Towel fees;
7. Locker fees; and
8. Fees for TEXTBOOKS.

See also: FUNDS.

Feinberg Law. See ANTI-SUBVERSIVE LAWS; ASSEMBLY; CONSTITUTIONAL RIGHTS OF TEACHERS AND ADMINISTRATORS.

Felony. A felony is a crime which is generally punishable by a severe penalty such as imprisonment for a period in excess of six months.
See also: MISDEMEANOR.

Field Trips. See GOVERNMENTAL IMMUNITY; NEGLIGENCE; RULES.

Fifth Amendment. See CONSTITUTIONAL LAW; SELF-INCRIMINATION; SILENT, right to remain.

First Aid. See MEDICAL SERVICES.

First Amendment. See ASSEMBLY; CONSTITUTIONAL LAW; CONSTITUTIONAL RIGHTS OF TEACHERS AND ADMINISTRATORS; RELIGION; STUDENT RIGHTS.

Flag Salute. As long ago as 1943, the Supreme Court of the United States held that to compel a student to salute the flag or say the PLEDGE OF ALLEGIANCE violated the First Amendment of the U.S. Constitution. The Court said:

> **If there is any fixed star in our constitutional constellation, it is that no official, high or petty, can prescribe what shall be orthodox in politics, nationalism, religion, or other matters of opinion or force citizens to confess by word or act their faith therein. *West Virginia State Board of Education v. Barnette*, 319 U.S. 624, 642 (1943).**

In the above quoted case, the PLAINTIFF students were Jehovah's Witnesses, but the Court did not rely on the students' religious convictions; instead, it based its decision on the students' right of free speech. The Court explained that:

> **To sustain the compulsory flag salute we are required to say that a Bill of Rights which guards the individual's right to speak his own mind, left it open to public authorities to compel him to utter what is not in his mind. (319 U.S. at 634).**

As a result, the Court did not sustain the compulsory flag salute.

It also follows that teachers cannot be forced to salute the flag if this violates his or her religious beliefs or moral convictions. However, it is clear that where the school requests to have the students salute the flag or say the pledge of allegiance each morning, the teacher can be required to appoint one of his or her students to lead the exercise, and the teacher must sit or stand respectfully during the flag salute or pledge. If the school chooses, it may relieve the teacher of a homeroom assignment where the flag salute or pledge takes place, so long as this is not meant as a punishment to the teacher.

Foreseeability. "Foreseeability" is a legal term relating to NEGLIGENCE. Whether or not an injury is foreseeable as a result of a defendant's conduct is a fact question that the jury will look at in deciding if liability should be imposed.

There are times when a person is obligated to foresee an event occurring. For example, if there is a banana peel on the floor, it is foreseeable that someone might slip and be injured. If two boys are fighting, it is foreseeable that one might get hurt. If glass is on the playground, someone might get cut, and that is also foreseeable. These are clear examples.

When a teacher or administrator foresees or reasonably could foresee that an injury might occur if a particular condition is not corrected or preventative action is not taken, he or she has a duty to do something about it prior to the injury occurring. If he or she does not, liability may be imposed for negligence.

Just when can an injury be foreseen? This is a QUESTION OF FACT and it depends on the individual facts and circumstances. However, it is clear that it is foreseeable that an injury will occur if a large group of young students are gathered without supervision; where a teacher is absent from class for long periods of time; or where there are particularly hazardous activities taking place in shop, science, or physical education classes. The REASONABLE AND PRUDENT teacher or administrator would be able to foresee that an injury is likely to occur in any of these situations, and once an injury is foreseeable, the condition causing the danger should be eliminated. Where the group of young students has gathered, the reasonable and prudent teacher or administrator would provide supervision or not permit them to gather. If the teacher is going to be absent from class, he or she must generally provide substitute supervision and have RULES governing student conduct while he or she is absent. In shop classes and the like, it is imperative that the teacher have rules of safety that are communicated, learned and enforced.

The teacher or administrator has a higher standard of care and should be able to foresee an accident more than could the average "man on the street." Sometimes there are unique situations where a teacher or administrator "knows" there is a hazardous condition but there does not seem to be anything he or she can do about it. For example, assume that a shop teacher has a class that is overcrowded and therefore dangerous because it is difficult to supervise the class properly. Or assume that an elementary teacher knows that there is a post sticking out of the playground and that it therefore is dangerous. Or assume that a principal knows that part of a building is unsafe because of a fire hazard. What can these people do? If someone is injured and that person is in charge, it is very likely that he or she would be named as a DEFENDANT for failure to exercise due care in rectifying the hazardous condition. In order to possibly relieve themselves of liability, the teacher or administrator in each of these instances should notify his or her immediate supervisor in writing. This notification should point out that the condition is dangerous, that an injury is foreseeable, that he or she wants the condition to be corrected, and that there is nothing the teacher or administrator can do about it without help. A copy of the letter should be saved. Then, should an injury occur, the injured party will not be able to hold the teacher or administrator liable for negligence, assuming that person had done all that could be done in order to eliminate the condition. (See also GRIEVANCE.)

There are certain supervisory duties which the teacher or administrator is required to perform, and it is the school board's duty to provide that teacher or administrator with the equipment, facilities, and staff necessary to carry out these duties properly. If the board does not, and the board has notice, there are occasions when the board could be acting in a negligent manner. For example, if there are three hundred young students playing outside and only one teacher is assigned to supervise, the teacher should point out in writing that such circumstances are not safe for students. The teacher must supervise as adequately as he or she can, but should an injury occur, which might otherwise have been prevented if adequate supervisory personnel had been provided, the liability, after their having been notified, would rest with the school district and its administrators—not with the individual teacher.

Students have a right to a safe environment, and teachers, administrators, and the school board have the duty to provide this safe environment within the limits of their capabilities.

Fourteenth Amendment. See CONSTITUTIONAL LAW; CONSTITUTIONAL RIGHTS OF TEACHERS AND ADMINISTRATORS; DUE PROCESS; EQUAL PROTECTION; EXPULSION OF STUDENTS; STUDENT RIGHTS.

Fraternities. See SECRET SOCIETIES; STUDENT RIGHTS.

Free Speech. See ACADEMIC FREEDOM; BIBLE READING; CONSTITUTIONAL LAW; CONSTITUTIONAL RIGHTS OF TEACHERS AND ADMINISTRATORS; OBSCENITY; PRAYERS; STUDENT RIGHTS.

Fundamental Interest Theory. The fundamental interest theory is a method of testing the validity of aid to parochial schools. Under this theory, education is perceived as being a fundamental interest. The benefits derived by granting certain aid to parochial schools in furtherance of this fundamental interest is then balanced against the First Amendment's "Establishment of Religion Clause." If the main effect of the aid is furtherance of this fundamental interest in education, and the benefit to RELIGION is merely incidental, the aid will be upheld. On the other hand, if there is a significant benefit to religion, and there exists no overriding benefit to the state's fundamental interest in education, the aid will be judged impermissible.

Funds, school.

1. *Administration.* Expenditures of school funds are frequently governed by states STATUTES. As a result, what is a proper expenditure of school funds in one state may be found to be improper in another. However, as a general rule, the school board is granted a great deal of discretion in this area and has the power to make expenditures which are necessary to give effect to the powers, duties, and authority granted to it. The legislature may designate procedures for expenditure of school funds, and may designate who has the authority and responsibility for the funds; if the legislature does so, these provisions must be strictly complied with. As a general rule, school funds may be deposited in a bank.

Some state statutes appropriate money for special purposes (e.g. CONSTRUCTION). The funds established to accomplish these purposes must be administered separately of the general school fund. Also, when school districts receive federal funds, these funds must be spent according to the terms of the grant, and in accordance with the rules of administration and expenditure specified by federal regulations. (See also ELEMENTARY AND SECONDARY EDUCATION ACT OF 1965.)

2. *Authorized Expenditures.* Aside from these few administrative problems, most of the questions concerning school funds are concerned with the kinds of particular expenditures which the school board may lawfully make. In many states, the statutes will expressly state the purposes for which school funds may be spent. Along with the expressly authorized purposes of expenditure, the board will have the power to spend school funds on certain implied purposes. For example, where the school board is expressly authorized to establish various education programs, the power to make related expenditures is deemed to be implied (e.g. school purchase of athletic facilities and equipment).

A school board may employ doctors, nurses, or dentists to *diagnose or inspect* students to see if health regulations have been complied with. However, in the absence of statutory authorization, the board cannot employ such persons to *treat* students. This is subject to the rule that the board can and frequently must incur the expense of providing first aid services or emergency MEDICAL SERVICES. Also, where a student is injured due to the NEGLIGENCE or willful acts of school personnel, the school may incur liability for medical services. Many statutes specifically authorize school districts to purchase liability insurance for its employees. (See GOVERNMENTAL IMMUNITY.)

By statutory or implied authority, school districts are generally deemed to have the power to purchase group medical, dental, disability, and life insurance for the employees. In addition, the school board may employ legal counsel to advise the board members on problems related to the school district.

School districts have the implied power to insure school property, but generally it must do so by conventional means. Mutual association forms of insurance have been invalidated where the contingent liability of the district was not limited.

The school district may not use school funds for a solely private mercantile purpose which is unrelated to education. The operation of cafeterias is educationally related and is for the benefit of the students; therefore, this expenditure of school funds is legally permissible. The same rationale has upheld the establishment of school bookstores which sell school books, supplies, stationery, etc., so long as the stores are not operated for a profit and the items are sold at cost plus an amount necessary to cover operating expenses.

Several miscellaneous expenditures have at times been the subject of dispute. Band uniform purchases have been held to be proper expenditures under some state statutes. Expenditure of school funds to cover the costs of board members' attendance at various school related conventions has also been upheld. The school district also may employ architects and pay a commencement speaker's expenses. Whether or not a school district may purchase campsites for use by students and residences for school personnel has not received a wide acceptance, and a split of authority exists on this issue.

The most talked about expenditure of school funds involves TRANSPORTATION. Spending school funds for the transportation of students is allowed under most statutes. However, where the statutes are silent as to the costs of transporting students, most COURTS hold that the parents are responsible for getting their children to school, and school boards may not use public funds for this expense.

Some state statutes require that transportation be furnished to *all* school age children, including students attending non-public schools. These statutes have withstood constitutional attack by being recognized as a benefit to the general public welfare and as only an incidental benefit to RELIGION. (See also PRIVATE AND PAROCHIAL SCHOOL AID.)

Most statutes are broad enough to permit school boards to provide transportation to students participating in extracurricular activities. However, the board is not allowed to use school funds to supply transportation to the students' parents or to patrons of such events.

If the school board is in doubt as to what school funds may be spent on, it should seek an Attorney General Opinion on the scope of authorization granted in the statutes of the state in which the board is located. In this manner, the school board would have the right to make expenditures pursuant to the opinion, without fearing possible personal liability or public condemnation.

3. *Persons Allowed to Authorize Expenditures.* Occasionally, questions arise as to who may authorize the expenditures of school funds. A board of education may not delegate its discretionary authority to make expenditures to employees of the district or to a single member or committee of the board. A few state statutes specifically authorize school boards to delegate some of its purchasing authority, but in the absence of such authority, the school board may not delegate the authority to purchase goods and services for the school district to the district superintendent, principals, teachers or other employees. This means that the board of education will not be bound by purchases made by persons other than the board, *unless* the purchases are ratified by the board.

In nearly all districts, school district personnel make purchases for the school. Final approval is left to the board's discretion, however, and the board may ratify such purchases by accepting and paying for the goods or by voting to accept a contract to that effect. If the board does not ratify the purchase, the supplier must try to recover the goods or sue on an unjust enrichment principle.

Most states have statutes requiring an annual reporting and publishing of school district financial reports. These statutes must be strictly complied with. A board of education may employ an accountant to audit the district's financial records.

See also: ACTIVITY FUNDS; FEES.

G

Gifts, acceptance of. See DONATIONS.

God, an act of. There exist certain legal defenses which at times will protect persons from liability. One such defense is "an act of God." If an injury occurs and it can be shown that the proximate cause of the injury was an act of God, liability will not be imposed. This is true even though the party being sued might have been negligent to a minor degree. For example, assume that the school district erected a flagpole on the playground and that this flagpole was weak and poorly constructed. If the pole broke and a student was injured as a result, liability would be imposed for NEGLI-GENCE. However, if a bolt of lightning struck the pole, causing it to break, and a student were injured as a result, no liability would be imposed because the proximate cause of the injury was an act of God.

Acts of God come in many forms: lightning, hurricanes, floods, blizzards, hail, storms, etc. If school district personnel reasonably can foresee that "God" is brewing up a storm, they must take reasonable precautions to avoid subjecting students to an unreasonable risk of harm, or liability will be imposed for their negligence. For example, assume that a school district schedules a field trip in which the students are going to the desert to study the plant life and animals which live there. If the field trip takes place and, without warning, a flash flood occurs, the school district would generally not be held liable if a child were injured in the flood. However, if weather reports had forecast possible rain and flash flooding in the desert, and the school district personnel ignored these warnings and took the students on the scheduled field trip, liability probably would be imposed if a child were injured. The distinction is that in this latter example, God had warned the school personnel of the danger, they ignored it, and, therefore, they were the ones who subjected the students to an unreasonable risk of harm and resulting possible injury.

If the injury sustained is in fact proximately caused by an act of God, the injured party has no legal recourse and cannot recover DAMAGES. After all, who would the injured party sue? God? No one has ever been reported to have sued God—that is, no one except for Canary Harris.

In the 1800's, a woman named Canary Harris lived in a little town called Amity. The house she lived in had a porch which had been built by her dear departed husband. Canary was very fond of the porch, not only because her husband had built it with his own two hands, but because it was needed for rocking and visiting with the neighbors on warm summer nights.

One sad day, a meteorite falling from the sky destroyed the porch of Canary's house. Canary couldn't understand how such a thing could have happened. Had it been a hurricane or a flood, she could have understood, but in this instance, God had singled her out. Why? She didn't know. She had always been a good, God-fearing, Christian woman. Canary thought and thought and made certain in her mind that this wasn't a punishment for some transgression she had committed. She concluded that there was only one explanation—God had made a mistake. Canary figured that God had intended the meteorite for a man down the road who made corn liquor, but the meteorite had missed its mark.

Canary reasoned that there was only one thing she could do—sue God. She spoke to the local attorney, who, after the shock wore off, suggested that such a suit was fallacious—after all, God has no legal standing. Canary pointed out that when a company is located out of town a lawyer sues his local representative, so why not do the same in this case. They did. Canary sued God's local representative, the Reverend Farr.

The Reverend Farr felt very bad about the incident, but he refused to accept responsibility for the damage. There was only one alternative left— Canary appealed to a higher authority, Bishop Tuttle.

God's flock, the local Amity townspeople, were quite upset with Canary's actions. Nevertheless, Canary was resolved to stick it out, and none of the ripe tomatoes or invectives leveled by the local flock were going to cause Canary to give up her belief that God had made a mistake and had a duty to rebuild the porch.

Finally, Bishop Tuttle arrived in town. He had come to settle on behalf of the Lord. The Bishop had found that Canary's appeal was a just one, and he reversed the decision of the local Reverend. By the authority vested in him by God, the porch was rebuilt. To Canary, the porch was proof of God's justice.

Governmental Immunity. Governmental Immunity means that the state or federal government, and their governmental agencies are immune from suit and cannot be held liable for any injuries caused while carrying out their governmental functions. In the past, it was a well-accepted rule of law that a person could not sue City Hall. Governmental immunity still exists in many states. This is changing to some extent, but governmental immunity still has important implications to all teachers and administrators in the United States. (For purposes of this section, the term "teachers" includes administrators as well.) If a student is injured as a result of a teacher's negligence, the student has recourse against only the teacher. That is, the teacher will be solely liable unless the student can also name the local school board as a party defendant. The school board is a governmental agency of the state. Therefore, it is immune from suit unless the state has waived its immunity and given permission for its citizens to sue.

It seems strange that a rule of law exists which prevents a person from suing a governmental agency that has wronged him or her in some way. In some states, it is felt that the "king can do no wrong," and in these states, the laws remain rigid, and the legislatures insist that an innocent victim has no recourse against the state or its agencies. For example, assume that a person is visiting City Hall and a ceiling lamp falls because of loose brackets and the person is injured. If the injury occurred in a state under complete governmental immunity, there would be no recourse against the city for the injuries sustained. There is a possibility that the person could sue the contractor, but, realistically, it is the city that should be responsible for maintaining a safe environment for people to visit. This example reflects the situation existing within the schools, and therefore, teachers need to know where their own schools stand in relation to this concept for their own welfare.

First of all, it is necessary to understand how immunity will affect a teacher's liability. The school is an arm of the state, and teachers are AGENTS of the school. Whether or not the school can exercise its right to immunity depends, as earlier stated, on the laws of that particular state. The same does not hold true for teachers. Teachers are liable for their own torts and cannot defend themselves on the basis of immunity. They will be saved from personal liability only if the school (state) deems it appropriate.

The doctrine of governmental immunity can be broken down into four categories with distinctions that must be made within each. Each state's position with regard to these categories is detailed in the chart following this section. In the first category are those states which exercise the *complete right to immunity*. This means that if a student is injured by a teacher acting within the scope of his or her duty, the student has recourse only against the teacher. The teacher cannot look to his or her employer for indemnification, and must therefore pay any DAMAGES incurred from his or her own pocket. This means that it is imperative for a teacher within this category to carry liability insurance through his or her local educational association or to obtain coverage through a "rider" to a homeowner's or renter's insurance policy.

In category two are those states *which distinguish between "governmental" and "proprietary" acts*. A governmental act is one which is for the purpose of fulfilling the school's obligation to teach children. A school district within this category will not be liable for injuries sustained while the school is performing a governmental act. If the school district is involved in an activity that is not in the furtherance of its duties as required by law, and is involved in an activity which is for its own convenience, or an activity which could be provided by a private third party or corporation, it is involved in a "proprietary" act and can be held liable. It should be noted that most acts in which a school is involved could automatically be deemed governmental, depending upon the viewpoint taken, but a helpful test is to ask:

1. Is the activity required by state law? If so, it is governmental.

2. Can the activity be done by a third party, or is it for the purpose of saving or raising extra money? If so, it is proprietary.

For teachers who work within category two, school district liability will depend upon the nature of the act which causes the injury. For example, if a teacher negligently injures a student while teaching him swimming (a governmental act), the teacher would be solely liable. On the other hand, if the school requested a teacher to transport students to football games in his or her private car, and if a student was injured when the teacher negligently drove into a ditch, the teacher and the school district would both be liable. Realistically, the school district would be the ultimate bagholder of the debt because the school district has the deeper pocket or assets from which to draw. However, this does not necessarily provide the teacher with too much protection. The school board could force the teacher to pay his or her share, because the teacher is jointly liable with the school district. For this reason, the teacher working within a district in category two should also carry liability insurance.

In the third category, liability will be dependent upon whether or not the school district purchases liability insurance. In the first two categories, school districts are not generally allowed to buy insurance (with the possible exception of liability insurance in specific areas such as bus transportation). For those teachers within category three, however, they can be saved from liability if they have acted or omitted to act in an area covered by school district insurance. Here, school districts have the discretionary power to decide whether or not to buy insurance (with the possible exception of bus TRANSPORTATION insurance which is mandatory in some states). In other words, should the district decide to buy insurance covering the negligence of its employees, an injured student could name the school district as a party defendant along with the teacher. Although this would generally make the school district the ultimate bagholder, there are seldom any clauses barring a later suit for contribution by the teacher to the school district. It should also be noted that liability exists only to the extent of the insurance coverage. Thus, should a judgment come down for $50,000 and the school district is insured for only $25,000, the remaining $25,000 would be the teacher's burden. Again, private insurance by the teacher is recommended.

In category four, there are those states which have waived immunity for the negligent acts and sometimes for the INTENTIONAL TORTS of its teachers committed while the teachers are acting within the scope of their employment. Here, the teacher will be saved from liability to the extent that the state has waived immunity. For example, if the state has waived immunity up to $50,000, the teacher would not have to pay for anything except that which is over the maximum amount. This is not necessarily an absolute protection for the teacher. There are some states which *must* defend and pay the teacher's costs, and there are other states where it is discretionary. In the latter case, should the district choose not to defend the teacher, the teacher is left on his or her own. This does not mean that the teacher is left helpless. The school district must still pay for its own defense and must pay a portion of the judgment; the teacher simply has to contribute his or her own share. This share can be substantial, and should a judgment be rendered for more than what is waived by the state, the excess is the sole responsibility of the teacher.

Where each state stands in relation to the aforementioned immunity provisions is detailed in the following chart. Some of the states have an asterisk before them. This means that there is something unique about the statute involved, and there is an explanation following the chart.

GOVERNMENTAL IMMUNITY IN PUBLIC SCHOOLS IN THE UNITED STATES

(as of June 1, 1973)

	Category One	Category Two	Category Three	Category Four
Alabama	X			
Alaska				X
Arizona				X
*Arkansas			X	
California				X
*Colorado				X
*Connecticut				X
Delaware		X		
*Florida			X	
*Georgia			X	
*Hawaii				X
*Idaho				X
Illinois				X
Indiana				X
*Iowa				X
*Kansas			X	
Kentucky	X			

	Category One	Category Two	Category Three	Category Four
*Louisiana		X		
Maine		X		
Maryland			X	
*Massachusetts				X
Michigan		X		
*Minnesota				X
*Mississippi			X	
Missouri				X
Montana			X	
*Nebraska				X
Nevada				X
New Hampshire			X	
New Jersey				X
*New Mexico			X	
*New York				X .
North Carolina			X	
North Dakota			X	
*Ohio		X changing →		
Oklahoma			X changing →	
*Oregon				X
Pennsylvania				X
Rhode Island		X		
So. Carolina	X			
So. Dakota				X
*Tennessee	X			
*Texas		X		
*Utah				X
*Vermont			X	
*Virginia			X	
*Washington				X
Washington, D.C.				X
West Virginia			X	
*Wisconsin				X
*Wyoming			X	

Arkansas:	School districts are not forced to carry insurance on anything except motor vehicles.
Colorado:	The school may buy insurance and the defense of the teacher is discretionary.
Connecticut:	School districts protect and "save-harmless" the teacher for negligence and intentional torts.
Florida:	Immunity of the school district is waived to the extent of insurance coverage.
Georgia:	School districts *may* buy insurance for children riding *in* buses to and from school.
Hawaii:	Immunity waived for negligence but not intentional torts.
Idaho:	Immunity waived for negligence but not for intentional torts.
Iowa:	Immunity waived for negligence and intentional torts committed within the scope of the teacher's duty.
Kansas:	School districts must purchase liability insurance for transportation accidents and may buy liability insurance for torts of teachers.
Louisiana:	School districts may carry insurance for buses.
Massachusetts:	School districts may purchase liability insurance providing for the indemnification of teachers.
Minnesota:	The school districts "save-harmless" the teacher.
Mississippi:	Injured persons can sue the school district only for transportation accidents.
Nebraska:	Immunity waived for negligence but not for intentional torts. Permits the school district to sue the teacher for his or her act or omission.
New Mexico:	School may insure itself for negligence and some intentional torts, but may seek indemnity from the teacher.
New York:	Teachers shall be "save-harmless."
Ohio:	Ohio is in a state of flux, and has gone back and forth. The law as of April, 1973 is that legislative consent must be granted before immunity will be waived. A case is pending before the U.S. Supreme Court, however, and with that outcome or by legislative enactment, Ohio should go into category three or four.
Oregon:	School districts may "save-harmless" the teacher for negligence and intentional torts.

Tennessee:	School buses must be insured. School districts are immune otherwise.
Texas:	School has the authority to insure for injuries arising out of transportation accidents.
Utah:	Immunity waived for negligence but not for intentional torts.
Vermont:	School districts must "save-harmless" the teacher to the extent of policy limits.
Virginia:	School districts must carry insurance for transportation of pupils.
Washington:	School districts may purchase liability insurance for teachers.
Wisconsin:	Immunity waived for negligence but not for intentional torts.
Wyoming:	Insurance does not have to be purchased. If it is, the board may "save-harmless" the teacher for negligence or other acts that are within the scope of the teacher's duty.

Governmental immunity protects the state while forcing teachers and injured students to fend for themselves. The injustices do not arise out of merely obscure incidents of an occasional broken back, but are daily occurrences of broken arms, lost fingers, and partial blindness. Students are injured. They are injured by breaches of the school's duty to provide for the students' safety. Yet, although the injuries occur, and students remain uncompensated, many states continue to remain immune from suit. Some states have waived immunity to a limited extent. Others have waived immunity through "save-harmless" statutes to a point where most if not all injuries will be compensated. The teacher stands on soft sand, and will remain so until "save-harmless" statutes are made mandatory in all states, and until the causes of action are limited in their amount. This would protect both the teachers and the students while still being realistically workable. As many writers have analogized, for a state to remain immune from suit in cases involving wrongful injuries committed against its citizens is like saying that a ship may carry anyone but its builders.

See also: ALLOCATION OF LIABILITY.

Graduation Requirements. See CURRICULUM; DIPLOMAS.

Grievance. A grievance is a statement of dissatisfaction, usually made by an individual, but sometimes made by an employee organization or by management, concerning interpretation of an agreement or of a work related matter relating to the internal operations of the school.

The method of dealing with grievances arising out of the interpretation of the terms of a contract AGREEMENT are generally specified in the contract or in a memorandum of understanding. These kinds of grievances are frequently resolved by binding ARBITRATION.

Where the grievance involves a personal complaint of a school district employee regarding the internal operations of the school, most school districts have established their own local grievance procedures. These grievance procedures are extremely important to the district's employees for two reasons:

1. These procedures provide a forum for employees to air their views. They allow school district personnel to resolve quickly and equitably their complaints at the lowest possible administrative level. At the same time, they protect the parties to the dispute against undesirable publicity and legal expenses.

2. When a school district employee's grievance merely involves the internal operations of the school, he or she is allowed to take the complaint to the courts or to the public.

Local grievance procedures may be used by teachers and other district employees to present their complaints regarding everything from textbook selections and personnel policies to personality conflicts and possible unsafe conditions existing on school premises. These procedures also are beneficial to the school board and its administrative staff as it provides a quick and inexpensive solution to possible serious problems. For example, assume that a physical education instructor believes that the school board's failure to provide padding for a wall which is three feet from the basket presents an unreasonable risk of danger to students engaged in a basketball game. Also assume that this teacher puts in a requisition for padding, but the school board fails to provide funding in its budget for this equipment. What can the teacher do? File a grievance. In this manner, the teacher is able to bring a better understanding of the situation to the school board, and the teacher's actions are likely to protect the teacher from being sued for NEGLIGENCE if a student suffers an injury during a basketball game. If the board fails to remedy the situation, the school district may be held liable. Also, having exhausted the school's grievance procedure, the teacher would be free to make his or her complaint public.

H-I

Handicapped Children. See EQUAL PROTECTION; PREGNANT STUDENTS; SPECIAL EDUCATION; STUDENT RIGHTS.

Health Programs. See ATHLETICS; FUNDS; MEDICAL SERVICES; SEX EDUCATION; VACCINATION.

Hearings. See CONSTITUTIONAL RIGHTS OF TEACHERS AND ADMINISTRATORS; DUE PROCESS; EXPULSION OF STUDENTS; STUDENT RIGHTS.

Hearsay. Hearsay consists of statements made by a witness the validity of which is not based on the witness' personal observations or knowledge but on the observations or knowledge of someone else not in the courtroom or hearing room.

Home Instruction. See COMPULSORY EDUCATION; PRIVATE SCHOOLS.

Homosexuals. To date, no court has directly held that homosexuals must be permitted to teach in the public schools. However, several COURTS have rendered important legal opinions involving homosexual teachers. As

149

many states liberalize their laws to provide that homosexual relationships between consenting adults are not crimes, and as the gay liberation movement gains greater acceptance, legal questions involving homosexual teachers are being asked with greater frequency.

In 1969, California's highest court ruled that a teacher who had engaged in a limited non-criminal homosexual relationship could not have his teaching *certificate* revoked. The court said that in order to prohibit a homosexual from accepting a teaching position, it must be shown that he or she is *unfit as a teacher*. In explaining how a school board may meet the test of demonstrating that a particular homosexual is unfit to teach the court said:

> **In determining whether the teacher's conduct thus indicates un-fitness to teach the board may consider such matters as the likelihood that the conduct may have adversely affected students or fellow teachers, the degree of such adversity anticipated, the proximity or remoteness in time of the conduct, the type of teaching certificate held by the party involved, the extenuating or aggravating circumstances, if any, surrounding the conduct, the praiseworthiness or blameworthiness of the motives resulting in the conduct, the likelihood of the recurrence of the questioned conduct, and the extent to which disciplinary action may inflict an adverse impact or chilling effect upon the constitutional rights of the teacher involved or other teachers. These factors are relevant to the extent that they assist the board in determining a teacher's fitness to teach. *Morrison v. State Board of Education*, 461 P.2d 375, 386-387 (Cal. 1969).**

When asked by school officials, a school teacher admitted that she was a homosexual. The teacher was immediately dismissed on the grounds of immorality. Word leaked out about her sexual preference, and the community became terribly aroused. The teacher sued the school district. In 1973, the case was decided, and the court ruled that immorality as a grounds for dismissal is unconstitutionally vague. However, although the judge awarded the wrongfully dismissed teacher DAMAGES, the teacher was not reinstated. As a result, this case is being appealed. Unfortunately, the judge in this case failed to face directly the issue of whether or not a homosexual must be allowed to teach. Nevertheless, he did suggest in a footnote that there must exist a nexus between the conduct complained of and the teacher's fitness to teach before the courts will uphold his or her dismissal. *Burton v. Cascade School District Union High School No. 5,* 353 F.Supp. 254 (U.S. Dist. Ct. Ore., 1973).

In further development of these legal questions, a U.S. District Court Judge ruled in 1973 that the right of a homosexual school teacher to continue teaching is protected only so long as he or she does not publicly discuss his or her sexual preferences; (i.e. as long as a homosexual teacher is discreet, he or she may remain teaching). In this case, the judge upheld the transfer of an eighth grade science teacher to a desk job, after the teacher discussed his homosexuality on a nationally televised program of "60 Minutes." The judge stated that:

> ... [T]o some extent every teacher has to go out of his way to hide his private life. . . . [A] homosexual teacher is not at liberty to ignore or hold in contempt the sensitivity of the subject to the school community.
>
> A sense of discretion and self-restraint must guide him to avoid speech or activity likely to spark the added public controversy which detracts from the educational process. U.S. Dist. Judge Joseph Young. Capitol Journal (Salem, Ore.), June 1, 1973, sec. 3 at p. 18, col. 5.

The judge further noted that although society's intolerance for homosexuality is ebbing, public disclosure contributes to the likelihood of deleterious effects occurring to the educational process.

On appeal, the court ruled that the teacher's media appearance was protected by the First Amendment. However, the court upheld the transfer on the grounds that the plaintiff had intentionally withheld facts about this affiliation with a homophile organization when he applied for his teaching position. *Acanfora v. Montgomery County Board of Education,* 491 F. 2d. 498 (4th Cir. 1973). This case is on appeal to the Supreme Court

The next logical step in this legal progression would seem to be a clear holding that the dismissal of a teacher based on the conduct of his or her personal life may form the basis for removal from his or her teaching position only where such conduct affects the teacher's fitness as a teacher. But note carefully that a ruling such as this would not allow *unfit* persons to teach. If a person has had a homosexual relationship with a minor, it is clear that this would affect his or her fitness to teach. It is also clear that if the teacher's status as a homosexual, conduct as a homosexual, or whatever, has caused the teacher to lose the respect of and rapport with his or her students and has resulted in the teacher's inability to teach effectively, the teacher may be dismissed and all courts would uphold the dismissal.

See also: CONSTITUTIONAL RIGHTS OF TEACHERS AND ADMINISTRATORS; TEACHERS, dismissals.

Illness. See SICK LEAVE.

Immorality. See CONSTITUTIONAL RIGHTS OF TEACHERS AND ADMINISTRATORS; HOMOSEXUALS; TEACHERS, dismissals.

Immunity. See GOVERNMENTAL IMMUNITY.

Immunization. See VACCINATION.

Implied Authority. Implied authority is the power or right to act which is expressed indirectly. It is often clear that a granting of certain EXPRESS AUTHORITY necessarily incorporates a granting of implied authority to carry out additional acts. For example, if a teacher is given the express authority to control student conduct within the classroom, it necessarily follows that the teacher has the implied authority to make and enforce reasonable rules and regulations governing that conduct.

Implied Contract. An implied contract is a contract in which the promise by the obligor is not express, but is inferred by his or her conduct or is implied in law.

Imputed Negligence. Imputed negligence is NEGLIGENCE which is not directly attributable to the person himself, but which is the negligence of a person who is in privity with him, and with whose fault he is charged. Through the doctrine of imputed negligence, an employer is often held liable for the acts of his employees.

See also: GOVERNMENTAL IMMUNITY.

In Loco Parentis. *In loco parentis* is a Latin phrase which literally means "in the place of parents." This legal doctrine was established by the COURTS in order to give school officials the necessary authority to regulate student conduct. In essence, *in loco parentis* means that when a student is within the jurisdiction of the school, school officials may discipline students as if the students were their own children.

Until the late 1960's, the doctrine of *in loco parentis* was available for use by the school in defending nearly any manner of discipline or punishment. This doctrine also was used as a basis for upholding school RULES. However, since the advent of COMPULSORY EDUCATION laws, the idea that parents voluntarily delegate unrestricted authority to school officials lacks realism. It is now recognized that parents entrust their children to school officials for a specific educational purpose. Therefore, school officials have authority over their charges only for the purpose of accomplishing that education.

This is not to say that the doctrine of *in loco parentis* is fading into history, as some people suggest. The COURTS are not abolishing this concept, they are merely defining its perimeters. Education of children imposes three duties which teachers and other school officials owe to their students: (1) instruction; (2) supervision; and (3) safety. School officials necessarily must have a certain amount of authority in order to fulfill these duties. As a result, when acting in performance of these duties, school officials are recognized to have the authority to enact reasonable rules governing student conduct and to use reasonable disciplinary action in controlling students. In these matters, school officials' authority is much like that of the students' parents. Moreover, parents do not have the right to prevent school officials from exercising this authority. On the other hand, school officials may be prevented or punished for exceeding their authority. For example, unreasonable rules may not be enforced (see STUDENT RIGHTS); and unreasonable or excessive punishment may result in liability for injuries a student suffers.

Frequently, questions arise as to when does the student come within the jurisdiction of the school such that school officials have the right to exert their legal authority. In the past, school officials were felt to have the authority to regulate student conduct from the moment the students left home until the moment they returned. However, in nearly all states, the law presently is that a student comes within the school's authority only when he or she is on school premises or is attending school sponsored activities or school related functions. Therefore, among other things, the school's jurisdiction extends to: (1) field trips; (2) school club activities; (3) school athletic events; (4) the playground, classroom, and other school property; and (5) school buses and bus stops.

This also means that the school is not responsible for the students' actions or safety going to and from school. However, a student must be provided safe TRANSPORTATION if the school operates buses, and the student must be released at a safe bus stop. Nevertheless, if the school bus driver has deposited a student at a safe bus stop, the school will not be liable if the student is injured in an accident on his or her way home from the bus stop.

The fact that the school is not responsible for the students' actions or safety outside of the school's jurisdiction also means that school officials do not have any legal authority to regulate the students' conduct. For example, if a teacher observes a group of students smoking on their way to school, the teacher can ask the students to put out the cigarettes, but would have no authority to compel the students to do so.

See also: CORPORAL PUNISHMENT; EXPULSION OF STUDENTS.

Incompetency. See TEACHERS, dismissal.

Indebtedness. See BONDS.

Injunction. An injunction is a mandatory or prohibitive writ issued by a court. This is a court order which restrains individuals or groups from committing acts which, in the court's opinion, will do irreparable harm. In some special kinds of cases the court will issue what is termed a mandatory injunction which compels an individual or a group to do an act which, in the court's opinion, is necessary to prevent irreparable harm. Failure to comply with the court's injunction order is a CONTEMPT OF COURT.

See also: STRIKES.

Injuries. See CORPORAL PUNISHMENT; GOVERNMENTAL IMMUNITY; INTENTIONAL TORTS; NEGLIGENCE.

Innoculation. See VACCINATION.

Insubordination. See TEACHERS, dismissals.

Insurance. See FUNDS, school; GOVERNMENTAL IMMUNITY.

Intelligence Testing. As used for a great many years, and even up to the present time, intelligence is measured for the most part through the use of a standardized intelligence test. The most commonly used tests are the Stanford-Binet I.Q. test and the Wechsler Intelligence Scale for Children. Many school districts use the results of such tests as a basis for grouping students into various "tracks" or ability groups. Such tests, as presently used, are not able to measure the innate intellectual ability of youths of varied racial, cultural, or disadvantaged backgrounds. The reason is that the standards which are used to validate such tests are those of a white, middle-class society, and the questions selected also represent those values.

The educational and psychological effects of grouping on this basis is being subjected to in-depth studies. The coming years should find an increasing number of legal challenges to the use of such tests as the basis for assigning students to different CURRICULUM levels. The COURTS do not like to interfere with school matters which are discretionary in nature because they realize that educators are far more competent to decide the merits of various school policies. But where such policies are discriminatory or are in other ways in violation of constitutional rights, they become a matter for judicial determination.

Ability grouping based on standardized intelligence testing could in the future prove to lead to a system of racial segregation. Recognizing this, the testing procedures hopefully will be revised before the courts are forced to declare them totally invalid as a violation of constitutional rights. Court interference would definitely be an inadequate solution to the problem. For example, in the District of Columbia, students were being placed in ability groups ranging from what was termed "basic track" to "honors track." In grouping the students, school officials relied primarily on standardized intelligence test scores. The court found that such tests measured intellect gained through cultural experience, not innate intelligence; and the court totally abolished the track system of ability grouping in the District of Columbia. *Hobson v. Hansen*, 269 F.Supp. 401 (D.D.C. 1967); aff'd 408 F.2d 175 (1969).

The results of a challenge to a California system of ability grouping are much more heartening. Linguistic bias in intelligence tests was charged by a group of California students. These Mexican-American students sought an order preventing the board of education from placing children in educable mentally retarded classes on the basis of standardized intelligence tests, because the tests were shown to place a heavy emphasis on verbal skills and as a result placed a disproportionate number of bilingual students in the mentally retarded classes. In settling the case, the parties agreed to stipulate to four things:

1. Through the use of interpreters, intelligence testing would be made in the students' native language.
2. Mexican-American and Chinese students in the educable mentally retarded classes would be retested.
3. A special effort was required to help students found to have been misplaced re-adjust.
4. An effort would be made to design an appropriate I.Q. test.

Diana v. State Board of Education, Civil #C-70 37 RFR (N.D. Cal., Jan. 1970).

The stipulations made in this case were later used as a basis for several federal laws as well as for state-wide laws in California relating to intelligence testing. Cal. Educ. Code § 6902.06, .07, .085, .095 (West Supp. 1972).

In a final case involving ability groupings, a federal court allowed the school district to continue tracking students so long as several safeguards were instituted. The court ruled that:

1. The school board must demonstrate a valid educational purpose for ability grouping: i.e. show that it is beneficial to maximize education.
2. The basis for the grouping must be based upon actual ability: i.e. the board must consider external factors in judging performance on I.Q. tests.
3. The school program must provide remedial education which enables the slow student to catch up if possible.
4. Mobility between tracks must exist: i.e. the board must provide for re-evaluation of students in order to allow slow students to move up in tracks where remedial education has enabled him or her to do so.

Moses v. Washington Parish School Board, 330 F.Supp. 1340 (U.S. Dist. Ct. La., 1971); aff'd 456 F.2d 1285 (5th Cir. 1972).

This area of education cannot adequately be solved by the courts. Educators must bear the burden of providing equal educational opportunity for all students. As a starting point, the court requirements in the above cases should be carefully examined.

Intentional Tort. An intentional tort exists when an injury is wrongfully caused and the person causing the injury intended the act. The intentional torts which educators need to be aware of are:

1. ASSAULT.
2. BATTERY.
3. DEFAMATION.
4. FALSE IMPRISONMENT.
5. MENTAL DISTRESS.
6. TRESPASS TO PERSONAL PROPERTY.

See also: GOVERNMENTAL IMMUNITY.

J-L

Jehovah's Witnesses. See FLAG SALUTE; PLEDGE OF ALLEGIANCE; RELIGION; STUDENT RIGHTS.

Kindergartens. Whether or not a state legislature is forced to establish kindergartens depends upon the wording and intent of the state's constitution. Where the necessary language is missing, the legislature is free to determine if kindergartens will be established.

Most state constitutions do not specify the range of ages of students for which schools must be established, and instead have a general provision that the legislature shall establish and maintain a system of free public schools. As a result, where the range of ages are not specified, the legislature makes the determination.

Of the states which do provide age ranges, Wisconsin is the lowest and requires that free public schools be provided for children between the ages of four and 20. Six years of age is the most common specified minimum in state constitutions. The COURTS have held that the legislature has the authority to go beyond the minimum constitutional requirements. Therefore, where free public education is required by the state constitution to be provided for children between the ages of six and 20, the legislature is allowed to establish kindergartens. The same rule applies to the other side of the age range. As a result, where a state constitution required free public schools for children between the ages of five and 18, the legislature was held to have the authority to provide free public schools for persons between the ages of five and 21.

Knives. See ASSAULT; BATTERY; RULES; TRESPASS TO PERSONAL PROPERTY.

Labor Unions. See AGENCY SHOP; ASSEMBLY; COLLECTIVE BARGAINING; CONSTITUTIONAL RIGHTS OF TEACHERS AND ADMINISTRATORS; UNION SECURITY.

Lease of School Property. See BUILDINGS; PROPERTY.

Leaves of Absence. There are a number of different types of leaves of absence. SABBATICAL LEAVE, SICK LEAVE, MATERNITY LEAVE, MILITARY LEAVE, and PEACE CORPS LEAVE are the most common. Some of these leaves are mandatory and must be granted to the teacher or administrator. Others are left to the discretion of the local school boards. Even when the leave is mandatory, local boards still have some discretion to promulgate rules and regulations governing the procedure for taking the leave of absence. These rules and regulations should be clearly stated in SCHOOL BOARD policies, and cannot be arbitrary or in violation of a person's constitutional rights.

Sometimes a leave of absence is granted with pay, and sometimes it is not. Generally this depends on state statutes, and possibly school board policies. Although the state sets out minimum requirements in regard to leaves of absence, there is generally nothing to prevent the local board from increasing a teacher or administrator's right to a leave of absence. For example, if the state says a teacher has the right to ten sick leave days a year, there is nothing to prevent the board from adopting a policy of granting 11 days. Also, state statutes may be silent as to "personal" or "professional" leaves of absence. If so, the local board could adopt a policy that each teacher or administrator is entitled to one or two days leave for personal business or professional endeavors. Bereavement leave and family sickness are also examples of leaves commonly granted by local board policy.

As earlier stated, local boards can adopt rules or regulations governing sick leaves. Typical rules include requiring a doctor's certificate in cases of long absence, or requiring the teacher or administrator to make an application for leave within a certain period of time. The rules must generally have an educational purpose and, of course, cannot be discriminatory.

See also: EQUAL PROTECTION; PATERNITY LEAVE.

Letters of Intent. See CONTRACTS; NONRENEWAL; RENEWALS.

Liability.
1. *Contracts:* see BUILDINGS; CONSTRUCTION; CONTRACTS.
2. *Insurance:* see FUNDS, school; GOVERNMENTAL IMMUNITY.
3. *Principals:* see PRINCIPAL.
4. *School boards and school board members:* see GOVERNMENTAL IMMUNITY; SCHOOL BOARDS, liability.
5. *Students:* see STUDENTS, liability.
6. *Superintendents:* see SUPERINTENDENTS.
7. *Teachers:* see GOVERNMENTAL IMMUNITY; NEGLIGENCE.

See also: ALLOCATION OF LIABILITY.

Libel. See CONSTITUTIONAL RIGHTS OF TEACHERS AND ADMINISTRATORS, freedom of speech; DEFAMATION; STUDENT RIGHTS, freedom of speech.

Local School Boards. See SCHOOL BOARDS.

Lockers, searches. See SEARCH AND SEIZURE; STUDENT RIGHTS.

Loyalty Oaths. During World War II, SCHOOL BOARDS zealously sought to keep subversives from teaching in the public schools. In doing so, many loyalty oaths were enacted which prohibited membership in various organizations, and which forbade teachers from making certain kinds of statements within and outside the school.

Loyalty oaths came under fire in the 1950's, and many decisions have been handed down since. In 1952, the Supreme Court of the United States was faced with its first loyalty oath case, and held by a unanimous decision that it was unconstitutional to disqualify a person from teaching based on his having been a member of a subversive organization when that person did not know the nature of the organization's activities or its philosophy at the time he had been a member. *Wieman v. Updegraff*, 344 U.S. 183 (1952).

Since this 1952 case, the Supreme Court upheld some loyalty oaths and struck down several others. In 1966, the Court set forth the test which must be applied in determining if an oath is valid. It said that a person cannot be punished for being a member of an organization *unless* it can be shown that he or she has the *intent* to further the unlawful aims of the organization or participates in carrying them out. This test was reiterated in a case involving three instructors at the University of New York who had refused to sign a statement that they were not Communists and that if they had ever been Communists they had communicated that fact to the president of the university. The Court explained that "guilt by association" cannot be allowed under the U.S. Constitution, and therefore, the teachers were reinstated. *Keyishian v. Board of Regents*, 385 U.S. 589 1967).

This is not to say that all loyalty oaths are invalid. The Supreme Court has merely said that teachers may be disqualified from public employment only where the can be shown to have the specific intent to further the unlawful objectives of the controversial organization. Therefore, teachers and other school employees should be willing to sign a loyalty oath such as the following one which the Supreme Court upheld in 1968:

> **I do solemnly swear (or affirm) that I will support the constitution of the United States of America and the constitution of the State of New York, and that I will faithfully discharge, according to the best of my ability, the duties of the position of** . . . . , **to which I am now assigned.** *Knight v. Board of Regents*, **269 F.Supp. 339 (U.S. Dist. Ct. N.Y., 1967); aff'd 390 U.S. 36 (1968).**

It should also be noted that the membership of the Supreme Court has changed and the philosophy of some of the decisions reflects this. A loyalty oath case decided in the early 1970's, although strongly criticized by legal commentators, suggests that the Court has taken a new stand in regard to loyalty oaths. It is presuming that such oaths are valid. In a 1972 case, the Court went so far as to uphold a Massachusetts loyalty oath for state employees which reads:

> **I do solemnly swear (or affirm) that I will uphold and defend the Constitution of the United States of America and the Constitution**

of the Commonwealth of Massachusetts and that I will oppose the overthrow of the government of the United States of America or of this Commonwealth by force, violence or by any illegal or unconstitutional method. *Cole v. Richardson,* 92 S.Ct. 1332 (1972).

Note that this oath uses the terms "uphold and defend" and "oppose." This is the present state of the law and public employees should be willing to sign a loyalty oath similar to the above. Whether or not the Court will reverse its stand on loyalty oaths remains to be seen, but it is unlikely to occur for a good number of years.

See also: ANTI-SUBVERSIVE LAWS; ASSEMBLY; CONSTITUTIONAL RIGHTS OF TEACHERS AND ADMINISTRATORS.

M

Malpractice, suits against teachers. In 1972, an 18-year-old California youth sued teachers and school officials for $1 million, claiming that the defendants had been guilty of graduating him from high school with B-minus grades, even though he was able to read at only a fifth grade level. The theory behind this kind of malpractice suit was that the student's teachers were negligent for failing to supervise the process of education: i.e., failing to diagnose an obvious learning problem or prescribe a clearly needed therapy. It was also alleged that the school was guilty of fraud for telling the student that he would learn to read if he came to school, and for leading his parents to believe that he was learning to read.

This effort at forcing ACCOUNTABILITY through a lawsuit is not going to be effective. Legislative efforts, moves by teachers to set goals for themselves, and demands by citizens for wider educational choices will be necessary for accountability to become a reality. Nevertheless, this widely publicized case has been effective in creating greater attention to the existing problems.

This case was dismissed by the court in 1974. Students cannot use teachers or administrators as scapegoats for failures of the educational process. There are a great many possible legal defenses to this kind of malpractice suit. Among them:

1. Teachers are not responsible because they have little say in the funding, equipping, or organization of the schools.
2. There is no constitutional guarantee to literacy.
3. Education is indefinable.
4. The parents and the students themselves may be guilty of CONTRIBUTORY NEGLIGENCE for participating in the failure to learn.
5. Schools are only one of many factors that influence learning in children, and the other factors—physical, emotional, social, etc. must also be considered.
6. No one has been able to isolate the effect schooling has on learning.
7. Parents may not have the legal standing to sue the state in this kind of case.

Some of these defenses are, of course, less persuasive than others. But the most important defense of all is that education is not always a product as much as it is a process. What is gained through years of schooling cannot always be measured in standardized terms.

Malice. Malice is an expression of hatred or ill will. Basically, in malice, there is an intent to cause injury to another through the use of an express or implied plan of doing an unlawful or tortious act.

Mandamus. Mandamus is a writ which issues from a court having higher authority, directing an official or inferior court to perform a designated legal duty. A writ of mandamus is used, for example, to compel a school district to issue a CONTRACT where it is the district's legal duty to do so. If the deadline for RENEWAL has passed, or if there is an improper teacher dismissal, the legal course of action is generally through a writ of mandamus. If the teacher or administrator is successful in convincing the court that the school board should be required to perform a certain legal duty, the court will order that the writ of mandamus be issued.

Mandatory Education. See COMPULSORY EDUCATION.

Marriage. See MARRIED STUDENTS; MATERNITY LEAVE.

Married Students. (For a preliminary introduction, see STUDENT RIGHTS.) As long ago as 1929, a school board rule which permanently prohibited a married student from attending a public school was found to be invalid. The court suggested that such a rule would be reasonable only if there was a showing of immorality, misconduct, or a deleterious effect on the other students.[62] Some schools attempted to get around this rule by merely "suspending" students for various periods of time, rather than forcing the student to permanently withdraw. A clear majority of the COURTS have declared such RULES to be unreasonable and arbitrary. For example, a school rule requiring withdrawal from school for a period of one year subsequent to marriage was invalidated,[63] and in another case, a rule requiring withdrawal from school after marriage for the remainder of the school year was also invalidated.[64]

In addition, a case involving a 16-year-old mother established the rule that a married student has the right to attend school even though she has a child.[65] However, marriage emancipates a minor from COMPULSORY EDUCATION laws, and therefore, the courts hold that a married minor cannot be compelled to attend school against his or her will.

Prohibitions on a married student's right to engage in extracurricular activities has not met with such firm opposition from the courts. Most courts have upheld these rules, based on a belief that they are reasonable because the school board has an interest in:

1. Discouraging teen-age marriages.
2. Preventing students from losing interest in or dropping out of school.
3. Protecting the student's marriage by having the student spend more time at home.
4. Protecting the moral welfare of other students.
5. Maintaining discipline and avoiding disruption.

The validity of these arguments is subject to question. This is not to say that school officials are not rightfully concerned about these interests; but it is doubtful that preventing married students from participating in extra-

---

[62] *McLeod v. State*, 122 So.737 (Miss. 1929).
[63] *Board of Education of Harrodsburg v. Bentley*, 383 S.W.2d 677 (Ky. 1964).
[64] *Anderson v. Canyon Independent School Dist.*, 412 S.W.2d 387 (Tex. 1967).
[65] *Alvin Independent School District v. Cooper*, 404 S.W.2d 76 (Tex. 1966).

curricular activities does in fact protect any of the above stated objectives.

Extracurricular activities have often been viewed as special privileges which the board may grant or withhold at its discretion. However, modern judicial reasoning has resulted in tests which suggest that denying such privileges amounts to a denial of EQUAL PROTECTION and such a denial can only be upheld if there is a valid state purpose and the denial does in fact accomplish such a purpose. It is extremely doubtful that restrictions on married students can be justified under these tests.

In addition, one court has spoken of marriage as a constitutionally protected right. Infringement on this right would be permissible only where it is "necessary to promote a compelling state interest." [66] Since education has also been seen as a fundamental right, limiting educational opportunities would infringe on the student's right to marry and right to an education. If such rules are intended to punish a student for exercising this protected right, they are in violation of equal protection, deny DUE PROCESS, and are not based on a compelling state interest. This case involved a young girl who was suspended from school for five days because she got married. When she returned, she was not allowed to engage in extracurricular activities. Discouraging teen-age marriages could perhaps be seen as a compelling state interest but rules of this type do not accomplish the purpose, and in addition, are often intended more as a means of punishing the student.

In another similar case, a high school senior honor student married a 16 year old girl who was pregnant. This young man was also an excellent baesball player and was sought by several colleges and major league teams. A district rule prohibited married students from participating in school sponsored extracurricular activities. Under this rule, the boy was denied the opportunity to play varsity baseball. He sued, and the court invalidated the rule and held that such a rule puts an undesirable strain on the student's marriage and constitutes an invasion of marital privacy. The court also stated that:

> [E]xtracurricular activities are, in the best modern thinking, an integral and complementary part of the total school program. The rule which plaintiff attacks cuts him off from a part of the education which under the Ohio statutes he has a right to receive. . . .[67]

---

[66] *Holt v. Shelton*, 341 F.Supp. 821 (U.S. Dist. Ct., Tenn. 1972).
[67] *Davis v. Meek*, 344 F.Supp. 298, 301 (U.S. Dist. Ct., Ohio 1972).

These cases suggest that school rules barring married students from participating in extracurricular activities will no longer be upheld by the courts.

See also: CONSTITUTIONAL LAW; DISCRIMINATION; EQUAL PROTECTION; PREGNANT STUDENTS; STUDENT RIGHTS.

Mass Resignation. Mass resignation involves the simultaneous submission of resignations by a large group of teachers. The purpose of a mass resignation is to force the school board to accede to the teachers' demands. Frequently, the teachers' employee organization will hold the resignations and use them as a threat, but do not necessarily submit them to the board.

A STRIKE is defined as any concerted refusal to work. Mass resignations are often looked upon by the COURTS as a form of a strike. If seen as being a truly valid resignation of the teachers involved, the teachers have no obligation to return to work and the court will not compel them to do so. On the other hand, if the resignations are treated as being valid, the school board would have no obligation to "rehire" the teachers. Moreover, under a few state STATUTES, TENURE and seniority rights are granted on the basis of continuous service, and an interruption (such as a resignation) might adversely affect these rights.

Maternity Leave. Maternity leave is a LEAVE OF ABSENCE granted to tenured and nontenured teachers and administrators due to pregnancy. Today, we take much of this for granted. However, there was a time when marriage and pregnancy were considered grounds for dismissal. Teachers even signed CONTRACTS which said that they would not be secretly married or date young men "except insofar as it may be necessary to stimulate Sunday School work." Of course, this restriction was only directed towards the female gender of our society who, it was felt, could be adversely affected by "falling in love, becoming engaged, or by tolerating any familiarity on the part of men."

Eventually, things began to change. Teachers were allowed to be married. However, the slide to the left-wing of liberalism was not without its splinters. Although a teacher could be married, it was felt that pregnancy verged on immorality, and certainly constituted a breach of contract. By statute, most local school boards may dismiss teachers only on specific grounds. As a result, one board went so far as to try to dismiss a teacher for giving birth because, the board asserted, it constituted an act of

"NEGLIGENCE." The court refused to uphold the board's reasoning, and ordered that the teacher be reinstated. *In re Leakey*, 43 Lack. Jur. 41 (Pa. Com. Pleas 1943).

The EQUAL PROTECTION Clause of the Fourteenth Amendment has been used as a basis for striking down arbitrary policies disallowing maternity leave. For example, a school board may not refuse a nontenured teacher a maternity leave, particularly where such a leave is granted to tenured teachers. In addition, the CIVIL RIGHTS ACT OF 1964 makes it clear that a teacher may not be dismissed due to her pregnancy. As a result, the right to be pregnant is assured, but questions still remain regarding: when must the teacher take maternity leave, may she be paid during the absence, and when may she return?

The teacher must leave her teaching duties when her pregnancy affects her educational effectiveness or when she and her doctor determine that her health necessitates such a leave. This general rule began in the early 1970's, and has received reinforcement in nearly all of the cases deciding this issue. In January of 1974, the Supreme Court of the United States settled the issue when it ruled that schools could not force pregnant teachers to take a leave of absence after the fourth or fifth month of pregnancy. Although the court did not close the door on the possibility of mandatory leave during the last few weeks of pregnancy, the basic rule is that the teacher must be allowed to remain teaching until she and her doctor determine that her health necessitates her taking the leave. *Cleveland Board of Education v. LaFleur*, 94 S.Ct. 791 (1974).

Many school boards have changed their policies to conform with these requirements, and the state of New York has liberalized its maternity leave policies for state workers to allow pregnant employees to continue working during the pregnancy as long as they desire. The law permits payment of accumulated sick leave for the absence, and allows unpaid maternity leave for up to two years. This type of law complies with the E.E.O.C. requirements and guidelines.

School boards may, of course, enact reasonable rules governing the procedures for maternity leave. It is reasonable to require that the teacher make a written application for maternity leave at least one month prior to the date the leave is to take effect. Submission of a doctor's certificate would also be a reasonable rule.

School boards have asserted a number of different arguments as to why a teacher should not teach beyond a certain month. These arguments, such as increased liability, inability to carry out responsibility in fire drills, increased absence on the part of the teacher, and impact on students, have all been frustrated by court decisions. The pregnant teacher should continue to remain as long as she is qualified and capable of performing her duties.

When, then, may she return to the classroom? Court decisions have opened the door to modern trends in this area. Courts will generally hold that the period of a woman's post-delivery absence, as with her pre-delivery absence, is up to the teacher and her doctor. If she is physically and mentally able, the teacher may return immediately. The school board may require a certificate from a doctor as to her physical fitness. In addition, the Supreme Court has suggested that a board rule requiring the teacher to wait for return until the beginning of the following school term *might* be valid.

The rules on maternity leave policies affect tenured and nontenured teachers alike. New York law requires that teachers should be paid during the absence for accumulated sick leave days. There is some dispute in this area, but the trend is that pregnancy constitutes an illness and not a disability, and that therefore, teachers should be paid sick leave benefits. Otherwise, it is discriminatory and in violation of her constitutional rights.

See also: PATERNITY LEAVE.

Mechanic's Lien. A mechanic's lien is a statutory lien allowed to the materialman for work performed or materials furnished for the improvement of real property. Generally, a mechanic's lien will not be allowed to a subcontractor for improvements made to school property. School PROPERTY is not owned by the local board but by the state. A lien can attach to the CONSTRUCTION contract itself provided money is owed on that contract. In order to prevent unjust enrichment or inequitable results, statutes generally provide that a bond shall be had prior to construction. This bond is for the purpose of ensuring that the subcontractor shall be paid for services or materials rendered.

See also: BUILDINGS.

Mediation. Mediation is the effort by a third party to reconcile the parties in a labor dispute so that a settlement can be reached. Where parties are negotiating, but are unable to reach AGREEMENT, COLLECTIVE BARGAINING laws frequently provide that a mediator is to be provided by an impartial state agency which is created to administer the negotiation laws. This mediator tries to get the parties back on the road leading to a solution of the dispute by making suggestions, advising the parties, and by trying to get the parties to modify some of their demands. Occasionally, some mediators will recommend terms for a solution, but the mediator has no power to force a solution.

See also: MEET AND CONFER BARGAINING LAWS.

Medical Services. Medical services as used in this context is meant to refer to the medical facilities, diagnostic, and first-aid treatments which are provided by the school district for students. The school board has the authority and the right to hire professional doctors and nurses in order to diagnose and inspect students to see if health regulations have been complied with. These medical services, however, are limited. In the absence of statutory authorization, the school district cannot provide free medical *treatment* for such things as communicable diseases, operations, or dentistry. Emergency treatment must be REASONABLE AND PRUDENT, and first aid may be administered by unlicensed laymen if the circumstances are such that immediate aid is necessary.

School board authority in this area is limited. Each state has minimum health requirements for students and teachers. Thus, under the guise of its police power, the state may require VACCINATIONS and reasonable physical examinations. In addition, schools have the right to check teeth, eyesight, and hearing in cooperation with the local board of health. Should a student wish to be excluded, he or she would need a doctor's certificate. A question might arise as to whether or not medical services can be imposed upon a student in violation of his or her constitutional rights. The answer to this would depend on the form of the treatment and the religious convictions or other constitutional provisions asserted by the child. The COURTS would have to balance the constitutional rights with the school's duty to maintain a safe and healthy atmosphere in which to attend school. If the circumstances are such that by not allowing oneself to be treated, he or she would endanger others, the treatment can be a prerequisite to entering school.

See also: FUNDS.

Medication. Teachers and administrators cannot give medication to students except in cases of emergency. Should an emergency arise, the medication given must be REASONABLE AND PRUDENT under the circumstances then and there existing.

See also: MEDICAL SERVICES.

Meet and Confer Bargaining Laws. Meet and confer laws provide a method of determining wages, hours, and conditions of employment through discussions between the school board and the employee organization. These parties are required to meet and discuss employment relations and try to reach an agreement.

An exact definition of meet and confer bargaining is hard to nail down because there are differences in the wording of these laws. Proponents of COLLECTIVE BARGAINING laws criticize meet and confer laws and argue that meet and confer STATUTES force an employee organization to engage in collective begging rather than collective bargaining. There is some justification for this view, but it is much too simplistic because most laws do not follow the *pure* meet and confer concept.

The pure meet and confer concept was founded on the notion of complete sovereign authority. Under this concept, the public employer retains broad managerial discretion, subject only to recall. The outcome of employer-employee negotiations is dependent more on school board determinations than on bilateral decisions by equals at the bargaining table. Employees have the right to discuss, but the school board retains the right to act unilaterally on any matter pertaining to wages, hours and conditions of employment. The board must consider the presentation made by the employee representative, but after giving it reasonable consideration, the board may act unilaterally. Only about three states have retained the pure meet and confer approach to public employee bargaining.

Other jurisdictions having meet and confer statutes define the meet and confer obligation as ". . . the process whereby the representatives of a public agency and representatives of recognized employee organizations have the mutual obligation to meet and confer in order to exchange freely information, opinions and proposals to endeavor to reach agreement on conditions of employment." This kind of law requires bargaining with an eye toward reaching agreement. In addition, some of these laws require the parties to "meet and confer in good faith." This is even more explicit in requiring the employee to approach the discussions with an open mind and to try and agree. Arguably, although this kind of meet and confer law suggests at first glance that the parties do not meet as equals, in reality, the employees are granted many bargaining rights which are not far from approaching the right to collective negotiations.

Meet and confer laws are in the process of being exchanged for collective bargaining laws. Each year, more and more states examine the need for improvement of employer-employee relations in the public sector, and most of them recognize that meet and confer laws have been beneficial but such laws may have lost their ability to meet the needs and demands of public employees.

Meetings. School board meetings, student meetings, and teacher meetings are regulated either by state law or by RULES of the local administration or school board. The first of these, school board meetings, is regulated by state law, and a thorough discussion of the law and procedures in this matter can be found under the section SCHOOL BOARDS.

Student meetings are not regulated by law but are governed by rules of the local administration and school board. Regulation of student meetings is subject to the rules relating to STUDENTS' RIGHTS. Generally, rooms do not have to be provided for any meeting not approved of by the administration or school board. Attendance at student meetings such as assemblies may be required. On the other hand, attendance at meetings involving extracurricular activities after school hours may not be required. Of course, the conduct of the students at any meetings may be regulated by teachers and administrators.

As for teachers' meetings, the school district must provide for these. Board members may attend formal teachers' meetings, and may voice their opinions on the topics discussed. The school administration may require teacher attendance at regularly scheduled meetings, but must allow for absences with valid excuses.

Mental Distress, infliction of. Infliction of mental distress is a tort involving conduct which exceeds all bounds tolerated by a decent society, which is especially calculated to cause and does cause mental distress of a very serious nature. This is a tort which can be intentional or the result of NEGLIGENCE. Not much is heard about mental distress because it is a relatively new tort. In the past, mental distress generally had to be accompanied with some sort of physical injury. This was true because proof of mental injury was difficult to achieve, and without physical injury, fraudulent claims could be asserted. Today, no physical injury is usually necessary for *intentional* infliction of mental distress; however, for *negligent* infliction of mental distress, a physical injury generally still has to be present.

Teachers and administrators have the right to discipline students, but they cannot do so in a manner which is calculated to cause severe emotional distress. In one instance reported to the authors, a teacher took a rocket ship that had been used in a school carnival, and hung it from the ceiling in her classroom. Whenever a child got "carried away," the teacher would have the student stand under the rocket ship as she lowered it over the student in front of the class. There, the student would stand in the dark until he or she was ready to fit into the classroom activities.

In another instance, a fifth grade student was "clowning around." Therefore, the teacher took her lipstick, painted a clown's face on the child, and told him to return after school was out in order that she might make certain that he hadn't removed the mask.

None of these cases ever went to court. In each of these cases, the teacher might have been sued, and might well have been liable for any emotional distress the children suffered. These are actions the reasonable teacher or administrator would not tolerate, and they are actions especially calculated to cause severe mental distress.

This does not mean that a teacher or administrator cannot admonish a student in front of his or her peer group, and isolating a student into a separate part of the classroom or out of the classroom entirely is on many occasions appropriate discipline. However, these things must be done in a reasonable manner. If a teacher or administrator takes action which is calculated to cause or does cause mental distress of a very serious nature, and a student suffers such distress as a result, the teacher or administrator may be held liable.

Mental Examinations. A teacher or administrator can be required to take a physical and mental examination to determine fitness to perform the required teaching or administrative functions. The mental examination that can be required is one which relates to fitness, and not the intelligence of the teacher or administrator. The local school board of the past had the power to require a teacher to take an intelligence test, but such a test could not be required today. Today, the teacher's CERTIFICATE is prima facie evidence of competence.

Mergers. See REORGANIZATION.

Merit Pay. Merit pay is a system by which a teacher is or is not promoted to higher pay scales based upon his or her performance or educational achievements. It is clear that school districts can determine annual increments on the basis of merit. This has come into some controversy, but the controversy is generally based upon the EVALUATIONS and their procedures. The COURTS have held that local boards have a great deal of discretion in the area of merit pay increases. So long as the determination of pay increases is not discriminatory and is based upon relevant criteria, the merit pay schedule will be upheld. Professional growth requirements are examples of proper criteria. Although a teacher may have met the minimum state requirements for CERTIFICATION, it is within the school board's authority to require further educational qualifications.

Methods. A teacher's teaching method is within his or her own discretion. This method may be evaluated and subjected to some changes where it is necessary for improvement. However, so long as the teacher is adequately fulfilling the duty of instruction, the methods should be of no concern to the school board.

Military Leave. Military leave is leave granted to a teacher or administrator who has been drafted or is required to perform duties for the National Guard or military reserve training. Military leave is mandatory and must be given if the teacher or administrator has been employed for more than six months. The teacher or administrator is not entitled to his salary during the time of the absence, but does have the right to his same position upon return. However, there is generally a time limit on the length of time a person can be absent, and if that time is overextended, the board has the right to hire a replacement.

Ministerial Acts. Local school districts are obligated to perform certain duties. Many of these duties are governmental in nature and cannot be delegated. For example, duties that involve the exercise of discretion cannot be delegated. However, duties that are private in nature or that can be carried out by anyone without having to make a decision between various factors, are ministerial in nature and can be delegated. For example, the local board has the duty to hire teachers and administrators. That duty involves decisions and the exercise of discretion. Therefore, this duty cannot be delegated to someone such as the SUPERINTENDENT. The superintendent may make recommendations, but the final decision rests with the board. On the other hand, taking minutes at board meetings, or taking a survey to determine how many students are enrolled for the coming year can be done by almost anyone. These acts are therefore ministerial and can be delegated.

See also: GOVERNMENTAL IMMUNITY.

Minutes, school board. See SCHOOL BOARDS, meetings.

Misdemeanor. A misdemeanor is a crime which is generally punishable by a fine or imprisonment for less than six months or both. A misdemeanor is an indictable offense which is less serious in nature than a FELONY.

Mitigation. See CONTRACTS; DAMAGES.

Money. See ACTIVITY FUNDS; BONDS; FEES; FUNDS.

Moral Turpitude. Moral turpitude is conduct which is contrary to honesty or good morals. This is a very imprecise term which must be considered by judging the individual's conduct in relation to the surrounding facts and circumstances.

See also: DECERTIFICATION; TEACHERS, dismissals.

Mothers. 1. *Students.* See MARRIED STUDENTS; PREGNANT STUDENTS; STUDENT RIGHTS.

2. *Teachers.* See CONSTITUTIONAL RIGHTS OF TEACHERS AND ADMINISTRATORS; MATERNITY LEAVE.

Municipal Corporation. A municipal corporation is a corporation for a particular place that is formed to carry out political purposes at a local level. The school board is a municipal corporation. It is an arm of the state government and it has certain delegated authority but no inherent power of its own. Its power comes from the state and it cannot exceed the authority which is granted.

Music. Allocation of school FUNDS for music classes and instruments is within the power of the school board. Students may be required to deposit FEES for breakage, but generally not for sheet music unless the class is extracurricular in nature and not a part of the general CURRICULUM.

N

Negligence. Negligence is the unintentional doing or not doing of something which wrongfully causes injury to another. (For an explanation of liability for intentionally caused injuries, see INTENTIONAL TORTS.) In our schools, teachers and administrators should constantly be on the alert in order to avoid negligent injuries to students or to themselves. Of all the lawsuits filed against teachers and administrators, negligence is the most prevalent. Because this is so, it is necessary to thoroughly understand the elements that constitute negligence.

Negligence is a tort, involving four elements:

1. Duty;
2. Violation;
3. Cause; and
4. Injury.

If any of these four elements is missing, there can be no liability for negligence.

First of all, there is "duty." All people owe all other people the "duty" of not subjecting them to an unreasonable risk of harm. If a dangerous condition exists, and a teacher or administrator is or should be aware of it, it is his or her duty to eliminate the condition before someone is injured.

Because a student is a "ward" of the teacher or administrator when in school, there exists a legal duty to eliminate dangerous conditions, to protect students, and to come to their aid. If a person is walking down the street and sees someone being assaulted, he or she has no legal duty to render aid. However, if a teacher or administrator is on the playground and sees a student being battered, he or she is legally obligated to render any possible aid. Along the same lines, if an ordinary person sees children swinging in a high tree with a thin rope, there is no duty to stop them. However, should a teacher or administrator see students doing the same thing, during the school recess, there is a duty to stop the activity if it is foreseeable that a child could be injured.

The teacher's or administrator's duty can be put in one word: "safety." It is the teacher's and administrator's duty to maintain a safe environment in which the students can learn. Safety in the classroom, on the playground, and on any school sponsored activity must be maintained.

Before a person is held liable for negligence, he or she must have "violated" the duty owed. The test for whether or not a person has violated his or her duty is: Did the person act in the way a REASONABLE AND PRUDENT teacher or administrator would have acted in the same or similar circumstances? The test is not that complicated, but is very important. The reasonable and prudent teacher or administrator is simply an "ordinary" teacher or administrator.

Would the ordinary teacher or administrator consider it reasonable to leave a college-prep high school English class unsupervised for five minutes? Probably yes. Would it be reasonable to leave a woodshop class unsupervised for ten minutes? Probably not. Would it be reasonable to let children play on a trampoline without supervision? No. These questions were answered with a "probably yes," "probably not," and "no"—but now let us change the facts. Suppose the English class consisted of "hard learners," who become unmanageable without constant attention. Would it be reasonable to leave them now? Probably not. Suppose the woodshop class was finished working and all that the students were doing was cleaning the shop. Could the teacher leave them for ten minutes now? Probably yes. Suppose the children on the trampoline were the state AAA gymnastic champions. Could the teacher leave them to practice together? Probably yes.

As one can see, by changing the facts, we have changed the potential outcome. As this demonstrates, whether or not a person has been negligent is a QUESTION OF FACT for the jury to decide. The jury must consider all of the facts and all of the circumstances, in order to reach a proper conclusion. First, the jury will decide if there was a duty. Next, it will decide if that duty was violated.

In addition to duty and violation, negligence must have the element of "cause." If a person violates his or her duty, and it "causes" injury, there will be liability for negligence. "Cause" can present some complicated problems. Generally, an accident is caused by a number of facts and circumstances working together. If a person throws a rock in the air and another is injured thereby, it is easy to see what caused the injury. However, if two students are left unsupervised and they begin fighting, it is difficult to determine if the cause of an ensuing injury would be lack of supervision or the students' own voluntary acts.

In the law, it is generally said that an injury must be "proximately caused" by an act before there is liability. If an act or omission produces an event, or if the event would not have occurred without the act or omission, that event is proximately caused by that act or omission. In other words, did an act occur because of something the teacher or administrator did or did not do?

As mentioned before, there may be contributing causes to an injury. If there are contributing causes, the question is whether or not those causes supercede, or intervene, and take over the original cause. If the causes are concurrent, the original cause still exists, and the defense would be forced to try to prove CONTRIBUTORY NEGLIGENCE, or ASSUMPTION OF RISK. On the other hand, if the other causes are intervening and they supercede the former cause, the original cause will disappear and there will be no liability. An example might help to clear this up.

In one case, a Maryland teacher left her physical education class unattended while the students continued to do "push-ups." One of the students left his position, and his foot hit a girl's head. The girl's front teeth were badly damaged, and the teacher was sued for negligence. The lower court found in favor of the injured student, but was overruled. Granted, the teacher may have been negligent in leaving the class unattended, but the court found that her absence was not the proximate cause of the injury. The court said:

> **If a rule can be developed from the teacher liability cases, it is this: a teacher's absence from the classroom, or failure properly to supervise students' activities, is not likely to give rise to a cause of**

action for injury to a student unless under all the circumstances the possibility of injury is reasonably foreseeable. . . .

The point is that a teacher could be liable to an injured student, whether or not the teacher could have prevented the injury, if the injury is a reasonably foreseeable consequence of absence or failure to supervise. Under such circumstances, the intervening force does not become a superceding cause which breaks the chain of causation, but becomes a part of the original tort. *Segerman v. Jones,* 259 A.2d 794, 804 (Md. 1969).

In other words, the teacher's absence may have been a partial cause of the injury, but it was superceded by the actions of the student causing the injury. The student's action was the proximate cause and, therefore, the teacher was not liable. If the teacher should have reasonably foreseen that his or her absence from the classroom might lead to this kind of conduct, the teacher's negligence would not have been superceded.

So far, we have talked about (1) duty; (2) violation; and (3) cause. The fourth necessary element for negligence is (4) injury. Without an injury, there can be no liability. The extent of the injury determines the amount of DAMAGES that will have to be paid. Punitive damages are seldom allowed, and if the injury is slight, nominal damages would probably be awarded. The most common award is compensatory damages, or those damages which make the injured party "whole" again.

Negligence has to do with safety. Because safety is so important, it is necessary for teachers and administrators to make reasonable RULES that govern the students' conduct. Emphasis is placed on the fact that these rules must be communicated to the students and must be consistently enforced. A rule that is not enforced does not really exist.

Even with a knowledge of the elements of negligence, injuries will continue to occur. Some injuries will be unavoidable. Others will be foreseeable, and still others will be the result of ignorance or carelessness. (See FORESEEABILITY.) If a teacher or administrator is careless, that does not necessarily mean he or she is negligent. It is careless to be absent from class, but it is not negligent unless the absence is unreasonable. (See ABSENCE FROM CLASS.)

Even though a person might be negligent, there are some defenses. Assumption of risk and contributory negligence are the most common defenses and save many people from being held liable. GOVERNMENTAL IMMUNITY is a defense for some school boards, but if that

immunity is waived, there may be some assistance given to the teacher or administrator. Also, an act of God is a defense. (See GOD, act of.)
See also: IMPUTED NEGLIGENCE.

Negotiable Issues. See SCOPE OF BARGAINING.

Negotiations. See COLLECTIVE BARGAINING; MEET AND CONFER BARGAINING LAWS; SCOPE OF BARGAINING.

Neighborhood Schools. See COMPULSORY EDUCATION; VOUCHERS.

Newspapers. During the 1960's and early 1970's, the schools were confronted with many issues involving newspapers. One of these issues involved the question of whether or not teachers had the right to criticize school officials or the school system in local newspapers. For an explanation and discussion of these issues, see CONSTITUTIONAL RIGHTS OF TEACHERS AND ADMINISTRATORS.

Another of the issues which troubled educators involved student publications. For an explanation and discussion of the problems surrounding student newspapers, see STUDENT RIGHTS. One of the special problems involved in student newspapers is the question of whether or not school officials may exercise prior restraints on these newspapers. This is a highly controversial area, and one which has not been settled completely.

School officials have the power to establish reasonable regulations on the time, place, and manner of distribution of student publications. These are recognized as being "conditions" on freedom of the press, not "prohibitions." School officials also have the power to prohibit the students from distributing obscene or libelous material. (See DEFAMATION; OBSCENITY.) However, the more controversial issue which has not been decided clearly is whether or not the school has the power to require prior approval of the content of student publications before the students will be allowed to distribute them.

A heavy presumption of invalidity exists against RULES providing for prior restraints on freedom of speech. Therefore, the school policy must be narrowly drawn to advance the social interests which justify it without unduly restricting protected free speech. A majority of the COURTS will uphold a school rule requiring prior approval of student publications if it meets with the following suggested requirements:

1. The policy should specify that it is applicable only to distribution of materials on school property and at school-related functions.

2. The policy must spell out clearly what kind of materials are forbidden in order to allow the student to be able to ascertain what he or she may or may not write. In addition, in prohibiting certain kinds of materials, school officials must not violate the students' right of free speech. (See STUDENT RIGHTS.)

3. The policy must establish a procedure for submission of materials for approval. The essential elements of this procedure which are necessary to satisfy the requirements of the Constitution are:

   a. "Distribution" must be defined in order to make it clear that the policy is directed at a substantial distribution and not at the passage of a note, paper or magazine from one student to another.

   b. The policy must specify to whom the materal should be submitted, how the submission is to be accomplished, and who is responsible for granting or denying approval.

   c. A definite, brief period of time must be specified for approval or disapproval of what is submitted. (Prompt review generally should be made within 24 hours.)

   d. The policy should state that if school officials fail to act within the period of time set pursuant to paragraph "c" of this section, the students have the right to distribute the materials.

   e. The policy must provide an adequate and prompt appeal procedure.

   f. The policy should state that it is not operative until each school establishes its review procedure and informs its students.

Keep in mind that this is a policy regarding prior approval of "speech." It perhaps will prevent some "speech" from taking place. This is why it is necessary to meet such stringent constitutional requirements. If prior approval is not required, or even if prior approval has been granted, once the "speech" has taken place, if it proves to be disruptive, libelous, etc., school officials certainly do have the authority to punish the students who were responsible for it.

Non-Public Schools. See PRIVATE AND PAROCHIAL SCHOOL AID; PRIVATE SCHOOLS.

Nonrenewal. Unlike a teacher dismissal, nonrenewal is a type of discharge "after" a contract has expired. The word "discharge" can be a bit misleading—legally, the person is not discharged, he or she is just not rehired. The outcome remains the same—the teacher or administrator is out of a job.

Most state statutes cover nonrenewal of nontenured teachers or administrators. Unlike dismissals, it is generally stated that a nonrenewal can be based on any just cause and sometimes on no cause at all, so long as it is not an arbitrary or capricious decision. As one can readily see, there are not a great many protections against nonrenewal. Of course, the nonrenewal may not be in violation of the teacher's or administrator's constitutional rights, and strict nonrenewal procedures must be followed. Generally, notice of nonrenewal must be received on or before a certain date, the notice must sufficiently inform the teacher or administrator of the intent not to renew, and it must be delivered in the manner prescribed by statute. If the statute says that the notice must be sent by certified mail to the last known address, it would be insufficient to put the notice in the teacher's or administrator's mailbox at school. If the notice is sent late, it has no legal effect. If the statute says that the reasons for nonrenewal must be in the notice, the reasons must be there or the notice is inadequate. All aspects of nonrenewal must be followed exactly.

If improper notice is received, the teacher or administrator would be well advised to consult an attorney or his or her educational association. Quick and accurate steps must be taken, or there is a possibility that the courts will hold that proper notice has been waived.

See also: CONTINUING CONTRACT LAWS; DUE PROCESS; RENEWAL; TEACHERS, dismissal.

Nonresidents, admission to school. Whether or not a nonresident may be admitted to a school depends on varying state statutes. Generally, the states say that this decision is discretionary and that admission is mandatory only where a nonresident does not have proper facilities within his or her own school district. If there is room within the district for the nonresident, the nonresident may be admitted and may be required to pay a TUITION payment.

Notice. See DUE PROCESS; NONRENEWAL; RENEWALS; TEACH-ERS, dismissals.

Nurses. See MEDICAL SERVICES.

O

Oaths. See LOYALTY OATHS.

Obscene Literature. See OBSCENITY.

Obscenity. Case law as well as statutory law relating to obscene material is applicable in the school environment as well as in the community. The age, intelligence, and experience of the students are all relevant factors to be considered when trying to determine whether or not certain literature is obscene or is unsuitable for the students' instruction.

Over the years, various tests have been used in an effort to provide a uniform standard for making a determination of whether or not certain material is obscene. Prior to 1973, the test for obscenity was whether or not the material was "utterly without redeeming social value." In making this determination, national standards were to be used.

In 1973, the Supreme Court of the United States rejected the prior test and applied a new test to be used in making a determination of obscenity. The Supreme Court ruled that:

1. Material may be declared obscene if "(a) . . . 'the average person, applying contemporary community standards', would find that the work taken as a whole, appeals to the prurient interest, and . . .

(b) . . . the work depicts or describes, in a patently offensive way, sexual conduct specifically defined by the
applicable state law, and

(c) . . . the work, taken as a whole, lacks serious literary,
artistic, political or scientific value."

2. The determination of "prurient interest" and "patently offensive" may be made in light of forum community standards rather than on the national standard.

3. Exhibiting obscene material in places open to the public is
not protected as a constitutional right of privacy.

4. States may find a nexus between antisocial behavior and
obscene literature and may regulate its exhibition and com-
merce in public places.

Miller v. California, 93 S.Ct. 2607, 2615 (1973); and *Paris Adult
Theatre I v. Slaton,* 93 S.Ct. 2628 (1973).

Through the Supreme Court rulings of 1973, the states are given much
greater latitude and power to regulate literature. However, the state regulations must be specific. As the Court said:

> **State statutes designed to regulate obscene materials must be care-
> fully limited. . . . [W]e now confine the permissible scope of such
> regulation to works which depict or describe sexual conduct. That
> conduct must be specifically defined by the applicable state law, as
> written or authoritatively construed. A state offense must also be
> limited to works which, taken as a whole, appeal to the prurient
> interest in sex, which portray sexual conduct in a patently offensive
> way, and which, taken as a whole, do not have serious literary,
> artistic, political, or scientific value. *Miller v. California,* 93 S.Ct.
> 2607, 2614-2615 (1973).**

The Supreme Court gave several examples of what could be defined for
regulation:

> **(a) Patently offensive representations or descriptions of ultimate
> sexual acts, normal or perverted, actual or simulated.
> (b) Patently offensive representations or descriptions of mas-
> turbation, excretory functions, and lewd exhibition of the genitals.
> (93 S.Ct. at 2615.)**

These examples are among the more obvious types of regulations which the states will make. It is possible that state STATUTES may tend to be far more restrictive with regards to obscenity than they have ever been. But, it is not necessarily the state statutes themselves which will inhibit freedom of speech. The publishers' fear of being punished or subjected to numerous lawsuits in different states and different cities over the same materials will necessarily force them to exercise strict censorship over the materials they publish.

Thus, in a 5-4 decision, the Supreme Court has taken a giant step—backwards. The Supreme Court is now allowing obscenity to be judged in terms of community standards. School administrators, teachers, and students, as well as publishers and book distributors, are left not knowing what constitutes obscenity. They are left without clear guidelines as to the kinds of materials which may be used in the classroom. It has always been an accepted basic rule of law that when people of normal intelligence are forced to guess as to what conduct is or is not prohibited, the rule or the law is unconstitutionally vague, and no punishment will be allowed. Not knowing what kinds of classroom materials are prohibited or allowed is bound to wreak havoc with freedom of speech within the schools. The chilling effect which will spread throughout the classroom will remain until this Supreme Court ruling is overruled or modified.

Offer, contract. Every contract in order to be valid must be offered and accepted. The offer to enter into a contract must be clear and definite, and with the present intent to have the offer accepted and to become binding. Generally, the offer should state the time to begin and the time to finish the services to be rendered, and the consideration to be paid. The offer continues to exist for a reasonable time, or for a stated period of time, and must be accepted in order to be considered valid prior to the time the offer is extinguished. Prior to acceptance, the offer may be revoked, unless the person has paid (such as earnest money) for the offer to last for a certain time period.

See also: CONTRACTS.

Officers. See PRINCIPAL; SCHOOL BOARDS; SUPERINTENDENT; TEACHERS; VICE-PRINCIPAL.

Omission. An omission is simply failing to act when there is a legal duty to do so.

Open Hearing. An open hearing generally becomes an issue at teacher or administrator dismissals. Whether or not a person has a right to an open hearing depends upon state statutes. The teacher or administrator involved has the right to ask for a closed hearing; but it is not clear whether or not he or she has the right to a hearing that is open. The better view is that a teacher or administrator involved does have the right to an open hearing or else it violates DUE PROCESS. If there are proper reasons for dismissal, the board should have nothing to hide; and if the teacher or administrator involved wants to bring these reasons into the public forum, he or she is exercising a valid right.

Oral Contracts. See CONTRACTS.

"Outside" Employment. The question sometimes arises as to whether or not a teacher or administrator has the right to work at something other than the school position. Antiquated rules of local boards have said that teachers and administrators must spend 24 hours a day working or thinking about their school and their job. These rules are no longer valid. A teacher or administrator may accept outside employment so long as that employment does not interfere with or affect the school position. If the outside employment creates a CONFLICT OF INTERESTS, or causes the teacher or administrator to lose effectiveness within the school, the employment may be curtailed. Otherwise, a person's private life should be of no concern to the local board.

See also: CONTRACTS.

P

Parental Authority. Parents, like any other citizens, have the right to vote for school budgets and for members of the board. This is just about the extent of their legal authority over school functions and policies. Legally, when the child enters school grounds, the parents' control ends, with relation to most school matters. The parent as a rule has no right to determine the CURRICULUM, who will teach, how a subject will be taught, or what RULES should be enacted and enforced. This means that a parent does not have the right to observe a teacher in order to evaluate the teacher's effectiveness. That is an administrative function. On the other hand, parents do have a right to see their child's records and to discuss problems with school personnel. This right is limited. As far as *direct* authority over the school's duty of instruction, SUPERVISION and safety, the parent has no control except with his or her voting power for members of the local board.

There is some case law that, although the parent has no control over the school curriculum, there are instances wherein the parent has the right to determine whether or not his or her child shall participate in certain classes or activities. If the objections are reasonable or are based upon the parent's or student's constitutional rights, they should be adhered to. If they are not, they may be ignored without any remedy being available to the parent. (See CURRICULUM; SEX EDUCATION; STUDENT RIGHTS.)

See also: STUDENT RECORDS.

Parental Liability. Parents are liable for their own TORTS, but not for the torts of their children unless such liability is imposed by statute. Most states have enacted such legislation, but have limited the liability to anywhere between $200 and $2000. Any judgment for over that amount would generally be up to the child to pay. Because the child is usually "judgment proof" (unable to pay), the injured party will either get no compensation or will receive compensation through another source, such as personal injury insurance.

Parking Lots. See AUTOMOBILES; FUNDS.

Parochial Schools. See PRIVATE AND PAROCHIAL SCHOOL AID; PRIVATE SCHOOLS.

Paternity Leave. Paternity leave is a LEAVE OF ABSENCE granted to a father after the birth of his child. This type of leave has been unknown in the past, but seems to be gaining some momentum as more DISCRIMINATION cases are decided.

In one case, the father of a new child applied for paternity leave for six months in order to care for the new infant in his family. Women had been allowed such a leave, but the same right was denied to the male teacher. The teacher filed a complaint and the court ruled that he stated a valid cause of action. *Danielson v. Board of Education of the City University of New York*, 4 Employment Practice's Decision 7773, U.S.D.C.S.D. (New York 1972). Thereafter, the school board adopted a policy granting male teachers the right to take this type of absence.

In this case, MATERNITY LEAVE for women teachers had been granted whether or not the teachers were ill or healthy. In other words, if they asked to leave for up to three semesters to care for the child, they were given that right irrespective of their physical condition. It was contended by the teacher that, because of this fact, the father had the same right or else denial would constitute discrimination.

Maternity leave irrespective of health is not the same as maternity leave due to the physical demands of pregnancy. If female teachers are granted maternity leave for health reasons, denial of the same to men would not constitute discrimination, for obvious reasons. Technology and women's lib have not yet advanced to the point where there is a complete reversal of roles. Unless men can become pregnant, maternity or paternity leave due to illness will not become one of their constitutional rights. However, leave based on something other than the demands of pregnancy should be granted to men as well as women.

Peace Corps Leave. Peace Corps leave is a LEAVE OF ABSENCE that is mandatory. Under federal law, a teacher who joins the Peace Corps is assured of his or her right to the teaching position upon return. However, the teacher must have worked in the district for a certain period of time, and the maximum allowable period of absence is generally two years.

Peace Symbols. See CONSTITUTIONAL RIGHTS OF TEACHERS AND ADMINISTRATORS; STUDENT RIGHTS.

Performance Bonds. See BUILDINGS; CONSTRUCTION.

Personal Property. See TRESPASS TO PERSONAL PROPERTY.

Personnel Records. Personnel records do not have the same quasi-public status as STUDENT RECORDS. These records are not public, and they are not open to inspection by the school district employees. A 1968 case event went so far as to hold that a grand jury was not entitled to inspect personnel records. As stated by the court:

> . . . [T]he personnel records of the district are maintained as confidential files; it is common knowledge that such matters are among the most confidential and sensitive records kept by a private or public employer, and their use remains effective only so long as the confidence of the records, and the confidences of those who contribute to those records, are maintained. It does not matter that here the employees themselves sought disclosure of the records; the records are the property of and are in the custody and control of the district, not of the employees. *Board of Trustees of Calaveras Unified School District v. Leach,* 65 Cal. Rptr. 588, 593 (1968).

Personnel records must be distinguished from the teacher's permanent file which is kept open for inspection by the teacher and his or her agents.

All evaluations are placed in this permanent file, and it is kept separate from the personnel records kept by the teacher's superior.

Petitions. See GRIEVANCE.

Physical Disability. See LEAVES OF ABSENCE.

Physical Educaton. See ATHLETICS; CURRICULUM; NEGLIGENCE.

Physical Examinations. See COMPULSORY EDUCATION; MEDICAL SERVICES; VACCINATION.

Physicians. See MEDICAL SERVICES.

Picketing. See STRIKES.

Plaintiff. A plaintiff is a party to a lawsuit. The plaintiff is the one who is suing for some injury or wrong he or she has suffered due to the alleged wrongful acts of the DEFENDANT.

Playground. It is the duty of the school and the teachers in charge of playground SUPERVISION to make certain that the play area is safe and free from hazardous conditions. If a teacher is assigned to supervise a playground, he or she is not expected to be in all places at all times. However, the teacher must be REASONABLE AND PRUDENT, and should circulate in and about the students present in order to determine whether or not any hazardous activities are being pursued.
  See also: NEGLIGENCE.

Pledge of Allegiance. Neither a teacher nor a student may be compelled to recite the Pledge of Allegiance to the flag. As long ago as 1943, the Supreme Court of the United States held that to compel a student to salute the flag or say the Pledge of Allegiance violates the First Amendment to the U.S. Constitution. The Court explained its holding by saying:

> **Words uttered under coercion are proof of loyalty to nothing but self-interest. Love of country must spring from willing hearts and free minds, inspired by a fair administration of wise laws enacted by the people's elected representatives within the bounds of express constitutional prohibitions. These laws must, to be consistent with the First**

Amendment, permit the widest toleration of conflicting viewpoints consistent with a society of free men. *West Virginia State Board of Education v. Barnette*, 319 U.S. 624, 644 (1943).

Subsequent to this case, several COURTS ruled that teachers also have the right to refuse to recite the Pledge of Allegiance or lead his or her students in the recitation. One case involved a father-son situation (teacher and student) who refused to salute the flag or say the Pledge of Allegiance. *State v. Lundquist*, 278 A.2d 263 (Md., 1971).

School officials can require the teacher to instruct one of the students to lead the Pledge. In addition, the teacher can be expected to remain sitting or standing respectfully while the Pledge is recited. Unless such action is taken as a form of punishment, school officials could provide that a teacher who refuses to lead a "homeroom" class in the Pledge may be relieved of the homeroom assignment.

Some people object to the words "with liberty and justice for all." They do not believe that this reflects the true quality of life in America. The objection does not have to be based on RELIGION. Under the American Constitution, these people have a right to their beliefs and may not be forced to utter words contrary to these beliefs. True loyalty and patriotism cannot be demonstrated merely by reciting the Pledge by rote memory without any conviction or meaning.

The better rule is that the Constitution will protect a teacher or a student who refuses to salute the flag or recite the Pledge of Allegiance as a matter of personal conscience, even if other teachers or students follow their example. However, there is some split of judicial authority on this point.

See also: BIBLE READING; CONSTITUTIONAL RIGHTS OF TEACHERS AND ADMINISTRATORS; FLAG SALUTE; PRAYERS; STUDENT RIGHTS.

Police. School officials have the right to cooperate with police in regard to crimes or investigations of students. However, school officials would be well advised to consider such things as DEFAMATION and the students' constitutional rights. For example, STUDENT RECORDS are confidential in many areas. Also, it is frequently asserted that a teacher or an administrator stands within the shoes of a parent. If a student is being questioned by police, ordinarily a parent would want to be present. Therefore, although there may be no legal duty, it seems that a student's parent should be called before allowing police to question the child. If that is impractical, the teacher or administrator should try to be present, and at least make certain that the student knows that he or she has the right to remain silent, has the right to have counsel present, and that anything he or she says can and will be used against him or her. Actually, the proper place for the police to question students is not within the schools. It may be more convenient for the police to do it there, but the better place is at the student's home or at the police station.

See also: SEARCH AND SEIZURE.

Policies, school board. See SCHOOL BOARD, policies.

Political Activities. See ANTI-SUBVERSIVE LAWS; CONSTITUTIONAL RIGHTS OF TEACHERS AND ADMINISTRATORS; PUBLIC OFFICE.

Prayers. The New York Board of Regents recommended the reading of the following prayer in the public schools:

> **Almighty God, we acknowledge our dependence upon Thee, and we beg Thy blessings upon us, our parents, our teachers, and our country.**

The reading of this prayer was challenged on the grounds that it was contrary to the beliefs and RELIGION of some of the students and violated the First Amendment to the U.S. Constitution. In 1962, the Supreme Court ruled that this prayer was religious in nature and therefore violated the "establishment of religion" clause of the First Amendment. The Court explained that:

> **. . . [I]n this country it is no part of the business of government to compose official prayers for any group of the American people to recite as a part of a religious program carried on by the government.** *Engel v. Vitale,* **370 U.S. 421, 425 (1962).**

The Supreme Court's decision was written in such a manner that it seemed to apply only to prayers which constitute a religious exercise. As a result, some teachers continued the practice of "prayer" recitation in a modified form. In one case, a kindergarten class was required to recite the following verse before "snack time:"

> We thank you for the flowers so sweet;
> We thank you for the food we eat;
> We thank you for the birds that sing;
> We thank you for everything.

The word "GOD" had been eliminated from the original last line. This did not prevent a Federal Court of Appeals from recognizing that this was in fact a prayer and therefore was unconstitutional. *DeSpain v. DeKalb County Community School District*, 384 F.2d 836 (7th Cir., 1967).

See also: BIBLE READING; FLAG SALUTE; PLEDGE OF ALLEGIANCE.

Pregnant Students. Courts have held that MARRIED STUDENTS may not be prohibited from attending school. This rule holds true even though the student has a child; but while a girl is carrying the child, many schools have RULES which prohibit her attendance at school. Some of these rules require pregnant students to withdraw from school immediately upon becoming aware of the pregnancy, or at a specified month of the pregnancy. Like similar rules involving pregnant teachers, these rules are being challenged. The main arguments advanced are that these rules deny the student EQUAL PROTECTION and are arbitrary and capricious and therefore in violation of the student's right to DUE PROCESS of law.

The COURTS are becoming increasingly willing to declare such rules invalid. Although several of the earlier cases held that mandatory withdrawal from school during an advanced stage of pregnancy would be upheld, the modern trend of judicial reasoning would be that such rules are unreasonable and unconstitutional. Rules which are necessary for a student's health, safety, or welfare are, of course, reasonable, and the courts will uphold them. However, rules which specify, for example, that a girl must withdraw from school after the fifth month of her pregnancy are arbitrary and capricious. If it is safety the schools are concerned about, the early stages of pregnancy have been shown to be the most hazardous and critical. It is also possible that absence from school would cause more serious harm to the girl than her attendance at school. For example, in 1971, an unwed, pregnant high school girl was reinstated to her classes by a Massachusetts court. Several doctors testified that the girl's condition would not be an obstacle, and absence from school would cause depression and mental anguish. The court explained its decision in the following words:

... [N]o danger to ... [the student's] physical or mental health resultant from her attending classes during regular school hours has been shown; no likelihood that her presence will cause any disruption of or interference with school activities or pose a threat of harm to others has been shown; and no valid educational or other reason to justify her segregation and to require her to receive a type of educational treatment which is not equal to that given to all others in her class has been shown.[68]

As the preceding case also suggests, the fact that a pregnant student is unwed is not a sufficient reason to deny her attendance at a public school. However, one court has given judicial status to the rule that if, after a fair and impartial DUE PROCESS hearing, it is found that such a student is so lacking in moral character that her presence in school will "taint the education of the other students," she may be barred. This is a difficult test to comply with, but unless such a finding is and can be made, it would clearly be unfair to forever brand such a person as a scarlet woman.[69]

Again, it should be pointed out that only a minority of cases, and a few state statutes, provide that the school must allow pregnant students to attend. However, this is a rapidly growing minority and it will eventually become generally accepted law. Many educators have recognized the need to aid student mothers and, fortunately, have no intention of waiting for the law to force them to recognize the plight of the student mother. Some have demonstrated their concern by setting up special programs for married and pregnant students.[70] Such an enlightened response to the problem is encouraging, and long overdue.

In addition, rules necessary to implement the provisions of the CIVIL RIGHTS ACT OF 1964 have been adopted by the Department of HEW. These rules prohibit the denial of any benefits or participation in any programs administered by an agency receiving federal funds based on reasons which discriminate on the basis of race, sex, religion, etc. Suits brought under these rules, contending that denying a pregnant student the right to attend school is discriminatory, have a strong chance of success.

Pregnant Teachers. See MATERNITY LEAVE.

---

[68] *Ordway v. Hargraves*, F.Supp. (U.S. Dist. Ct. Mass. 1971); quoted from Nolpe Notes, vol. 6, #6, p. 4 (June, 1971).
[69] *Perry v. Grenada Municipal Separate School District*, 300 F.Supp. 748 (Miss. 1969).
[70] Richard Woodbury, "Help for High School Mothers," *Life*, April 2, 1971, p. 34.

Preponderance of Evidence. A preponderance of evidence is the greater weight of evidence, or evidence which is more credible and convincing to the mind. The greater number of witnesses has nothing to do with the preponderance of evidence.

See also: TEACHERS, dismissals.

Press, freedom of. See CONSTITUTIONAL LAW; CONSTITUTIONAL RIGHTS OF TEACHERS AND ADMINISTRATORS; NEWSPAPERS; STUDENT RIGHTS.

Presumption. A presumption is a conclusion or inference that if fact "A" exists, fact "B" necessarily follows. A presumption may be either "conclusive" or "rebuttable." If it is a conclusive presumption, the proof of fact "A" makes it mandatory for the court or the jury to find that fact "B" exists, and evidence to the contrary is inadmissible. On the other hand, if it is a rebuttable presumption, the proof of fact "A" permits the jury to find fact "B" (sometimes forces the jury to find fact "B") but evidence is allowed to show that fact "B" does not, in fact, follow from fact "A."

For example, at COMMON LAW there was a conclusive presumption that a child under the age of seven could not be contributorily negligent. Therefore, evidence to show that a six-year-old child did, in fact, contribute to his or her own injury would be inadmissible. On the other hand, there was a rebuttable presumption that a child from age seven to age fourteen was not capable of CONTRIBUTORY NEGLIGENCE. Therefore, evidence to show that a thirteen-year-old child did, in fact, understand a dangerous condition and therefore, contributed to his or her own injury would be admissible.

Another example is that it is presumed that a school board decision is proper and within the scope of the board's authority. However, evidence would be admissible to prove otherwise, thereby rebutting the presumption.

Principal. A principal is an employee of the school district and is not an officer of the school board. The principal is in charge of the day-to-day operation and management of the school, and therefore, has a certain amount of discretion and authority to make and enforce reasonable RULES governing the school, teachers and students. These rules should be written, communicated, and followed as closely as possible. Of course, the rules may not conflict with SCHOOL BOARD policy or with state law, and they must not violate contract rights or constitutional rights of the teachers or students.

The principal serves a very important function within the school system. However, he or she does not enjoy the immunities or rights to indemnification that many officers of the board or board members themselves enjoy. (See SCHOOL BOARDS, liability and GOVERNMENTAL IMMUNITY.) Instead, the principal is personally liable just like any teacher for acts done within and without the scope of his or her authority.

Principals often wonder whether or not they can be held liable for the tortious acts of the teachers. The general rule is that a principal may not be held liable for an injury unless it can be shown that there was NEGLIGENCE on the principal's part which contributed to the injury. The principal cannot, nor is he or she expected to, supervise every activity in which students are involved. Teachers have the duty to supervise the specifics. However, if a principal participates in the activity in a negligent manner, or if the principal knows or should know that a teacher is incompetent to fulfill the supervisory duties, the principal is then liable for his or her own negligence. In such a case, both the teacher and the principal would be named as defendants, and would be jointly liable.

It should be noted that the principal's duty to ensure safety inures not only to students, but to teachers as well. If the principal knows or should know that a certain student has dangerous propensities, it is the principal's duty to do something about it. If the principal does not, and a teacher is injured as a result, it is quite possible that the principal could be liable for negligence in not having removed or properly disciplined the child.

Privacy. The right of privacy is occasionally raised as a basis for preventing dismissal or punishment of a teacher for activities he or she engages in out of the public view and on his or her own time. This right of privacy is not mentioned in the Constitution. However, there is some judicial authority suggesting that a right of privacy does in fact exist and that it is protected under the Constitution.

The initial birth of this concept occurred in 1965. At that time, the Supreme Court of the United States invalidated Connecticut's ban against the dissemination of information about contraception and birth control devices. *Griswold v. Connecticut*, 381 U.S. 479 (1965). The law was declared invalid because it invaded a zone of privacy which extends beyond the matrimonial bedroom. The Court explained that the right of privacy exists within the "penumbra" of the first ten Amendments and it is safe-guarded by the Constitution's seldom used Ninth Amendment: "The enumeration in the Constitution, of certain rights, shall not be construed to deny or disparage others retained by the people."

In another important case, the Supreme Court held that the private and personal use and viewing of obscene material may not be made a crime. As the Court stated:

> **Whatever the power of the state to control public dissemination of ideas inimical to the public morality, it cannot constitutionally premise legislation on the desirability of controlling a person's private thoughts.** *Stanley v. Georgia,* 394 U.S. 557, 566 (1969).

This right of privacy will not protect the importer or distributor of obscene material, however.

These two cases are not directly in point for teachers and administrators. However, they do apply by analogy to public employee's private lives. The great weight of judicial opinion is rapidly shifting to suggest that the private conduct of a person who also happens to be a teacher may not be used as grounds for dismissal except where such conduct affects his or her fitness to be in the classroom. In other words, there must exist a nexus between the conduct complained of and the teacher's ability to perform his or her teaching duties.

The implications of the right of privacy are extremely broad. The COURTS have only begun to touch on the protections granted under this constitutional right. Hopefully, the Supreme Court will not shift into reverse and declare that the framers of the Constitution never intended to reserve to citizens of the United States a right to conduct their personal lives in privacy.

See also: CONSTITUTIONAL RIGHTS OF TEACHERS AND ADMINISTRATORS; HOMOSEXUALS.

Private and Parochial School Aid. This is an extremely complex area of the law, one which has traditionally been subjected to a great deal of litigation. Over the years, many attempts have been made to directly or indirectly aid private and parochial schools. Some of these attempts have been successful, but a great many have not. The cases resulting from attempted aid to these schools have frequently been decided by the Supreme Court of the United States. This Court has enunciated various tests which are to be used in judging the constitutionality of the state or federal government aid. These tests, though often difficult to understand and apply, are extremely important because the COURTS need a tool which they can use to break down the many varied kinds of attempted aid into categories. Once this has been done, the courts can take a closer look at who or what is actually benefitting from the aid, i.e. the students, parents, schools, or the state. This is crucial in helping the courts apply uniform standards.

The importance of categorizing aid and applying various tests to determine constitutionality can best be demonstrated by mentioning just a few of the kinds of aid programs which have been established or attempted: free TEXTBOOKS, bus TRANSPORTATION, tax refunds, tax credits, tax deductions, VOUCHERS, school lunches, public health services, use of state owned facilities by religion instructors, teachers' salaries paid by the state, TUITION reimbursements, and a host of others. Many of these aid programs are new. The ingenuity of persons attempting to obtain government aid for private and parochial schools, or children attending those schools, seem limitless, and there is no reason to expect that many new forms of possible aid will not be developed.

The following explanation of private and parochial school aid is intended to give the reader a general overview of legislative and court history in this complex area. A brief explanation will be made of some of the tests the courts have used in determining the validity or invalidity of government aid, and in this manner, the reader will be able to understand the court rulings, and in many cases, will be able to judge for himself or herself the kinds of aid which are permissible under the U.S. Constitution. Keep in mind that some state constitutions may impose even greater restrictions on aid to non-public schools. The term "parochial schools" will be used in the subsequent parts of this section, and it is meant to mean both private and parochial schools.

The First Amendment to the U.S. Constitution established a two-pronged prohibition on government action with regard to RELIGION. In what has come to be known as the "establishment of religion" clause, the Constitution provides that: "Congress shall make no law respecting an establishment of religion or prohibiting the free exercise thereof. . . ." Through the Fourteenth Amendment of the Constitution, the Supreme Court holds that the states are also subject to the requirements of the establishment of religion clause. Note that this clause requires the state and federal governments to maintain a policy of strict neutrality towards religion. While they may not directly aid religion, neither may the state or federal governments discriminate against or inhibit religion.

Not until 1947 was the establishment of religion clause clarified. At that time, the United States Supreme Court said:

> The "establishment of religion" clause of the First Amendment means at least this: Neither a state nor the Federal Government can set up a church. Neither can pass laws which aid one religion, aid all religions, or prefer one religion over another. Neither can force nor influence a person to go to or to remain away from church against his will or force him to profess a belief or disbelief in any religion. No person can be punished for entertaining or professing religious beliefs or disbeliefs, for church attendance or nonattendance. No tax in any amount, large or small, can be levied to support any religious activities or institutions, whatever they may be called, or whatever form they may adopt to teach or practice religion. Neither a state nor the Federal Government can, openly or secretly, participate in the affairs of any religious organizations or groups and *vice versa*. In the words of Jefferson, the clause against establishment of religion by law was intended to erect "a wall of separation between Church and State."[71]

In 1925, it was firmly established by the Supreme Court that although compulsory attendance laws obligate parents to send their children to school, the parents have a constitutional right to send them to private or parochial schools.[72] This case substantiated the legitimacy of parochial education. Since parochial education had been legitimated, supporters sought to justify government aid to such schools. For many years, it seemed the courts' attitude was not whether the government should aid parochial schools, but "how."

Several state STATUTES provided that the state would supply free TEXTBOOKS to *all* students attending school. Students attending parochial schools were granted free secular textbooks under these laws. As early as 1929, this kind of law was challenged, but the court upheld it.[73] In this case, the court applied what has become known as the CHILD-BENEFIT THEORY. Under this theory, the court explained that where the state legislation is primarily for the benefit of the students themselves and the parochial school benefits only indirectly, the aid will be upheld. The state has the right to provide public aid to help all children learn about

71 *Everson v. Board of Education*, 330 U.S. 1, 15 (1947).
72 *Pierce v. Society of Sisters*, 268 U.S. 510 (1925).
73 *Borden v. Louisiana State Board of Education*, 123 So. 655 (La., 1929).

secular subjects, and in doing so, school children and the state alone are the beneficiaries, not the parochial schools.

Thus, the courts had established one theory which could be used to validate aid even though it might indirectly benefit parochial schools. The child-benefit theory requires the court to examine two questions: (1) What is the legislative intent? and (2) Who receives the aid, the parochial school or the parent and child?

In 1947, the Supreme Court of the United States reiterated some of the logic upholding indirect forms of aid. In this case, a New Jersey statute provided for reimbursement to all parents for money spent for bus TRANS-PORTATION of students to their schools. The Court explained that the establishment of religion clause prohibits the expenditure of any tax monies, large or small, in support of any religious activities or institutions. It went on to say that: "The First Amendment has erected a wall between church and state. That wall must be kept high and impregnable. We could not approve the slightest breach." [74] This means that the state must remain neutral towards the church, it may not aid it nor oppose it. Therefore, the Court upheld the bus transportation reimbursement and explained that this was public welfare legislation. By allowing public schools to provide transportation for *all* children, the Court said that the transportation regulation "does no more than provide a general program to help parents get their children, regardless of their religion, safely and expeditiously to and from accredited schools." Therefore, the "benefit" is to the child, and not to the parochial schools.

As a result of this line of cases, two legal principles evolved:

1. There can be no direct aid to church-related schools.
2. People may not be excluded from social welfare benefits because of their religion.

Therefore, it is clear that not all aid is impermissible. The test the courts adopted was one of *direct v. indirect aid*. Direct forms of aid, such as providing facilities for religious instruction or paying the salaries of religion instructors, clearly are not permissible under this test.

Several additional theories were also used by the courts in trying to determine the validity or invalidity of various forms of aid. Among these theories were the EXTERNAL BENEFIT THEORY and the FUNDA-MENTAL INTEREST THEORY. The fundamental interest theory seemed

---

[74] *Everson v. Board of Education,* 330 U.S. 1, 18 (1947).

to receive the most attention by the courts. Under this theory, in judging the validity of aid to parochial schools, education is perceived as being a fundamental interest. Aid to education is then perceived as aid granted in the furtherance of this interest. The court must then balance the benefit of furthering this interest against the requirements of the establishment of religion clause. If the main effect of the aid is furtherance of the fundamental interest in education, and the benefit to religion is incidental, the aid will be upheld. On the other hand, if there is a significant benefit to religion, and there exists no overriding benefit to the fundamental interest, the aid will be judged as being impermissible.

Along the same line of reasoning as uesd in the fundamental interest theory, in the early 1960's, the Supreme Court explained that, in making a determination of whether or not state or federal laws aid religion in violation of the establishment clause, the courts must look at the legislation and try to see what the *primary effect* is, and if there exists a *secular purpose*. This test was explained in the Supreme Court ruling which declared that reading the Bible or PRAYERS in the school was unconstitutional:

> The test may be stated as follows: What are the purpose and primary effect of the enactment? If either is the advancement or inhibition of religion then the enactment exceeds the scope of legislative power as circumscribed by the Constitution. That is to say that *to withstand the strictures of the Establishment Clause there must be a secular legislative purpose and a primary effect that neither advances nor inhibits religion.* . . . The Free Exercise Clause, likewise considered many times here, withdraws from legislative power, state and federal, the exertion of any restraint on the free exercise of religion. Its purpose is to secure religious liberty in the individual by prohibiting any invasions thereof by civil authority . . .[75] (Emphasis added).
>
> The place of religion in our society is an exalted one, achieved through a long tradition of reliance on the home, the church and the inviolable citadel of the individual heart and mind. . . . In the relationship between man and religion, the State is firmly committed to a position of neutrality.[76]

The child-benefit theory fits well into this kind of purpose and primary effect test. As a result, this theory was applied in a 1968 Supreme Court

---

[75] *Abington School District v. Schempp*, 374 U.S. 203, 222-223 (1963).
[76] *Id.* at 226.

case which upheld the constitutionality of a New York statute requiring local SCHOOL BOARDS to loan textbooks free of charge to children attending public, private and parochial schools. The Court examined the statute and found that the purpose and the benefit were secular in nature.[77]

Then, in 1970, the Supreme Court was faced with the question of whether or not property tax exemptions for religiously owned and used PROPERTY was in violation of the Constitution. The Court used the secular purpose and primary effect tests, and then added a new test for consideration: "We must . . . be sure that the end result—the effect—is not an excessive government entanglement with religion. The test is inescapably one of degree.[78] The Court upheld the tax exemptions because it reasoned that taxation would increase the degree of government involvement with religion. This "entanglement test" may become the courts' new approach in judging the validity of state aid.

In 1971, the Supreme Court outlined how the courts should determine the constitutionality of state aid:

> **In order to determine whether the government entanglement with religion is excessive, we must examine the character and purposes of the institutions that are benefitted, the nature of the aid that the State provides, and the resulting relationship between the government and the religious authority.[79]**

The secular purpose test was also added to the above outline. As a result, the courts must seek the answers to four questions:

1. Is there a secular legislative purpose?
2. Is the primary effect of the legislation a benefit or limitation on religion?
3. Does the legislation foster entanglement with religion?
4. Does the legislation prevent the free exercise of religion?

The Supreme Court's attitude in the early 1970's has been to restrict the possible forms of government aid which are constitutionally permissible. However, certain forms of assistance which meet the requirements of secular purpose, primary effect and government entanglement may be permissible. To withstand the test:

---

[77] *Board of Education v. Allen,* 392 U.S. 236 (1968).
[78] *Walz v. Tax Commission,* 397 U.S. 664, 674 (1970).
[79] *Lemon v. Kurtzman,* 403 U.S. 602, 615 (1971).

1. *All* children must benefit and be covered by the legislation;
2. No direct aid or payments may be granted to non-secular schools;
3. Aid granted must be for a secular purpose; and
4. Aid granted must not require the non-secular school to give up its religious instruction.

In applying the above tests, the Supreme Court has ruled that the state can provide parochial schools with secular, neutral, or nonideological services, facilities, or materials. Students attending parochial schools may be provided such things as bus transportation, school lunches, public health services, secular textbooks, and drivers' education courses which are supplied to *all* students in the state. SHARED-TIME and RELEASED TIME programs have also been upheld.

The Supreme Court has invalidated state laws which in essence provide direct financial aid to parochial schools. Such unconstitutional aid includes: tuition reimbursements to low-income parents of parochial school pupils; tax credits to middle-income parents; direct aid to parochial schools for maintenance and repair of buildings; granting of state funds to parochial schools for testing and record keeping; use of school owned or leased buildings for religious instruction; and many, many others.

The Supreme Court is suggesting that while the state may accept its obligation to see that children are educated, it has no obligation to assure the survival of church-connected school systems which help the state meet its obligation of providing education. However, this is not a final shutting of the door. Many indirect forms of aid are permissible, but the extent of permissible aid often depends upon the tests and theories which the court uses. If the court desires to liberalize its policy regarding aid to parochial schools, it will apply the tests and theories most conducive to supporting government aid. This is one of the main reasons why this is such a complex area of school law. There are many different tests and theories, and as the make-up and philosophy of the Supreme Court changes, the reasoning used in support of the case decision changes. However, it appears rather clear that for some time to come, the Supreme Court is going to take a fairly restricted view of state or federal aid to parochial schools. As a result, the aid programs will be forced to meet the requirements of the three-pronged "secular purpose, primary effect and government entanglement test."

Private Schools. Private schools must provide students with an education which meets the minimum CERTIFICATION requirements as set forth in state STATUTES or State Board of Education regulations. However, in nearly all other aspects, private schools are regulated privately and not by the state. A private school may be a parochial school or simply a private business enterprise. Problems do arise in relation to how "private" the private school may be, and to what extent does the state have authority over the private school's functions.

It is constitutional for a state to have COMPULSORY EDUCATION laws. However, even though a student may be compelled to go to school, he or she may not be forced into the public school system. That is, a student may not be forced to attend the public schools so long as a viable alternative is pursued.

There have been many constitutional challenges to the public school system based on religious grounds. Many parents have wanted to form their own schools or have their children attend "home school." Most home schools fail to meet the minimum state requirements. There must be a certified teacher, minimum CURRICULUM requirements must be met, and there is some authority to the effect that students should have free association with other students, thereby enabling them to learn through social interaction. If these requirements are met, then a private "home school" could be formed and certified by the state.

The liability of private schools is different from that of public schools. In a private school, the protections of GOVERNMENTAL IMMUNITY do not apply. The private school is liable for its INTENTIONAL TORTS and NEGLIGENCE just as any private individual would be. There is some authority to the effect that if the private school is a charitable institution, it comes within the cloak of "charitable immunity." Charitable immunity is a dwindling legal concept meaning that a nonprofit charity cannot be used and is immune from liability. This is thought to be an unfair law, and the better view is that this COMMON LAW immunity will be lifted.

Probationary Teacher. A probationary teacher is one who is not yet tenured or entitled to a continuing contract, but is serving a probationary period prior to obtaining TENURE or greater contract rights. During the time of probation, the teacher is observed and evaluated for the purpose of determining whether or not the district wants to keep the teacher on a more permanent basis. The probationary period is anywhere from one to three years, and if a teacher is renewed at the end of the probationary period, he or she automatically becomes tenured or entitled to greater contract rights under most state laws.

See also: CONTRACTS; DUE PROCESS; NONRENEWAL; RENEWAL; TEACHERS, dismissals.

Profanity. See CONSTITUTIONAL RIGHTS OF TEACHERS AND ADMINISTRATORS; OBSCENITY; STUDENT RIGHTS; TEACHERS, dismissals.

Professional Growth. See CONTRACTS; MERIT PAY.

Property. State legislatures have the power to grant local school districts the power to acquire and hold property, and in all states, local school districts are given this power. Nevertheless, property acquired by a school district becomes the property of the state. As a result, if the legislature decides to reorganize school districts, by consolidating some or abolishing others, it is free to do so because the legislature is not allowed to relinquish complete control over state property to local districts. This also means that the state has the right to take school facilities in one school district and give them to another district or to a state agency. Compensation to the local school district or consent of the local inhabitants is not required. All school facilities, including the land, BUILDINGS, and equipment, belong to the state and are subject to the will of the legislature.

The legislature gives local SCHOOL BOARDS the power, either express or implied, to acquire property and construct buildings which are necessary to efficiently operate the public schools. This is not an unlimited power. Several cases have prescribed the rule that the school board may not purchase property as a means of speculation or with the intent to make a profit. While the board has the right to purchase land for building sites, playgrounds and athletic events, it may not purchase land for use as a farm unless this is connected to the school program. The athletic sites, etc. which the board purchases do not have to be right next to the school grounds.

The school board may acquire property by a direct purchase, or if authorized by statute, through the use of eminent domain. The power of eminent domain allows the school board to condemn private property needed for school purposes. When private property is condemned, the school board must pay money based upon the property's fair market value to the landowner. The landowner must "sell" the property to the board. However, compliance with the state and federal constitutions is required. This means that the landowner has a right to DUE PROCESS. The public agency must give the landowner an opportunity to be heard, must demonstrate a public necessity for the property, and must pay a reasonable compensation.

Although most state STATUTES allow local school boards to acquire, by eminent domain, property within the district for school purposes, the board has no right to condemn property outside of the district. In addition, there is a split of authority as to whether or not the school board has the right to even *purchase* property which is located outside of the school district. This right will depend to a great extent upon the individual state statutes and court decisions. The courts will look closely to determine the purpose of the property acquisition. Keep in mind that in all cases, the property must be purchased in order to benefit the students' education and must be for the general public welfare.

Selection of a school site is within the local school board's discretion, and the board's decision will not be over-turned unless it is arbitrary and capricious. (See also REORGANIZATION; SCHOOL BOARDS, authority.)

Local school boards have the duty to maintain school property in a safe condition, and in a condition which meets building codes and safety standards. In nearly all jurisdictions, school boards have the power to insure school property against fire, vandalism, and disaster.

Disposal or sale of school property may be controlled by the state legislature because local school boards are deemed to be holding schools for the sole purpose of education of the state citizens. Therefore, even though a school might have been purchased and maintained solely by local FUNDS, if the legislature chooses, it can limit a local school board's discretion in the disposition of school property. When the school board does sell school property, the sale must be for an amount which is equivalent to the property's fair market value. The board cannot sell school property for a nominal sum, and it must receive the best price possible or the sale may be enjoined. School property may never be given away.

At times, questions arise regarding disposition of property which has been donated to the school district by a private party. Where such property has been donated to the district by a deed which conveys title in "fee

simple absolute" (i.e. free and clear of all restrictions), the board may
dispose of the property in the same manner as other school land. However,
there are times when property is donated to the district "only so long as
the property is used for school purposes." If this property ceases to be
used for school purposes, it will possibly revert back to the original donor
or his or her heirs.

See also: BONDS; BUILDINGS; CONSTRUCTION; REORGANI-
ZATION.

Proprietary. See GOVERNMENTAL IMMUNITY.

Protests. See CONSTITUTIONAL RIGHTS OF TEACHERS AND AD-
MINISTRATORS; STUDENT RIGHTS.

Provisional Certification. See CERTIFICATION; DECERTIFICATION.

Proximate Cause. See NEGLIGENCE.

Public Office, right to hold. In many cases, teachers and other school
officials are deemed to be holding an executive position in government.
As a result, the separation of powers clause of their state constitutions
prevents them from holding an additional public office. In addition, many
state constitutions have a "CONFLICT OF INTEREST" provision which
prevents legislators and other government officials from holding any
other office or position of profit. Under these constitutional provisions,
teachers and other school officials are prohibited from being members of
the state legislature. Recognizing this prohibition, several states amended
their constitutions to specifically allow teachers to serve in the legislature.

These constitutional provisions and the legal principles preventing office
holders from having a conflict of interest also apply to SCHOOL
BOARDS. School boards are prohibited from having contracts for services or materials with the individual board members and in some cases
with close relatives of board members.

A local school board member cannot hold another public office which
may present a conflict of interest with his or her position on the board.
As a result, a board member who accepts the position of mayor in the
city automatically vacates his or her school board position.

A local school board member is, of course, prohibited from being
employed as a teacher in the same school district over which the board has

jurisdiction. However, a teacher in one school district, who lives in another school district, is not prevented from being a member of the school board in the district in which he or she lives.

Publications. See CONSTITUTIONAL RIGHTS OF TEACHERS AND ADMINISTRATORS; NEWSPAPERS; STUDENT RIGHTS.

Punishment. See EXPULSION OF STUDENTS; GOVERNMENTAL IMMUNITY; IN LOCO PARENTIS; RULES.

Pupils. See STUDENTS.

Q

Qualified Privilege. See DEFAMATION; STUDENT RECORDS.

Question of Fact. A question of fact is an issue which is decided by the jury, whereas a QUESTION OF LAW is decided by the court. For example, if a person is on trial for illegal possession of drugs, it is up to the jury to decide whether or not that person is guilty. This is a question of fact. On the other hand, it is for the judge to decide whether or not the SEARCH AND SEIZURE for such contraband was legal. This is a question of law.

As to questions of fact, the jury weighs all of the evidence, decides what is true, and then communicates that decision to the court. If, for example, the jury decided that a teacher was assaulted by a student, that determination would be final and the student could not generally appeal the decision unless as a matter of law such a determination was impossible or there were other mistakes of law in the trial. Decision as to questions of fact are final, and the court will not change such a decision without exceptional circumstances being prevalent.

Question of Law. A question of law is an issue which is decided by the court (judge) and not by the jury which decides QUESTIONS OF FACT. For example, assume that the issue is whether or not a student's constitutional rights were violated when he was suspended for wearing a black armband. It would be for a jury to decide as a question of fact whether or not the student wore the armband; but it would be for the court to decide whether or not as a question of law, the wearing of the armband was a valid exercise of the student's constitutional right to free speech.

Quorum. A quorum is the number of persons needed to conduct the business of some official body. If a quorum is not present, any action taken or decision made is without legal effect. What constitutes a quorum can be set out by statute or by enabling rules of the official body. In the absence of statutes or rules in this area, a quorum generally constitutes a simple majority of the members needed to conduct business.

Quo Warranto. A quo warranto action is a suit brought to determine whether an officer has the right to exercise the duties of his or her office. For example, if a school board member took a position on the local board and it was believed that the election was not proper, or the board member was not legally qualified, a quo warranto action could be brought. An injunction of writ of MANDAMUS would not be the proper remedy. As one court said:

> **Quo Warranto is the Gibraltar of stability in government tenure. Once a person is duly elected or duly appointed to public office, the continuity of his services may not be interrupted and the uniform working of the governmental machinery disorganized or disturbed by any proceeding less than a formal challenge to the office by that action which is now venerable with age, reinforced by countless precedent, and proved to be protective of all parties involved in a given controversy, namely, *quo warranto*. In re Vacancy in Board of School Directors of Carroll Township, 180 A.2d 16, 17 (Pa., 1962).**

It might be noted that a private citizen has no right to bring a quo warranto suit unless that citizen can show that he or she is being injured differently from the public at large. Otherwise, it is for the state to bring suit against a person who is claiming a right to hold office for that state. If the state says that the officer has the right to be in his or her position, a private citizen cannot complain through a quo warranto suit without a unique type of injury.

R

Race Relations. See DESEGREGATON; DISCRIMINATION.

Ratification. Ratification is the making good of something which is invalid due to some existing deficiency. For example, if a contract with a teacher is invalid because it was not properly adopted at a regular school board meeting, the contract may be ratified and thus made good. If there are certain statutes or board rules prescribing procedures to be followed in ratification, these must be closely adhered to. Once the contract is ratified, it becomes totally binding and may not be breached by any party. The entire contract must be ratified and not individual parts. The effect of ratification can be illustrated in the words of an early court decision:

> **[B]y the very nature of the act of ratification, the party ratifying becomes a party to the original contract. He that was not bound becomes bound by it, and entitled to all the proper benefits of it.** *Hill v. City of Indianapolis*, **92 Fed. 467, 469 (Ind., 1899).**

There are many cases wherein school boards have needed to ratify otherwise invalid agreements. Ratification may be used, for example, where school BONDS have been issued without authority where the lack of authority is simply procedural. However, if the incurrence of the indebtedness is in violation of state laws, ratification would be impossible. In addition to teacher or administrator CONTRACTS and bonds, the school board may ratify CONSTRUCTION contracts as long as the construction is within the constitutional or debt limits of the state. The ratification must be explicit and binding on both parties. It is difficult to ratify by silence, but if the contractor is performing and nothing is said, there is a possibilty a contract will be found, even if the original is not ratified, under the theory of quantum merit.

Reapportionment of School Districts. See REORGANIZATION.

Reasonable and Prudent. A teacher or administrator is required to be "reasonable and prudent" in school related matters of instruction, SUPERVISION, and safety. Whether or not the teacher or administrator meets this standard is a QUESTION OF FACT for the jury to decide. The jury will look at all the facts and circumstances and then determine if, under the facts and circumstances, the standard of care was met.

For example, if a teacher was supervising the playground and a student was injured, the jury will look at all the facts to determine if liability will be imposed. If the teacher was walking around the playground and looking after the children, that would be reasonable even though a child was injured in a different area on the school grounds. However, if the teacher sat in one place reading a book without circulating to see what the children were doing, the failure to act would likely be considered unreasonable under the circumstances.

It should be noted that teachers and administrators are held to be a higher standard of care than the ordinary man on the street. The teacher or administrator is under the duty to possess more than the "ordinary" amount of intelligence in relation to students and their care. For example, it is the teacher's duty to "foresee" an injury when students are left unsupervised for long periods of time, or where large groups of students are gathered without adequate observation. The ordinary man does not have to foresee this, but the teacher does.

An educator's standard of care is not that of the ordinary reasonable and prudent man. Instead, the educator's standard of care is that of the reasonable and prudent teacher or administrator in the same or similar circumstances.

Recission. See CONTRACTS.

Records. See PERSONNEL RECORDS; STUDENT RECORDS.

Regulations. See EXPULSION OF STUDENTS; RULES.

Reinstatement. When a person is wrongfully dismissed or suspended, he or she may seek DAMAGES, reinstatement, or both remedies at the same time. Damages are awarded for past injuries sustained, and when reinstatement is not sought, damages are awarded for future losses where these losses are the necessary consequence of the breach of contract. Damages are generally for the purpose of "making one whole" again, or in other words, putting the person back into the same place he or she would have been in had the breach of contract not occurred.

Reinstatement is also a remedy. If a teacher or administrator is wrongfully dismissed or suspended, he or she might want the money lost during the dismissal or suspension, and also want the old position back. The courts have held that if there is authority to dismiss a teacher, there is authority to reinstate the teacher. However, reinstatement will only be allowed where the party can show that if there had not been a dismissal, there would have been a right to continued employment. For example, if a teacher was wrongfully dismissed, and if that teacher had TENURE or was to obtain tenure, then reinstatement along with damages would be allowed. On the other hand, if the teacher was on a one year contract that could be renewed or not renewed at the board's discretion, the only remedy would be for the damages suffered under the broken agreement. However, reinstatement will be granted a nontenured teacher who has been dismissed or nonrenewed based on reasons which are in violation of his or her constitutional rights.

It might be noted that, even though a teacher or administrator has the right to be reinstated, that does not necessarily mean that the reinstatement will be to the exact position previously held. If the position is available, and if there would be no hostile or adverse effect on the educational process, such a reinstatement would be necessary. However, if such were not the case, reinstatement to the same type of position at a different school and not an unreasonable distance away would be proper under the circumstances.

See also: CONTRACTS; DUE PROCESS; NONRENEWAL; RENEWALS; TEACHERS, dismissals.

Released Time. In the 1940's, it was a common practice in some school districts in the United States to allow non-secular education teachers to come into the public schools and teach RELIGION classes to students who voluntarily chose to be released from secular education classes to attend. All religious denominations were allowed to give such instruction, and the salaries of the non-secular education teachers were not paid by the public school system. Nevertheless, in 1948, the Supreme Court of the United States held that this practice was in fact a utilization of the public school system to aid religious groups spread their faith. As a result, the Court declared this system of released time to be a violation of the "establishment of religion" clause of the U.S. Constitution. *McCollum v. Board of Education,* 333 U.S. 203 (1948).

In 1952, New York's released time program permitting students to be excused from classes for one hour a week in order to obtain religious instruction off school premises was upheld by the Supreme Court. The Court distinguished this program from the released time program it had invalidated in 1948. It explained that this was not an "aid" to religion, it was merely an "accommodation" to the religious interests of the people. *Zorach v. Clauson,* 343 U.S. 306 (1952).

The "establishment of religion" clause of the Constitution requires the state and federal governments to remain neutral where RELIGION is concerned. Releasing students to attend religious instruction does of course allow such classes to continue, but this is in no way an expenditure of government funds in aid of religion. Allowing instruction in BUILDINGS owned or leased by the school district is an impermissible aid. It is also unconstitutional for the school district to pay the salaries of the religion instructors. In addition, if the school district were to pay the salaries of secular education teachers who go to the non-secular school to teach secular subjects, this would be an impermissible form of state aid.

Religion. (For a general introduction, see CONSTITUTIONAL LAW.) The First Amendment to the Constitution of the United States provides in part that "Congress shall make no law respecting an establishment of religion, or prohibiting the free exercise thereof; . . . ." Note carefully that this is a two-pronged test. In essence, it requires that the government must remain neutral towards religion. While it may not aid religion, neither may it discriminate against or inhibit religion. The "establishment of religion" clause expressly refers to "Congress." However, through the Fourteenth Amendment to the U.S. Constitution, the Supreme Court of the United States holds that the prohibitions on government action which are implicit in this clause are applicable to the states as well as applicable to the federal government.

The meaning of the establishment of religion clause was clarified some-what in 1947. At that time, the Supreme Court of the United States ex-plained what the mandates of this clause are:

> The "establishment of religion" clause of the First Amendment means at least this: Neither a state nor the Federal Government can set up a church. Neither can pass laws which aid one religion, aid all religions, or prefer one religion over another. Neither can force nor influence a person to go to or to remain away from. church against his will or force him to profess a belief or disbelief in any religion. No person can be punished for entertaining or professing religious beliefs or disbeliefs, for church attendance or non-attendance. No tax in any amount, large or small, can be levied to support any religious activities or institutions, whatever they may be called, or whatever form they may adopt to teach or practice religion. Neither a state nor the Federal Government can, openly or secretly, par-ticipate in the affairs of any religious organizations or groups and vice versa. In the words of Jefferson, the clause against establish-ment of religion by law was intended to erect "a wall of separation between Church and State." *Everson v. Board of Education*, 330 U.S. 1, 15 (1947).

As a result, the establishment of religion clause has wide implications with regard to the schools. Many cases and a great deal of publicity involve questions of state and federal aid for religious-oriented schools. (For an explanation of the issues and answers to many of these questions, see PRIVATE AND PAROCHIAL SCHOOL AID.) In the 1960's and early 1970's, much more attention has been devoted to the individual's right to freedom of religion. BIBLE READING and PRAYERS in public schools were held to violate the individual's right to freedom of religion. It was also ruled that teachers and students could not be compelled to engage in a FLAG SALUTE or to recite the PLEDGE OF ALLEGIANCE.

Freedom of religion also has varying implications with regard to COM-PULSORY EDUCATION and SEX EDUCATION. As the COURTS, the state legislatures, and the schools begin to demonstrate a stronger concern for the protection of the fundamental freedoms of each and every student, teacher, and administrator, the importance of recognizing the implications of the Constitution's freedom of religion provision becomes increasingly clear.

See also: CONSTITUTIONAL RIGHTS OF TEACHERS AND AD-MINISTRATORS; STUDENT RIGHTS.

Remedies. See DAMAGES; REINSTATEMENT.

Removal from Office. 1. *Board Member*, 2. *County Superintendent*, 3. *State Superintendent*.

1. Once a person has been appointed or elected to office, he or she does not automatically remain in that office without some limitations being imposed. School board members may be removed for such things as a CONFLICT OF INTERESTS; misappropriation of FUNDS; neglect of duty and failure to perform the duties of his or her office. In some states, the grounds for removal are designated by statute and certain procedures for removal are specified. In these instances, the statutory grounds must exist, and the procedures must be followed, or any attempted removal will be invalid.

In some instances, board members request or are asked to resign. Generally, a resignation cannot be implied by the conduct of the board member. That is, if a board member does not attend any meetings, his or her resignation will not be implied, but there will be grounds for legally removing the member. If a board member does resign, the resignation becomes effective when it is formally accepted. There is some authority to the effect that the resignation does not become effective until a replacement is elected and qualified, but such a situation exists in only a small minority of the states.

2. A county superintendent may be removed for the same reasons as a school board member. In addition, it has been held that a county superintendent may be removed for committing crimes involving MORAL TURPITUDE. Immorality has been ruled to be unconstitutionally vague in some cases, but it is clear that the commission of a FELONY constitutes grounds for removal. (See also TEACHERS, dismissals.)

If there are STATUTES listing the causes and procedures for removal, these statutes must be followed explicitly. Furthermore, there are statutes which prohibit certain types of conduct, and prescribe that any violation means that the superintendent automatically vacates the position. In that case, once it has been proven that there is a violation, the position is vacated. The board of education, however, cannot make that determination. The issue must be decided by the courts, and the superintendent is entitled to DUE PROCESS and fundamental fairness.

3. Whether a state superintendent is elected or appointed, the fact is clear that he or she can be removed for misconduct in office or failure to perform his or her duties. Generally, there is a QUO WARRANTO hear-

ing, and the state is the PLAINTIFF or the party having proper standing to bring the cause of action. Of course, there is a right to due process, and a removal in this instance would be before a court and generally not before an administrative agency.

Renewal, contract. Teaching CONTRACTS are subject to renewal when the initial term of the contract has expired. The renewal procedure is most important, and this is especially true when there is some question as to whether or not the teacher or administrator is to be rehired. Most state statutes set out the procedures, and the local board and the teacher or administrator must follow these procedures exactly.

In addition to the board having to follow proper procedures in delivering notice of renewal or NONRENEWAL of a contract, the teacher or administrator must follow proper procedures in accepting the contract. The acceptance of the contract must be clear and unambiguous. If the statute says the teacher must accept in writing, oral acceptance would not be binding. If the statute says the teacher must accept by writing the superintendent, then writing the principal would not be enough. The law assumes that the teacher knows the proper procedures for acceptance. As a result, teachers and administrators have a duty to familiarize themselves with the proper procedures, and act accordingly.

Many people are concerned with so-called "Letters of Intent." These letters generally state that the district "intends" to rehire the teacher or administrator, and then asks that he or she write a reply as to whether he or she will accept the position for another term. The letters of intent simply help the district project into the future. The letter says that the contract is forthcoming but is held up, generally due to negotiations or budget approval. If the teacher or administrator replies that he or she intends to accept, the acceptance becomes binding on the part of the board. That is, once the final contracts are issued, they must be sent to those who have accepted on the basis of the letters of intent.

Although the contracts must be issued by the board to the teachers and administrators pursuant to the letters of intent, final acceptance on the part of the teachers or administrators is not mandatory. Intent to accept based upon the letter of intent is tentative. The tentative acceptance is "subject to" the approval of the final terms of the contract. If the budget is not approved and salaries are lowered as a result, or if negotiations are not satisfactorily settled, the teacher or administrator may ignore his or her tentative acceptance and reject the contract offer.

Rather than send out letters of intent, some districts have the contracts signed prior to budget approval. If the budget fails, salaries as stated on the contract may have to be lowered. Generally, a party to a contract may not unilaterally change the terms of the contract after it has been signed. However, in this case, the courts imply that the board has the right to lower the salary stated on the contract, but the board cannot lower the salary below what the teacher or administrator had received the previous year. If the contract has been negotiated pursuant to a COLLECTIVE BARGAINING law, the board may not act unilaterally in changing the contract terms. Such a law generally provides for a reopening of negotiations upon the request of either party, where the legislative body or voters fail to provide sufficient funding to allow for compliance with the contract terms. Also, if because of the budget rejection, the contract terms (salary) are changed, the teacher or administrator may choose to either accept or to reject the new contract. This same option is not open to the board, because it is the party which is changing the contract terms. As soon as the teacher or administrator makes final acceptance, the contract becomes binding upon both parties.

Delays in issuing contracts are not unusual. There can be problems, however, where the contracts are not actually issued until school has finished for the preceding year and the summer session has begun. Many times, teachers and administrators are out of town during these months, and it is quite possible that they would not discover the final issuance and, thus, would be unable to fulfill their responsibility to accept within a stated or reasonable period of time. If this is the case, the teacher or administrator should notify the board of his or her final acceptance prior to leaving town. This protects the teacher or administrator and facilitates the local board's needs at the same time.

See also: CONTINUING CONTRACT LAWS; DUE PROCESS; TEACHERS, dismissals.

Reorganization. School reorganization is synonomous with such terms as "consolidation," "annexation," and "merger." Reorganization basically means that the boundaries of a school district are changed, or the organizational structure is altered in some manner. The extent of the power to reorganize and the delegation of this authority has caused some difficulty in the past.

Although the state board of education and local school boards share responsibilities in the management and operation of the schools, the ultimate authority to determine school district composition rests with the state legislature. This means that the state legislature may decide to create or abolish any school district without the consent of the citizens within that district. The decision as to whether or not the boundaries of a school district shall be changed is a discretionary function, and the exercise of that discretion will be upheld by the courts as long as it is based on some rational purpose consistent with the best interests of the state in providing a sound education for its children.

Many difficulties can arise in the reorganization process. Although a district may be reorganized, the reorganization may not impair contractual obligations of the existing district. Article I, Section 10 of the U.S. Constitution provides that no law shall be enacted which impairs the rights of parties under pre-existing contractual obligations. If a district is annexed to and becomes a part of a larger district, the first district does not totally disappear and become "one" with the second district. Even though the first district is no longer in existence per se, it remains liable for the debts and contractual obligations previously owed. Therefore, teachers' CONTRACTS would have to be honored, BONDS would have to be paid, and any other obligations would continue. However, if all of the assets are delivered to the annexing district by the old district, there are no sources from which to draw. Therefore, state STATUTES have been enacted wherein the law provides that the second district incurs the debts of the former. These statutes are uniformly upheld unless there are state constitutional provisions stating that no indebtedness will be incurred by a school district without the vote of the people. In this type of situation, the district should not be annexed without first providing for payment of all debts. If such payment is not made, the annexation would be unconstitutional, in that it would impair pre-existing contractual obligations.

The legislature may delegate administrative authority to the state board of education and to local school boards. However, when such authority is delegated, there must be some standards and guidelines defining the perimeters or limits of the power given to the delegated authority. This means that the delegated authority should know what facts it should take into consideration, the purpose for its creation, and the policies it may adopt.

In addition to the need for standards and guidelines, problems arise with respect to such things as selection of the school site, PROPERTY valuation and computing indebtedness, and dissolution of school districts. First of all, the selection of the school site is discretionary unless the state statute says that the school site shall be within a central location or located on a public road, etc. If the statute is silent as to school site selection, only the legislative guidelines and standards must be followed, in addition to good faith.

With regard to property valuation and incurrence of indebtedness, there are basically two limitations. The first limitation is that the district shall not be indebted in excess of a certain statutory percentage when compared with the value of the property within the district. Except for tax exempt property, all real property (land and buildings) will be included for valuation purposes. Some personal property is also includable, depending on state statutes with respect to taxation.

The second limitation is that a school district may not incur liabilities in excess of the revenue expected within the ensuing year. This means that the district cannot become indebted, using as collateral expected earnings within the distant future. If it does so, the debts would be void as to the district, but there is a possibility individual board members could be personally liable. The expectation of earnings in the immediate future should be reasonable, and if the revenue expected does not materialize, the indebtedness would be valid nevertheless. All districts are not bound by these limitations, but there may exist other limitations, depending upon the state in which the district is located. If the limitation is reasonable, then, of course, it must be followed.

Once a district is dissolved and becomes part of another, questions might arise as to the extent of the authority of the district's officers to act, and where the ownership of the district's assets goes. It is clear that the new district acquires title to the assets of the old, and the electorate in the old district automatically becomes voters in the new. The officers of the old district lose their authority to act, and the officers of the new district take over the responsibilities of managing and operating the new.

Residence. Residence is a person's actual place of abode. Domicile, on the other hand, is where a person intends to remain indefinitely. A person may have many residences, but he or she may have only one domicile in most instances.

At COMMON LAW, a child's domicile followed that of his or her father. Even though the child might be living with his or her mother in New Jersey, if the father lived in California, the child would be domiciled in that state. This has changed to some extent, and today, a child's domicile follows that of his or her legal guardian, or if the child is emancipated, domicile is where the child intends to remain indefinitely.

Intent is the important factor for determining domicile. Residence requirements for such things as voting, etc., are constitutional if they are reasonable and if there is a rational basis for such requirements. However, domicile exists the moment a person intends to remain indefinitely in a certain place, and where physical presence is established within the state's boundaries.

It has been held that a person cannot establish residence within a district for the sole purpose of attending school within that district. Such an opinion today is questionable if a "permanent" intent to establish residence is shown. If the student is actually living within the district with a reasonable degree of permanency, there is a duty to provide him or her with an education even though his or her guardian or parent might live somewhere else. For example, in one case, a mother agreed with the welfare department to place her child in a private home outside of the district in which the mother lived. The school district said that the student was not a "school resident." However, the Court of Appeals said that the child was a resident for school purposes, and that the mother did not need a court order for permanent placement into the private home. *In re Laricchiuta*, 243 N.E.2d 111 (Ohio, 1968).

As one early case said:

> **It is unquestionably true that . . . "in general, children whose parents are non-residents of a district are not permitted to attend the schools therein" . . .; and that children "temporarily" with relatives in one district yet have their school residence in the district where their only living parent resides.**

But, the court went on to say, the facts and circumstances must be applied to determine whether or not the residence can properly be called "temporary." *Fangman v. Moyers*, 8 P.2d 762, 763 (Colo. 1932). The court indicated that the sole purpose of the residence could present a different outcome. However, a close analysis of the facts and circumstances must be made before that criteria alone is used as a basis for denying a child the right to attend school.

See also: TUITION.

Resignation. See CONTRACTS.

Retirement. Teachers and administrators are generally required to retire upon reaching a certain designated age. In addition to mandatory retirement, most retirement plans allow for permissive retirement at a minimum age, and once these ages are met, the teacher or administrator is eligible for retirement benefits.

There are a number of retirement plans for teachers and administrators. Social Security is a federal plan that is sometimes used in place of state retirement plans. At other times, the state and federal plans work in conjunction with one another. In all plans, the purpose is to assure that there is money available at time of retirement, disability, or death.

There is no question but that a person may be forced to participate in a retirement plan. Constitutional objections have been raised and all have fallen to court decisions which state that the public purpose outweighs any constitutional arguments. Not only is it constitutional that a person may be forced to participate, but it is constitutional for states to contribute public monies to supplement contributions made by the public employee. It has been argued that state expenditures of this nature constitute gifts and are thus improper allocations. However, the COURTS have consistently held that such an allocation is not a gift from the public coffers, but is a deferred payment for services rendered over many years.

The amount of money a person receives from the retirement plan depends upon the amount of time he or she spent on the job and how much money has been contributed. Therefore, there has been some litigation as to whether or not a teacher or administrator may get credit for prior time served in other districts. The answer depends on individual state statutes. Generally, this credit is allowed for "full-time" related positions. However, this does not generally cover substitute teachers unless there is an affirmative statement to that effect within the retirement law. Either way, the teacher or administrator must comply with all of the requirements for prior credit or else he or she is precluded.

Different retirement plans are based on different theories. One theory is called a pension plan. Another is called an annuity plan. In a pension plan, money is withheld by the state and the teacher or administrator has no control over where it is spent. The money is not segregated and can be spent by or transferred from one agency to another. This has important implications because with this type of plan, the benefits may be reduced or raised without the teacher or administrator having a great deal of authority. On the other hand, if it is an annuity plan, the teacher or administrator has a vested contractual right and the plan cannot be changed or the monies improperly spent without breaching this contractual relationship. With an annuity plan, there is a property interest that cannot be divested without DUE PROCESS. Generally, a person elects to participate in this plan, and once the election is made, participation becomes a condition of employment. That is, the person must participate so long as he or she is working. If the participation ceases prior to retirement, all contributions plus interest are returned to the employee.

The state, as well as the teacher or administrator, contributes to the retirement plan. The teacher's or administrator's contribution is generally fixed by law and cannot be lowered. The state, on the other hand, may contribute less if there are no constitutional provisions or state STATUTES preventing such action. This points out the importance of whether or not the plan is a pension or an annuity plan. If it is an annuity plan, a lowering of the contribution by the state would constitute a breach of the teacher's or administrator's vested contract rights.

The actual date of when a person is entitled to retirement benefits has caused some difficulty. It is clear now that the right to benefits occurs upon the date a person reaches the age of retirement. It does not occur on the date a person applies. Some rights might be waived for waiting an unreasonable length of time, but generally a person is entitled to past benefits that have not been received. This is true so long as the teacher or administrator does not continue to work. Generally, the benefits do not begin if the teacher or administrator continues full-time in the same position.

Once a person elects to retire, there are a number of ways he or she can be paid. This is up to the teacher or administrator. A person may elect to be paid the maximum benefits until death and thereafter the benefits cease. Or a person may elect to take the ordinary benefits until death, and then if there is any balance, the remainder would go to the estate. The way a person chooses is a gamble, for if a person lives a long time, the maximum turns out to be the more beneficial; if not, the other alternative would have been best. In one case, a Pennsylvania teacher retired at the end of June in 1958. He elected to take the maximum and died less than two months later. He had contributed over $12,500, but the court held that his estate could not collect the remainder. *Ogden v.*

Public Schools Employee's Retirement Board, 182 A.2d 228 (Pa., 1962). Although the results seem harsh, that is the chance the teacher elected to take. Had he lived for another thirty years, he would have collected substantially more than what he contributed. However, in order to combat some of the more inequitable results, there are some statutes which provide that once the election to take the maximum has been selected, the participant must live at least another 30 to 60 days.

Rules. 1. *Of the State,* 2. *Of the Local Board,* 3. *Of the Teacher.*

1. The state legislature delegates the responsibility of education to a state agency generally called the State Board of Education. This agency is directly responsible to the legislature, but acts with a great deal of discretion. This agency, in turn, delegates some of its responsibilities to local SCHOOL BOARDS. Of course, the State Board of Education sets out minimum standards and rules under which the local boards must operate. Generally these standards are flexible and enable local boards to choose between a wide range of different alternatives. The state board controls the local boards; that is, local boards cannot make any rule which contravenes rules set out by the state legislature or by the State Board of Education. As a rule the State Board of Education retains authority (in a general way and sometimes specifically) over such things as TEXT-BOOKS, basic CURRICULUM, and evaluation of local districts.

2. Just as the state may make up rules, local boards may do the same thing in relation to their delegated duties. Lawful local school board rules (those which are not in conflict with the state laws or state board rules) control the operation of the local schools, and school administrators and teachers are obligated to follow these rules. Generally, the rules of the local board must be clearly set out in a published handbook of school board policies. The rules must be reasonable and within the scope of the board's authority. The rules must be properly adopted and published, and cannot conflict with constitutional or contract rights of the people the rules are directed to govern.

3. Teachers also have the authority to make up rules as long as they do not conflict with the rules of the state or of the local school board. As one court has said:

> Among the things a student is supposed to learn at schoool . . . is a sense of discipline. Of course, rules cannot be made by authorities for the sake of making them but they should possess considerable

leeway in promulgating regulations for the proper conduct of students. Courts should uphold them where there is any rational basis for the questioned rule. All that is necessary is a reasonable connection of the rule with the proper operation of the schools. By accepting an education at public expense pupils at the elementary or high school level subject themselves to considerable discretion on the part of school authorities as to the manner in which they deport themselves. Those who run public schools should be the judges in such matters, not the courts. The quicker judges get out of the business of running schools the better. . . . Except in extreme cases the judgment of school officials should be final in applying a regulation to an individual case. *Stevenson v. Wheeler County Board of Education*, 306 F.Supp. 97, 101 (U.S. Dist. Ct. Ga., 1969).

As the court mentions, the rules of the teacher or administrator must be reasonable and within the scope of the teacher's authority. (See TEACHERS.) The thing to remember is that not only must the rules be for an educational purpose but they must be:

1. In actual existence;
2. Communicated; and
3. Enforced.

The three main duties of a teacher involve instruction, SUPERVISION and safety. In order to carry out these duties, it is implied that the teacher may make up rules and may enforce them. In fact, it is the duty of the teacher to do just that. First, the teacher should write down rules. These rules should be clear and concise and ones that the student can readily understand. Next, the rules must be communicated to the student, and thirdly, the rules must be enforced. There are certain areas wherein these guidelines are especially important. Many teachers are sued and held liable for simply not having enforced rules regarding the health and safety of their students. It has been held that a teacher should have safety rules in vocational classes, where the teacher is absent from the classroom, and where large crowds of students are gathered. Remember, the rules must be reasonable, lawful, and cannot conflict with the student's constitutional rights.

See also: EXPULSION OF STUDENTS.

S

Sabbatical Leave. Sabbatical leave is a LEAVE OF ABSENCE granted to a teacher or administrator for rest, travel, or research without it affecting the teacher's or administrator's contract rights or TENURE status. Sabbatical leaves are generally not mandatory by state statute. However, such leaves are granted at the discretion of local school boards. This discretionary authority is proper so long as arbitrary decisions are not made; and there are some standards or criteria used to determine when such a leave shall be granted. Generally, the person involved must have been with the district a number of years. Furthermore, the purpose of the leave normally must be related to the teacher's or administrator's function within the school. The leaves are limited in number. When the person returns, he or she should return to the same or a higher position.

Safe Place Statutes. So called "safe place" STATUTES have been enacted in many states to partially combat the inequities of GOVERNMENTAL IMMUNITY. These statutes simply state that it is the duty of persons owning public BUILDINGS to make those buildings safe to visit and to work in. The statutes require insurance to be carried so that when an injury does occur due to an unsafe condition in the building, it will not go totally uncompensated.

Salary Schedules. Not all school districts have salary schedules. In districts that have such schedules, it is clear that the schedules may be altered or amended at the school board's discretion unless it is prohibited within adopted school board policies or a part of the teachers or administrators' CONTRACTS. Without an express provision in the contract, the schedules are not a part of the board's contractual obligations. This problem can be solved through negotiation AGREEMENTS.

It is possible for a local school district to adopt a salary schedule which will raise the salaries of some employees and decrease the salaries of others. However, such a decision must have a rational basis and cannot be unreasonable or in breach of any existing contractual obligations. *San Diego Federation of Teachers, Local 1278 v. Board of Education*, 31 Cal. Rptr. 146 (Cal., 1963).

See also: MERIT PAY.

Sanctions. Sanctions have been used primarily by the National Education Association (N.E.A.) and its local affiliates to censure or to condemn, formally and publicly, an agency, an organization, a school, or a community. Sanctions are imposed for alleged violations of standards judged by the N.E.A. as being essential for the maintenance of an adequate educational program.

In some instances, sanctions have precipitated positive changes in the quality of education provided by the schools and in employer-employee relations. However, many criticisms have been aimed at sanctions because some people believe that such tactics are ineffective in bringing about meaningful change.

As a general rule, sanctions are not illegal because they do not bring about an abrupt halt to the school operations. Sanctions frequently act more like a threat of a strike and seldom do they cause teachers to be absent from their positions. There have been several instances where sanctions have been enjoined, however.

See also: COLLECTIVE BARGAINING; MEET AND CONFER BARGAINING LAWS; STRIKES.

Save-Harmless Statutes. Save-harmless statutes have been enacted in a minority of states and will be enacted in more states as time passes. For those states which have waived GOVERNMENTAL IMMUNITY, save-harmless statutes simply say that if a teacher or administrator is sued for acts done within the scope of his or her duty, the school district will "save" the teacher or administrator and will hold the teacher or administrator "harmless." Some statutes state that school districts *must* save the teacher or administrator harmless. Others leave it to the discretion of the local school district. If such a decision is discretionary, teachers and administrators should negotiate that the discretion be eliminated by adopting school board policies to that effect.

School Boards. 1. *Structure.* 2. *Code of Conduct.* 3. *Meetings.* 4. *Policies.* 5. *Authority.* 6. *Discretion.* 7. *Liability.*

1. *Structure.* The local school board generally is made up of lay members of the community who are elected by the people within the school district. However, in some instances, members are appointed by the mayor or city council.

Education is a non-partisan commitment, and school board elections are handled accordingly. Most state laws require that members of the school board must be able to read and write and must live in the community in which they are a member. No board member may have personal business dealings with the board without a full disclosure (some statutes say not at all) and no person may become a member where it will create a CONFLICT OF INTERESTS. (See also STRUCTURE OF THE SCHOOL SYSTEM; ADMINISTRATIVE AGENCIES.)

2. *Code of Conduct.* The following is a typical code of conduct prescribing what a good school board member should do:

A Code of Conduct

A School Board Member Should:

Understand that his basic function is "policy making" and not "administrative."

Discourage subcommittees of the Board *which tend to nullify* the board's policy making responsibility.

Refuse to "play politics" in either the traditional partisan, or in any petty sense.

Respect the rights of school patrons to be heard at official meetings.

Recognize that authority rests only with the Board in *official meetings*.

Recognize that he has no legal status to act for that Board outside of official meetings.

Refuse to participate in "secret" or "star chamber" meetings, or other irregular meetings which are not official and which all members do not have the opportunity to attend.

Refuse to make committments on any matter which should properly come before the Board as a whole.

Make decisions only after all available facts bearing on a question have been presented and discussed.

Respect the opinion of others and graciously accept the principle of "majority rule" in board decisions.

Recognize the superintendent should have full administrative authority for properly discharging his professional duties within limits of established board policy.

Act only after hearing the recommendations of the superintendent in matters of employment or dismissal of school personnel at an official meeting.

Recognize that the superintendent is the educational advisor to the board and should be present at all meetings of the board except when his contract and salary are under consideration.

Refer all complaints or problems to the proper administrative office and discuss them only at a regular meeting after failure of administrtive solution.

Present personal criticisms of any school operation directly to the superintendent rather than to school personnel.

Insist that all school business transactions be on an ethical, and above board, basis.

Refuse to use his position on a school board in any way, whatsoever, for personal gain or for personal prestige.

Refuse to bring personal problems into Board considerations.

Advocate honest and accurate evaluation of all past employees when such information is requested by another school district.

Give the staff the respect and consideration due skilled professional personnel.

3. *Meetings.* MEETINGS of the board are very important. During board meetings, policy is adopted and decisions for school operations are made. Only at a meeting does the school board exist or have power. If the meeting is convened improperly, if proper procedures are not adhered to, or if a decision is made outside of a meeting, any action taken is without legal authority or effect. Various states have specific laws regulating the manner of calling and conducting local board meetings. These laws must be strictly followed. In some places, board policy regulates the meetings, and these policies must also be followed. For example, if state law says that meetings shall take place within the school district, any meeting held outside the district is invalid. However, there is a possibility that decisions made at an invalid meeting may be ratified at a later properly convened meeting.

Meetings of the board are generally held on regularly scheduled dates. The meeting is public and people have a right to hear most of the board's discussion and to discuss their own concerns with the board members. Generally, an agenda is prepared in advance of a regular meeting and should be available to school personnel and members of the public. The agenda should be followed closely and should provide for time in which to discuss old business, new business, and ordinary concerns of private individuals. Although members of the public have a right to express their views, they have no right to infringe on the school board's discretion. The board derives its power from the state and not from the people in each school district.

Assuming that the agenda has been properly prepared, the meeting should follow ordinary parliamentary procedure. The meeting should be properly convened with a QUORUM present. Most states say that decisions may be made by a majority of the quorum present and do not require a majority of the board as a whole to be present. However, this could depend on the type of decision being voted upon. If the decision is to hire a new superintendent or to acquire PROPERTY, it is quite possible that the law will require a majority of the whole. Either way, each board member has the right to actual or constructive notice of all meetings, and should also be given an opportunity to vote on all decisions.

After a meeting of the board, minutes should be made available to the schools and to the public. The minutes constitute the official record of the board and are the main channel of communication from the board to the school personnel and the public. Decisions, policies, RULES, and general opinions of the board should be clearly stated in the minutes and distributed to those who are interested or directly involved. These minutes are supposed to be public and open to public inspection at reasonable times. Because of their public nature, no secret decisions or policies should be adopted by the board. Such policies would have no legal effect, and would be evidence of arbitrariness or abuse of discretion.

In addition to "regular meetings" of the board, there are times when the board will have a "special meeting," or will call for an "executive session." A special meeting is simply a meeting that is not regularly scheduled and is generally held for a special purpose. A special meeting has all of the legal effect of a regular meeting, and once convened, it must follow the same adopted procedures of regular meetings. There must be notice of the meeting and the meeting must be in public. The special meeting should also follow any other regulations required by statute or local board or state board policy.

A special meeting is not an "executive session." An executive session is a private conference between members of the board. This conference is not public and is restrictive in its purpose. Executive sessions are supposed to be for matters involving property acquisition and personnel hiring or dismissal. The public does not have a right to know what transpires in a properly convened executive session, but it does have a right to know what the board members' opinions are in matters unrelated to property or personnel. These opinions should not be hidden under the cloak of an executive session. However, *decisions* made in an executive session have no legal effect until they are adopted at a properly convened public meeting. This does not mean that the discussion leading up to a decision, or even the facts relied upon in making that decision, must be made public. Only the decision itself has to be made known.

Although the general rule is that the board can only bind itself when it acts pursuant to a decision in a formal meeting, there are times when the COURTS will overlook the defect if it is necessary for justice and equity to result. Such action by the court is rare, however, and only takes place where there is absolute good faith on the part of those involved, or where an emergency absolutely requires the board to act without properly following necessary procedures.

4. *Policies.* School board policies are written statements indicating educational objectives and general methods by which these objectives are to be accomplished. They also include rules for the management and control

of schools. School board policies should be the primary concern of school board members. It is through their policy making power that board members direct the educational accomplishments and goals for the children within their district. Therefore, school policy is the single most important duty of local school boards.

Since the purpose of school board policy is to give direction, it stands to reason that the board members alone should not define policy without considering the opinions of teachers, students, and parents. The ultimate authority, of course, is with the board, but input from all interested groups should enhance communication and be conducive towards putting polices into practice.

Along with policy, the board makes up RULES which govern the management and conduct of the schools. In adopting these rules, the local board must make certain that the rules are reasonable, are within the scope of the board's authority, are adopted according to required procedures, are necessary or beneficial in accomplishing a proper educational purpose, and are not in violation of constitutional or contract rights of those involved. If the rules violate any of these principles, they are without legal effect and are not binding. However, in challenging an alleged unlawful rule, a person must follow appropriate GRIEVANCE procedures.

School board policies by their very nature must be communicated or made available to school personnel. It is advisable for each and every teacher and administrator to have access to a copy of school board policies. This is especially true in relation to those areas specifically directed at teachers' and administrators' duties, rights, and responsibilities. A copy of school board policies should be in the faculty lounge, in the school library, or in the main office of the school building. These written policies should not be hidden in the main administration building, nor should they be unorganized or difficult to read. Rules of the school board must be communicated or they will have no binding effect.

School board policies adopted "after" a contract has been signed bind the teacher or administrator as well as those adopted before the contract is signed. This is true unless the new policy goes to the very essence of the contract, thus substantially changing the contract terms, or unless it has been negotiated or adopted that the new policies will be binding only after a certain time has passed. (See CONTRACTS.)

All districts must follow the minimum standards set by the state board of education, but each district is allowed to adopt policies which are

conducive to accomplishing the district's particular needs. The fact that
policies differ from district to district is not illegal nor controlling. In fact,
state law may give certain districts the delegated authority to adopt policies
which other districts within the state cannot adopt. For example, it is
common for state laws to grant large districts more power than smaller
districts have in such areas as CURRICULUM, control, and management.

While the board creates school policies and steps for evaluating whether
these policies are followed, the board itself does not go into the school or
classroom to evaluate. This job is on the shoulders of the board's chief
executive officer, the SUPERINTENDENT. The superintendent and his
or her administrators carry out the executive requirements of the board
and then report back to the board and make various recommendations.
The board then acts on these recommendations by developing policies and
objectives.

All school boards should adopt policies to control action in the following
areas:

1. Rules covering the procedures and conduct of school board
   meetings.
2. Guidelines for school personnel in relation to their duties,
   rights, liabilities, curriculum requirements, EVALUA-
   TIONS, and grievance procedures.
3. Rules governing student conduct, rights and responsibilities,
   and grievance procedures.
4. Policies in regard to school PROPERTY, school services
   for the community, maintenance of school grounds and
   general purchasing procedures.
5. Rules governing release of STUDENT RECORDS and
   PERSONNEL RECORDS.

5. *Authority.* The authority of the local school board is delegated from
the state. A local school board is a state agency and a type of quasi-
MUNICIPAL CORPORATION with certain restricted duties and powers.
In performing its functions, the local board has express and implied rights.
Among these are the right to:

1. Enforce RULES of the state and State Board of Education.
2. Hire, dismiss, and determine the general duties of any
   school personnel.

3. Determine the CURRICULUM of students so long as it does not fall below minimum state standards.

4. Equip the district with the necessary materials for instruction.

5. Adopt reasonable rules governing the operation of the schools.

6. Adopt reasonable rules governing student and employee conduct.

7. Enter into binding CONTRACTS.

Local boards are not totally under rigid or inflexible controls of the state. The local board has the power to adopt certain TEXTBOOKS, to require certain courses of study, and to make reasonable rules in relation to instruction, supervision and safety. The local board may exercise these powers so long as (1) the state has not pre-empted the area; (2) the exercise of the power is reasonable and not arbitrary; and (3) the exercise is not in violation of a person's contract or constitutional rights.

It would be nearly impossible to list each and every right or limitation of the local school board. Basically, the local board has the authority to manage and control the schools. To "manage and control" means that the local board has the authority to give direction, to define school policy, to list educational objectives and to maintain an efficient educational system without *directly* participating in the transmission of knowledge. In other words, the local board has the power to adopt policies, but it does not have the power to implement those policies. For example, the board has the right to encourage the teaching of patriotism, but it does not have the power to enter a teacher's classroom to observe his or her methods and effectiveness. The local school board may adopt reasonable rules, but the administration and implementation of these rules is the responsibility of teachers and administrators.

6. *Discretion.* In exercising their express or implied authority, local boards have a great deal of discretion. So long as this discretion is not abused, the board or its members will not be subject to liability, nor will the board or its members be subject to judicial reversals of board decisions. It might be noted that the COURTS distinguish between the "power" of the board and the "discretionary" exercise of that power. If the board does not have the "power" to do something, that decision will automatically be reversed by the courts. However, if the local board does have the power, the court

will only look to see if the power was abused by an arbitrary or unreasonable action. This would be a QUESTION OF LAW and not a QUESTION OF FACT. If it is not clear whether the board has the "power," there will be a rebuttable PRESUMPTION against such power. On the other hand, if the board does have the power, there is a presumption that the discretion has not been abused, and the court will only look to see if the board's action was arbitrary or unreasonable. The problem lies in attempting to determine what constitutes an abuse of discretion. This can be partially solved by saying that so long as the board acts in good faith, has afforded the parties involved fundamental fairness or DUE PROCESS, and has acted pursuant to relevant standards, its actions will not amount to an abuse of discretion.

The courts are generally reluctant to interfere with local school board decisions. Even if the court does look into a board decision, it will seldom reverse that decision if it is based upon some reliable evidence and is not discriminatory in nature. However, if the decision is not within the scope of the local board's duty, if it is unconstitutional, if there is no evidence on which to base the decision, or if it is arbitrary or capricious, the court will not let the decision stand. Therefore, decisions must be analyzed objectively, and should not be based on personal bias or opinion.

7. *Liability.* In talking about school board liability, it is necessary to talk about the possible liability of the school board itself, and then examine the possible liability of individual members of the board. The local board is liable for the CONTRACTS properly entered into and any other legal acts granted to the board by statute. Because the board is an entity created by the state, there may be restrictions as to how much contractual liability the local board may incur. Furthermore, state statutes or local policies require that specific procedures must be followed if the board is to be bound by various contracts.

Many problems arise wherein a private party contracts with an individual member of the local board, thinking he or she is contracting with the board itself. The board can only act as a whole. Individual members cannot bind the board unless the board ratifies the actions taken. When one board member attempts to bind the board, there will generally be no remedy against the board itself. The general rule is that an individual contracting with the board has a COMMON LAW duty to inquire into the extent of the board's authority. This duty also requires that an individual must inquire into the extent of a board member's power to bind the board as a whole. Therefore, if inquiry is not made, and the board or a board member exceeds proper authority, any contract made is voidable.

Individual board members seldom incur personal liability for actions done or not done by the board. The board member is fulfilling a public function and is shielded by the corporate veil of the board as a whole. Again, if a person is dealing with an individual board member, he or she is under the duty to inquire into that member's authority. As a result, even if a board member exceeds his or her authority, there will generally be no personal liability unless the acts are gross, indicate bad faith, or are fraudulent or misrepresentative in nature. (See also GOVERNMENTAL IMMUNITY.)

School Buildings. See BONDS; BUILDINGS; CONSTRUCTION; PROPERTY.

School Calendar. The adoption of a school calendar is generally within the discretion of the local school board. However, if there are state STATUTES or state board of education rules governing the school calendar, these rules must be followed. Minimum requirements relating to the required number of teaching days are often prescribed by statute or state board rules. These requirements must be met if the school district is going to be eligible for state funds. However, in emergency situations, the state board has the power to waive these requirements. These minimum requirements may be exceeded by local school districts.

Questions frequently arise when the ordinary termination date for school is extended to make up for class days which were missed during the year due to inclement weather, etc. Teachers and administrators may be compelled to remain the extended period so long as that period is not unreasonable. This would depend upon the facts and circumstances. An extension of one or possibly two weeks is ordinarily not considered to be unreasonable. Beyond two weeks, authority to extend the year further seems questionable and may possibly be in breach of the teachers' or administrators' CONTRACTS. This problem can be solved before it ever comes into existence by spelling out the maximum termination date for school within the teachers' or administrators' contracts or within school board policies adopted by the local board. Where class days have been missed due to teacher STRIKES, the school board may in its discretion choose to make up the lost days. However, the teachers could not force the board to do so in an effort to make up the wages they have lost for teaching days which were missed.

School Closures. Schools may be closed due to inclement weather, holidays, emergencies, and when there is a health or safety hazard. Generally, teachers do not have to attend school on these dates. If the teachers and administrators do attend, the day is counted as part of their contractual days under the SCHOOL CALENDAR. If they do not attend, the day may be "made up" after the normal date for school closure would ordinarily expire.

School District, organization. See BONDS; BUILDINGS; REORGANIZATION.

School Funds. See FUNDS.

Scope of Bargaining. (For a preliminary introduction to this topic, see COLLECTIVE BARGAINING and MEET AND CONFER BARGAINING LAWS.) In the early stages of teacher negotiations, the emerging AGREEMENTS were limited to items of financial compensation for teachers (i.e. salaries, increments, dental insurance, etc.), summer school-work payment rates, and compensation for after-school coaching positions. These are "bread and butter" items. Teachers are still quite concerned about these issues, but they are also demanding a say in all items with which they, as professionals, are concerned. Teachers want to negotiate over items such as CURRICULUM, teaching aides and materials, class size, GRIEVANCE procedures, and an endless stream of other concerns.

Legislatures throughout the country are granting teachers the right to bargain. Some of these bargaining laws are in the form of "meet and confer" legislation, and many are in the form of collective bargaining laws. One of the main things which these laws tend to have in common is that most of them do not specify the mandatory scope of bargaining. As a result, most states are forced to take a case by case decision-making approach in trying to determine the mandatory scope of bargaining. This is vastly superior to a rigid legislative limitation on the mandatory scope of bargaining, because experience shows that if the court's or the "Public Employee Relation Board's" initial judgment was wrong, it is much easier to obtain a reversal. Nevertheless, it does leave many teachers and school board members arguing over what items may be negotiated.

The scope of bargaining is frequently defined as "wages, hours, and terms, and conditions of employment." This is rather broad, and phrases like "conditions of employment" are loosely interpreted by employee organizations to mean that everything is negotiable. SCHOOL BOARDS argue, and many bargaining laws provide, that matters of "inherent managerial policy" are not bargainable, and a reasonable limitation on the range of bargainable education problems and policies is necessary to preserve the school board's and administrators' discretion and to prevent compromises made in haste in the heat of a bargaining battle. This leads back, however, to what in essence is the same question—what items are within "inherent managerial policy" (i.e. what is bargainable)? As previously stated, most COURTS and labor employee management boards are defining the mandatory scope of bargaining on a case by case basis.

In essence, what this means is that the *mandatory* scope of bargaining has not been definitively decided. The mandatory scope will depend upon the wording of the state bargaining laws and case decisions. However, the *permissible* scope of bargaining is a completely different story. Here, it is held that the school board *may* negotiate with employees over all terms and conditions of employment except those which are specifically prohibited by law. In other words, the school board is free to bargain over *all* terms and conditions of employment and related issues unless a specific state law prevents the board from negotiating on certain matters. This should aid teachers in future negotiations over a broad range of subjects which in the past were sidestepped as being "non-negotiable."

Search and Seizure, unreasonable. The Fourth Amendment to the Constitution of the United States provides that:

> **The right of the people to be secure in their persons, houses, papers, and effects, against unreasonable searches and seizures, shall not be violated, and no Warrants shall issue, but upon probable cause, supported by Oath or affirmation, and Particularly describing the place to be searched, and the persons or things to be seized.**

This prohibition of unreasonable searches and seizures is made applicable through the Fourteenth Amendment to actions of those persons who are acting as arms of the state. The Fourth Amendment protections do not prevent evidence from being used to punish someone where the evidence is unlawfully seized by a person acting on his own and not acting on behalf of the state. In other words, if John, a salesman, broke into Joe's house and found a brick of marijuana and called the police, the marijuana could be used as evidence in a criminal proceeding against Joe, because John was not acting on behalf of the state.

In general, an unreasonable search and seizure is an examination without authority of law of a person's premises or person in order to discover contraband, illicit property, or some evidence of guilt to be used in prosecuting a crime. As a result of this prohibition, the question frequently arises as to whether or not school officials may search a student, a locker or a desk without probable cause or a SEARCH WARRANT. Since school officials are employees of the state, a reading of the Constitution would suggest that the Fourth Amendment's requirements are applicable in the school environment. However, the COURTS have generally refused to apply the Fourth Amendment to protect students from being punished, expelled, or prosecuted for a crime based on evidence seized by school officials in a desk or locker search, or even in a search of the student's person. Many of the courts which have refused to apply the Fourth Amendment protections revert to the theory of IN LOCO PARENTIS and suggest that the teacher or principal conducting the search is acting as an individual and not as an arm of the state. For example, in a case where school officials seized some marijuana in a locker search, the court held that the marijuana could be used as evidence in a criminal proceeding against the student. The court reasoned that:

> **The conduct of a person not acting under the authority of a state is not proscribed by the Fourth or Fourteenth Amendments of the Federal Constitution. . . . Therefore, acquisition of property by a private citizen from another person cannot be deemed reasonable or unreasonable . . . and a motion to suppress evidence so obtained cannot be made on the ground that its acquisition constitutes an unreasonable search and seizure. . . . *In re Donaldson*, 75, Cal. Rptr. 220 (1969).**

However, if school officials are acting as "agents of the police" in conducting searches of students or their lockers or desks, any evidence seized cannot be used to punish the students. Also, if the search is a joint operation of police and school authorities, the Fourth Amendment protections will apply. This same rule is true if the purpose of the search conducted by school authorities is to obtain evidence to be used in punishing the student.

It should be pointed out that in actuality there is no logical reason why the Fourth Amendment protections should not be applied in the school environment, and it is possible that in the future more courts will grant students these protections. Keep in mind that the Fourth Amendment does not prevent all searches, it only prevents unreasonable searches. As a result, school officials will always be held to have acted lawfully where they conduct a search which is necessary to protect the safety of the students or when they have probable cause to believe that a student is concealing illegal contraband. School authorities should strive to maintain an educational atmosphere which is safe and free from disruption, but they should also try to grant students some reasonable expectation of PRIVACY.

See also: CONSTITUTIONAL LAW; STUDENT RIGHTS.

Search Warrant. A search warrant is a written order, issued by a judge or a magistrate, in the name of the state, directing an officer to search a specified house or other premises for stolen or illegal property or contraband, or evidence of illegal acts. A valid search warrant is often required as a condition precedent to a legal search and seizure.

In order to obtain a search warrant, the affirming officer must show that there is probable cause to believe a crime is being committed, and that the evidence of that crime is at or in a particular place. Furthermore, the specific items to be seized and places to be searched must be listed with particularity or else the search warrant will be held invalid and any evidence wrongfully obtained will be inadmissible at the time of trial.

Secret Societies. Secret societies as used here is meant to refer to "exclusive" social clubs, which operate off campus but derive their membership from students of a school. These clubs may take the form of fraternities, sororities, or of other groups which are not open equally to all students.

Where statutory authority is given, schools may control membership in fraternities, sororities, or secret societies. It has been held that expelling students or prohibiting them from participating in extracurricular activities because they belong to a secret society is within the lawful discretion of the school board, and is neither discriminatory nor in violation of the students' rights.

In states which do not statutorily prohibit membership in such clubs or grant regulatory authority to local SCHOOL BOARDS, the school board has the IMPLIED AUTHORITY to regulate membership in such clubs. In only one state, Missouri, has this authority been limited. In that case, the Missouri court held that absent a showing of a detrimental effect on the school, membership in certain secret or socially elite clubs could not be regulated. *Wright v. Board of Education*, 246 S.W. 43 (Missouri, 1922).

"Special" clubs promote cliques and, although many clubs and societies are allowed and encouraged by school officials, RULES assuring that participation in certain clubs is not discriminatory and that the groups do not interfere with the other students' rights are advisable.

See also: DISCRIMINATION; EQUAL PROTECTION; STUDENT RIGHTS.

Segregation. See DESEGREGATION; DISCRIMINATION.

Self-Defense. Self-defense is the defense of one's person or property from an attempted injury by another person. The law of "self-defense" authorizes a person to act where he or she is acting under a reasonable belief of immediate danger. The law will allow the person to protect himself or herself to the extent necessary to prevent the threatened injury. However, once the threatened injury is prevented, the law will not protect further action or acts of aggression. When acting in justifiable self-defense, a person may not be punished criminally nor held responsible for civil DAMAGES.

See also: BATTERY.

Self Incrimination. Freedom against self incrimination comes from the Fifth Amendment of the United States Constitution. This right is not as all encompassing as many people believe. There is no right to "take the "Fifth" where the answers would incriminate another person; and there is no right to take the Fifth when the questions and answers are of a civil nature and do not indicate criminal activity is involved. Also, once "immunity" has been granted, there is no right to assert Fifth Amendment rights because there can be no criminal incrimination when such a cloak of immunity has been granted. Furthermore, even if there is a right to take the Fifth Amendment, that right can be waived by "opening the door" to questions and then trying to shut it again. In other words, once a witness starts answering questions that could be incriminating, he or she must continue answering the questions because the door has been opened and cannot be closed again.

In 1974, the Department of HEW proposed rules implementing the anti-discrimination provisions of the CIVIL RIGHTS ACT OF 1974. Among these rules was a requirement for integration of sexes in nearly all classes. Although many people feared that sex education classes would be forced into being coed, the department explained that such a result was not intended, and the sexes could be separated in sex education classes.

See also: EXPULSION OF STUDENTS; SILENT, teachers' right to remain.

Severance Payments. Severance payments are contract provisions converting accumulated and unused SICK LEAVE into a cash payment upon retirement or death. The formula used to compute the lump sum of these payments is: multiply the per diem rate times the number of accumulated sick leave days.

Where severance payments have been established as a part of a contract AGREEMENT for wages, hours, etc., these are not considered gifts and therefore, the board is not giving away school PROPERTY in violation of the law. Sick leave conversion plans are of benefit to the school district because they help to:

1. Reduce employee absences;
2. Curb or eliminate abuses of sick leave;
3. Reward faithful employees; and
4. Assure school administrators of sufficient teachers on the job.

Severance payments are fringe benefits which are negotiable items under most COLLECTIVE BARGAINING laws. School boards should be careful to provide that severance payments are available only to employees who have worked a specified number of years in the district. Contingencies such as death and dismissal should be covered. In addition, the policy should specify the maximum number of sick leave days which may be accumulated and at what rate. Failure to do so might lead to an open-ended liability and the COURTS might be forced to set it aside as being vague or unreasonable.

See also: MEET AND CONFER BARGAINING LAWS; SCOPE OF BARGAINING.

Sex, discrimination based upon. See ATHLETICS; CIVIL RIGHTS
ACT OF 1964; CONSTITUTIONAL LAW; CONSTITUTIONAL
RIGHTS OF TEACHERS AND ADMINISTRATORS; DISCRIMINA-
TION; EQUAL PROTECTION; MATERNITY LEAVE; PATERNITY
LEAVE; STUDENT RIGHTS.

Sex Education. No uniform legal rules or state policies have been adopted
with regard to the controversial matter of sex education in the public
schools. Some legislatures have enacted legislation providing for sex education instruction, but a few states expressly prohibit the teaching of birth
control. However, for the most part, the decision of whether or not sex
education shall be taught in the public schools rests with the state and
local SCHOOL BOARDS.

Parents have objected to sex education on many grounds. Among the
objections raised are that sex education:

1. Violates DUE PROCESS;
2. Prohibits parents from having a voice in selection of
   CURRICULUM;
3. Violates a right of PRIVACY;
4. Is an unlawful assumption of power by the school board;
5. Is an abuse of board discretion; and
6. Teaches the students more about sex than their parents
   know, and therefore, makes it difficult for parents to "scare"
   their children into being "virtuous."

Other than the last assertion, the validity of these arguments is doubtful.
Parents do not have any right to prohibit the teaching of sex education in
the public schools; however, they generally have the right to prohibit their
children from being forced to take such a course. As a result, the school
board and the school administrators should provide for two essential safeguards:

1. Explicit procedures for obtaining parental consent or objections for students enrolled in sex education courses
   should be established.
2. Only qualified instructors who have been adequately
   trained in the teaching of sex education should be allowed
   to instruct students on this controversial subject.

Where the above safeguards are provided, school boards may offer sex education instruction in the public schools. Teachers of sex education should be careful to treat this subject in an objective manner. They should not try to "frighten" students, nor should they try to "encourage" students. When asked about his or her feelings with regard to various sexual activities, the teacher is free to say what he or she believes. However, the teacher should not act as an advocate but should present objectively both the pros and cons of controversial sex topics. Sex should not be discussed in an oppressive or degrading manner, but where it is relevant to the subject being taught, the teacher's constitutional right of free speech allows for him or her to discuss the necessary topics relating to sex education.

See also: ACADEMIC FREEDOM; CONSTITUTIONAL LAW; CONSTITUTIONAL RIGHTS OF TEACHERS AND ADMINIS-TRATORS.

Shared-Time. Shared-time is often called "dual enrollment." Under the usual shared-time arrangement, a child regularly attends a parochial school for part of the school day, and also attends a public school for courses not offered or available in the parochial school. The courses taken are generally those which involve expensive equipment which the parochial schools cannot afford. Also, since parochial schools tend to be academic oriented, vocational education courses are often taken in the public schools.

Shared-time arrangements have become increasingly popular and necessary in some areas of the country because many parochial schools no longer have the financial resources to provide their students with a complete educational program. In addition, many U.S. Supreme Court decisions have drastically limited the kinds of public aid which may be granted to help students enrolled in religious-oriented schools. (See PRIVATE AND PAROCHIAL SCHOOL AID.)

At the present time, there is no definitive Supreme Court decision regarding shared-time arrangements. However, a clear majority of state COURTS have held that typical shared-time arrangements are constitutionally permissible so long as the subjects the student wishes to enroll in are not available in the parochial school, and so long as these arrangements are not in violation of the state constitution or STATUTES. It is clear, however, that public school teachers may not be allowed to "share" their education with students by going into the parochial school to teach.[80] (i.e.

---

[80] *Fisher v. Clackamas County School District*, 507 P.2d 839 (Ore., 1973).

Let Mohammed come to the mountain, but don't try taking the mountain to him—the Constitution will not allow it.) Although the parochial school student may be allowed to attend classes at the public school, such a student may only take classes which are available, and he or she may not demand that certain courses be offered at a specific time of the day.

The theory behind shared-time arrangements is that a parochial school student would normally have every right to attend the public school, so why should he or she be denied the right to attend classes which are not offered at the parochial school? This is a good argument. However, it is clear that by freeing the parochial schools from having to provide expensive classes in science, vocational education, etc., the state is helping such schools to remain in existence. There is nothing in the Constitution which does not allow for this. The state has an obligation to remain neutral, and cannot discriminate against certain students merely because they are attending a parochial school. As a result, if shared-time arrangements are challenged before the U.S. Supreme Court, the main question the Court will be forced to answer is: "Do these arrangements foster an excessive government entanglement with religion?" If so—they are unconstitutional. If not—they are permissible. This looks like a fairly close question, but the Supreme Court will probably uphold the validity of the typical shared-time arrangement.

It was previously stated that shared-time arrangements generally are not in violation of state laws. However, some state statutes provide that children are to "regularly attend, six hours a day" a public private or parochial school. In these instances, the enrollment is restricted to one school during the regular school day, and shared-time arrangements would be invalid. As one court explained:

> . . . [Where a school district] provided speech therapy for parochial school children in buildings maintained by the school board, and parochial children who desired such therapy were released from school for part of their regular six-hour day in violation of statutes which require all school children to regularly attend school six hours in [each] school day, [the] school district practice was invalid. . . .[81]

Where no such state statutes exist, most courts have upheld the practice of shared-time. As long ago as 1913, a public school in Pennsylvania was

---

[81] *Special District for Education and Training of Handicapped Children v. Wheeler*, 408 S.W.2d 60, 61 (Mo., 1966).

ordered to allow a parochial school student to attend a manual training class.[82] In New York, a parochial school student had a rheumatic heart condition which confined her in bed for one-half of a year. When the public school refused home teaching for the girl, the parents sought a court order compelling it. Justice prevailed, and the order was granted.[83]

See also: RELEASED TIME; RELIGION.

Shop Classes. See VOCATIONAL PROGRAMS.

Sick Leave. Sick leave is a LEAVE OF ABSENCE from school which is granted with pay and without loss of position or other employment rights for a certain period of time. Sick leaves are generally made mandatory by state statute. Under most sick leave provisions, a person is allowed a certain number of days absence each year, but most states and local school districts allow sick leave days to accumulate over the years up to a certain maximum number.

Whether or not sick leave days are transferrable from one district to another depends upon state statute or local board policies. Also, whether or not a person has a right to be paid for unused days depends, again, on state statute and local policies. (See SEVERANCE PAYMENTS.)

Sick leave days are to be used when the person is sick. However, a few states have statutes which are broad enough to allow for sick leave where an immediate member of the family is sick and in need of attention. "Not feeling good," headaches, physical injuries, cramps, and colds are all valid reasons for sick leave. The school board cannot require a teacher to present a doctor's certificate as proof of each and every illness, but a doctor's certificate can be required where the period of absence is for an extended period of time or where there is a detrimental effect on the classroom.

There are many RULES adopted by boards governing sick leaves. The rules must be reasonable. It is unreasonable to require that a teacher or administrator be bedridden or at home in order to receive sick leave benefits. If a teacher or administrator is seen at the grocery store during the day, that does not prove that he or she was not sick. However, if a pattern of behavior is developed, there is a possibility that it could be proved that

<hr>

[82] *Commonwealth v. School District of Altoona*, 88 Atl. (Pa., 1913).
[83] *Scales v. Board of Education*, 245 N.Y.S. 449 (1963).

the person was not really ill, and if the person was not ill, he or she should not be paid for the time absent.

Where the teacher or administrator is absent due to a prolonged illness beyond the sick leave time which he or she has accumulated, the contract between the teacher or administrator and the school district may be terminated. However, the length of time of the absence beyond the accumulated leave time must be substantial, and it is often prescribed by statute.

Silent, teachers' right to remain. The Fifth Amendment to the Constitution of the United States provides in part that: "No person . . . shall be compelled in any criminal case to be a witness against himself, . . ." Through the Fifth and the Fourteenth Amendments of the Constitution, a person has the right to refuse to make statements which may be used as evidence in a *criminal* proceeding *against himself or herself*. In other words, *in regard to incriminating statements*, people have a right to remain silent.

The COURTS have not only recognized that teachers have a right of free speech, the courts have indicated that such persons also have a right to remain silent. As a result, it would appear that a teacher may not be dismissed, refused employment, or threatened with discharge for refusing to divulge incriminating evidence. However, the history of the law in this area is not without some doubt to the contrary.

In a 1957 case, the Supreme Court of the United States held that a university professor could not be compelled to answer questions relating to the content of his classroom lectures or his knowledge of alleged subversive activities.[84] However, decisions of this nature were apparently limited by several subsequent decisions of the Supreme Court. Most notably, in 1958, the Supreme Court ruled that it was not an infringement on a teacher's rights to dismiss him for refusing to answer a school superintendent's questions concerning his membership in the Communist Party.[85] But the 1960's witnessed a dramatic change in public school law. The courts accepted the view that teachers do not shed their constitutional rights at the schoolhouse gates. The Supreme Court made a surprising reference to teachers when it was called upon to decide whether or not a lawyer could be disbarred for invoking the privilege against SELF-INCRIMINATION. In holding that the lawyer could not be disbarred for exercising this right, the Court said:

---

[84] *Sweezy v. New Hampshire*, 354 U.S. 234 (1957).
[85] *Beilan v. Board of Education*, 357 U.S. 399 (1958).

> Lawyers are not excepted from the words "no person . . . shall
> be compelled in any criminal case to be a witness against himself";
> and we can imply no exception. Like the school teacher . . . and the
> policeman . . . lawyers also enoy first-class citizenship.[86]

This suggests that the teacher's right to remain silent does in fact still exist, and as a result, he or she cannot bo dismissed for invoking the privilege against self-incrimination. However, the exact effect or nature of this right has not clearly been stated by the courts.

See also: ANTI-SUBVERSIVE LAWS; CONSTITUTIONAL LAW; CONSTITUTIONAL RIGHTS OF TEACHERS AND ADMINISTRATORS.

Slander. See DEFAMATION.

Smoking. Most states prohibit the sale of tobacco to minors, but only a few states make it unlawful for minors to smoke. As a result, local SCHOOL BOARDS have the authority to make their own RULES regarding smoking in the schools. In some instances, local fire ordinances prohibit smoking in public buildings, like schools, and if this is the case, the school board must respect these prohibitions.

There is no doubt that smoking is a health and safety hazard, and as such, rules relating to it are reasonable and will be upheld. There are only a few court cases involving schools' anti-smoking rules, and none of these cases have been forced to directly confront the issue. Nevertheless, the rules have been upheld by implication. For example, in 1970, a federal district court case mainly involved the DUE PROCESS rights of a student who had been expelled for smoking. By implication, the anti-smoking rule was upheld. *Davis v. Ann Arbor Public Schools*, 313 F.Supp. 1217 (U.S. Dist. Ct. Mich., 1970).

Since many states have lowered the age of majority to 18, the necessity of having a uniform school policy becomes increasingly clear. If the school board chooses to permit faculty members to smoke, it should not prohibit 18-year-olds from smoking if there is a safe place to do so.

All school board positions on the smoking issue have not been settled. Many schools have enacted clear rules explaining that since smoking is a health hazard, it is prohibited on school buses, in school BUILDINGS,

---

[86] *Spevack v. Klein*, 385 U.S. 511, 516 (1967).

and on school grounds. These rules are valid and may be enforced. Some schools have established smoking areas, some of which are on school grounds but not in school buildings. If smoking lounges are provided in school buildings, the school should be careful to supervise the area and make certain that it is safe.

School officials have no authority to regulate student conduct which is outside of the school's jurisdiction. As a result, if a teacher sees a student smoking several blocks from the school grounds, he or she would have no right to punish the student.

The school board should establish rules pertaining to smoking, and these rules should be written and enforced. The nature of the rules ideal-istically should be determined through involvement of all persons con-cerned: the school board, students, faculty, parents, and interested members of the public.

See also: EXPULSION OF STUDENTS.

Sororities. See SECRET SOCIETIES.

Sovereign Immunity. See GOVERNMENTAL IMMUNITY.

Speech, freedom of. See ACADEMIC FREEDOM; CONSTITUTIONAL LAW; CONSTITUTIONAL RIGHTS OF TEACHERS AND AD-MINISTRATORS; FLAG SALUTE; PLEDGE OF ALLEGIANCE; STUDENT RIGHTS.

Special Education. There have been questions raised as to whether or not school district FUNDS could be appropriated to private schools to help in the education of handicapped children. Such expenditures are proper if there are no facilities within the regular school system to provide for these children. Where there are facilities, the expenditure would be inappropriate.

It might be noted that a special education teacher is under a higher standard of care for the safety of his or her students due to the circum-stances of the position. The special education teacher should act as the "reasonable and prudent *special education* instructor." This means that more specific rules of safety must be communicated and enforced. Further-more, there is a higher standard of care in relation to the duty of SUPER-VISION. This is so because it is more foreseeable that a handicapped child is more likely to be injured without supervision than a normal child.

See also: NEGLIGENCE; PRIVATE AND PAROCHIAL SCHOOL AID.

Special Meetings, school board. See SCHOOL BOARDS, meetings.

Sports. See ATHLETICS; CURRICULUM; MARRIED STUDENTS.

Spring Notification. See ANNUAL OR LONG-TERM CONTRACTS; CONTRACTS; RENEWAL; TENURE.

Stare Decisis. Stare decisis is a legal doctrine which the COURTS tend to follow. Under this doctrine, when a court has once laid down a principle of law as applicable to a certain set of facts, other courts will adhere to that principle and will apply it to future cases where the facts are substantially the same. The "higher" the court, the more influence the decision will have.

Ωthis is an extremely important legal doctrine. Through this doctrine, uniformity and EQUAL PROTECTION are granted. It is the doctrine of stare decisis which allows people to predict with some certainty what a court's decision will or should be with regard to a given set of facts. Although courts will generally follow precedent, they are not *forced* to do so, and will not do so where changing times influence the courts to give a different consideration to the facts and circumstances.

State Board of Education. See STRUCTURE OF THE SCHOOL SYSTEM.

State Commissioner of Public Instruction. See CHIEF STATE SCHOOL OFFICER.

State Superintendent of Public Instruction. See CHIEF STATE SCHOOL OFFICER.

Statute of Limitations. The statute of limitations limits the time within which a cause of action can be brought. For example, if a contract is breached, there is a cause of action and any lawsuit filed must be filed within the statutory time limit. If it is not, then the right to bring the cause of action expires and there is no legal remedy available. Generally, for personal or property injury cases, the statute of limitations is two years. For contract cases, the limit is often six years.

Special statutes of limitation are not uncommon when there is a potential cause of action against a governmental agency. For example, in many states if a party in a personal or property injury suit intends to sue a city' or state agency, notice of the pending suit must be filed within 180 days of the injury. If the notice is not sent within the time limit, the lawsuit cannot be filed and would therefore be dismissed.

Statutes. Statutes are the written state laws. The written law should be distinguished from the "unwritten" law. The unwritten law is CASE LAW and the COMMON LAW. Whenever the state legislature enacts a new law, this law is written down and is known as a state statute. Statutes may not conflict with the state or the federal constitution. If a conflict does exist, the law as set forth in the state or federal constitution and as interpreted by the COURTS supersedes the state statutes.

Strikes. A strike is defined under most state STATUTES to mean a public employee's willful absence, in concerted action with others, from the full, faithful, and proper performance of his duties of employment for the purpose of inducing, influencing, or coercing a change in employment relations. A public employee has the right to express a complaint or opinion on any matter related to employment relations and this is not within the meaning of a strike.

In essence, a strike is any concerted refusal to work. A strike involves a group of persons and not just one individual. The refusal to work must be for the purpose of coercing the employer to accede to the employees' demands in regard to wages, hours, terms, or conditions of employment. A valid resignation amounts to a severance of the employer-employee relationship; a strike does not. However, in some cases, MASS RESIGNATIONS are equivalent to strikes.

Social and economic changes in America have contributed to causing teachers to resort to strikes. Persistent low salaries during periods of economic prosperity and inflation have forced teachers to take on a more "militant" attitude. During 1960, there were only three teacher strikes, but during the 1969-1970 school year, there were more than 60 times that number.

In an effort to minimize the problems caused by strikes, several different approaches have been tried. At one extreme, several states rely on severe anti-strike laws which include: the imposition of monetary penalties on strikers; removal of civil service status or other job rights; withdrawal of DUES CHECKOFF privileges from employee organizations; application of court INJUNCTIONS; and jail sentences and fines when court injunctions are defied. This is a very negative approach. It is unsound and out-of-date. Such laws do discourage some strikes, but they are more likely to produce labor-martyrs and headline-seekers, in addition to hindering harmonious labor relations.

At the other extreme, public employees could be treated like private ones, and therefore, would have an unlimited right to strike. No state has adopted this approach yet. However, in the early 1970's, several states adopted laws which allow teachers and some other public employees to strike provided that:

1. The parties have first followed an elaborate procedure of bargaining, including MEDIATION and FACTFINDING.
2. Strikes which present a clear and present danger to the public health, safety, and in some states welfare, may be enjoined.

By mid-1973, four states had adopted this "limited" right to strike approach. The effectiveness of this kind of COLLECTIVE BARGAINING approach will not be known for several years.

A majority of the states approach public-employee bargaining by combining a strike prohibition with an emphasis on collective bargaining, mediation and factfinding. Also, a great deal of well-deserved attention has been focused upon the benefits of ARBITRATION.

Under this majority of "in-between" states, strikes remain illegal, and the school board may seek injunctive relief from the COURTS. There are several legal bases for allowing injunctions to issue against public employee strikes:

1. Such strikes are in direct contravention of statute.
2. Public employee strikes are against public policy.
3. Public employee strikes interfere with and render the government incapable of performing its necessary duties and services.
4. Such strikes present a clear and present danger to the public health, safety or welfare in many instances.

Teachers have occasionally argued that injunctive relief gives the school board the power to compel involuntary servitude. This argument has been rejected. Teachers have CONTRACTS with the state. They cannot be

compelled to work, but they cannot lay claim to their positions and at
the same time refuse to perform contractual obligations.

Occasionally, a few courts have suggested that teachers *may* have a
de facto right to strike. This view has not been widely accepted, and it is
highly unlikely that it will be. Several judges have recognized that one of
the main purposes of a labor organization is to force management to
bargain fairly. If the employee organization is denied an effective bargaining weapon, like arbitration or the right to strike, freedom of association
amounts to little or nothing because the employee organization is incapable
of fulfilling its functions. As explained by one judge:

> . . . [T]he right to strike is, at least, within constitutional concern
> and should not be discriminatorily abridged without substantial or
> "compelling" justification. *United Federation of Postal Clerks v.
> Blount,* 325 F.Supp. 879, 885 (U.S. Dist. Ct. Dist. Col., 1971),
> Wright J. concurring); aff'd, 404 U.S. 802 (1971).

But even in the above case, an absolute ban on strikes of federal employees
was upheld.

It should be noted that in the absence of statutory authority, SCHOOL
BOARDS *cannot* impose penalties on strikers. The school board has only
one remedy available to it in these case—injunctive relief. The courts can
order the strike to be stopped. If it continues, the strikers may be found
in contempt of court, and if so, possible fines and jail sentences may be
assessed.

In recent years, more state legislatures have sought to cure the causes
for public employee discontent, rather than punish the result. This has
meant an ever increasing number of collective bargaining laws. Although
several of these collective bargaining laws have authorized a limited right
to strike, this is only an in-between measure. The final step is to authorize
binding arbitration. Through binding arbitration, employees and employers
will eventually benefit. But even more importantly, students will be assured that there will not be harmful disruptions in their school programs,
and the educational system will be the real winner.

Structure of the School System. Many of the laws which govern the operation of the schools are found in state STATUTES, the COMMON LAW,
and in CASE LAW handed down by the COURTS. However, these laws
are mainly general standards or apply only to specific kinds of situations.
The RULES and policies which govern the operation of the schools on

a day-to-day basis are enacted within the school system itself. The laws as provided by the constitutions, statutes, and courts are reflected in the policies of the school system.

Much like the courts, the school system has a hierarchy of authority. The structure of the school system, as explained in the subsequent part of this section, is important to recognize, because, as a general rule, the "lower" bodies in the school system may not enact rules or policies which are contrary to those specified by a "higher" body.

State Board of Education

The State Board of Education is the policy making body for the public schools within the state. The power, authority, and duties of this board vary somewhat among the states. Generally, the state board prescribes rules which are consistent with the state constitution and statutes for the operation of the public schools. The authority of the state board is just below that of the state legislature.

State Superintendent or Commissioner of Education

In many states, the State Superintendent of Education or the State Commissioner of Education, whichever he or she is called, is selected by the State Board of Education. In other states, this person is popularly elected by the voters. In a few states, appointment is made by the Governor.

The authority and responsibilities of this CHIEF STATE SCHOOL OFFICER vary among the states. As a general rule, he or she carries out the duties specifically designated for the State Superintendtnt or Commissioner of Education in the state constitution and statutes, as well as the plans and policies of the state board. This person is the executive head of the State Department of Education. In some states, most notably New York and New Jersey, the state commissioner is given the power and duty to render opinions on certain types of local educational employee relation controversies and disputes.

State Department of Education

The State Department of Education consists of professional workers and education specialists who carry out the administrative educational functions required to be performed on the state level. These persons must see to it that the laws relating to the schools are complied with. The State Department of Education frequently advises and consults with local school boards. In nearly all states, the state department handles teacher CER-

TIFICATION and DECERTIFICATION of teachers and teacher education programs and institutions.

An intermediate administrative unit which functions between the State Department of Education and local school boards exists in the majority of states. These units are frequently formed to serve individual counties. They often process reports and check to see if local school districts are complying with state laws and requirements. In many states, these intermediate units are used to provide specialized services which would be either too expensive for local school districts to perform, or which could be more effectively and efficiently handled through these units. Such programs frequently include: specialized education programs for teaching gifted, handicapped, or retarded students; trade and industrial arts; testing and counseling; and film and record services and libraries.

Local School Districts

The state legislature can create, reorganize, or dissolve local school districts in the manner it deems most beneficial to the educational interests of the state. Consolidation frequently occurs when school districts are too small to afford the kind of educational programs required to meet the needs of modern times. However, decentralization of extremely large school districts is also being carefully studied. (See also REORGANIZATION.)

Local School Boards

With the exception of Hawaii, which is run by one state-wide school district board, public schools are operated by local SCHOOL BOARDS. Although local school board members are elected or appointed on a local level, legally, school board members are deemed to be acting as state officials.

Most state statutes prescribe minimum qualifications for local school board members, but these are not very restrictive. For a detailed explanation of the powers and duties of local school boards, see SCHOOL BOARDS.

See also: ADMINISTRATIVE AGENCIES.

Student Records. The school has a clear right to collect and maintain student records. However, problems frequently arise in two areas: (1) Use of the records; and (2) Persons having access to the records.

A student's record generally contains information on his or her family background and relationships, health reports, attendance records, achievement and standardized test scores, and personality and behavior evaluations and observations made by teachers, counselors, and other school officials. The need for protection of the student's right to PRIVACY must be weighed against the school officials' and the public's need to know certain information. A few states have made an effort to specify guidelines and policies governing the kinds of information which may be collected and who may have access to the records under prescribed conditions. However, for the most part, there exists a complete absence of any uniform guidelines on the state or local levels. As a result, the State Board of Education and local SCHOOL BOARDS should take the initiative and accept the responsibility for establishing recordkeeping guidelines. Such established recordkeeping guidelines are necessary to curb abuses, to prevent needless resulting harm, and to protect teachers and school districts from liability. The necessary guidelines should:

1. Specify the types of information to be collected and the reasons for collection.
2. Designate a procedure for obtaining consent of the student and his or her parent for collection of certain personal information.
3. Establish a procedure for destruction of outdated, useless, or inaccurate information.
4. Establish reasonable rules as to who may have access to certain kinds of information and under what conditions the information shall be released.

In establishing the necessary guidelines, the following cases and legal principles should be considered.

The COURTS have not decided clearly whether or not student records are private or public, but the trend has been to grant to the student and his or her parents greater access to such records. Legally, student records are considered to be "quasi-public," and as such are available for inspection only by "real parties in interest." Parents have the right to inspect student records. This right of inspection is related to the right of citizens to inspect public documents of many kinds. School authorities sometimes refuse to allow parents to inspect student records involving special education or general education programs. They do so through delays in an attempt to discourage parents for pursuing their right of inspection. If the parents insist, school authorities usually comply. School officials should refrain from this kind of action. Parents should be granted access to these records, but the school should have established guidelines for release. During inspection of the records, appropriate personnel should be present to prevent misinterpretation of the records. This is particularly true of student behavior records because certain statements may not be properly evaluated or understood by the parents.

Students also have a sufficient interest to entitle them to inspect certain information in their own records. By statute, a few states give the power of release of student records to older students. Delaware, for example, grants this power to students who are 14 years of age or older. If the students have the power to release the records they need to know what is in them. Note that although students may have this right of inspection, guidelines for release may be lawfully established which provide for release of only certain kinds of information under proper conditions.

In one case, a Pennsylvania court held that student records relating to nonacademic matters could be released to higher education institutions. The court upheld the right of school officials to record a student's infractions of school RULES in his or her permanent file:

> **School officials have the right and, we think, a duty to record and to communicate true factual information about their students to institutions of higher learning, for the purpose of giving to the latter an accurate and complete picture of applicants for admission.** *Einhorn v. Maus*, **300 F.Supp. 1169, 1171 (U.S. Dist. Ct. Pa., 1969).**

However, if the school releases student records in violation of a state statute, the student can recover DAMAGES. Promiscuous circulation of information about which the public has no right to know, will subject school officials to liability.

Where there exists a professionally justifiable reason, school district officials and professional employees (e.g. principals, teachers, counselors and health personnel) have a right to inspect certain information contained in student records. In addition, some *general information may* at times be obtained by school board members. For example, a 1960 case held that a school board member could compel the superintendent to give him the names and addresses of students enrolled in certain schools. This information was needed for a particular purpose. *Wagner v. Redmond*, 127 So.2d 275 (La., 1960).

There have even been times where the courts have held that where a sufficient interest or need for inspection can be shown, an "outsider" may have a right to inspect certain school records. For example, in one case, a person who was not a student, parent, college admissions officer, or member of the school faculty sought to be allowed to inspect certain records. The court granted him this right, and explained that:

> **Where the defense of a person accused of a crime requires access to public records or even to records sealed from general examination, the right of inspection has a greater sanction and must be enforced.** *Werfel v. Fitzgerald,* 260 N.Y.S.2d 791, 798 (N.Y., 1965).

In view of the fact that many persons are entitled to inspect student records, the school district should try to protect itself from making improper disclosures. In order to do so, behavior records should be kept separate from academic records. Guidelines for release should be set forth in a clear and specific policy statement.

Student behavior records should contain information about disciplinary and counseling actions. This information should only be released:

1. to school personnel;
2. to persons outside of the school system who have the express consent of the student and his or her parents; or
3. under court order.

The school should provide that this information shall be released only in the presence of someone who is qualified to interpret it.

As this book was being printed, Congress established a policy regulating the keeping and release of school records. This law became effective on November 19, 1974 and is called the "Family Educational Rights and Privacy Act of 1974." (P.L. 93-380, § 438). If a school district fails to comply with this law, it is subject to forfeiture of federal funds which it receives. Among the requirements of this federal law is a provision mandating release of the records to parents who request to see them. The school district is given a short period of time to establish procedures for release of the records. This law also applies to colleges, and students will henceforth be allowed to inspect many of their records, including, perhaps, placement files and recommendations.

Teachers and administrators must be careful not to libel the student in the records. However, a carefully worded professional opinion made as a part of his or her duty as a teacher or administrator, made in good faith, and made as a part of the educational process and with regard for the student, will be held privileged against any libel suit.

See also: DEFAMATION.

Student Rights. (For a preliminary introduction, see CONSTITUTIONAL
LAW.) In 1967, the Supreme Court of the United States was called upon
to hear a case involving a fifteen year old boy who had been committed to
the state reform school for a period of up to six years. The boy had been
convicted of making an obscene phone call to a neighbor. Had the boy
been an adult, the maximum punishment he could have received for having
committed such an offense would have been a $50 fine and two months
in jail. Also, among other things, the boy had been denied a right to
counsel and a right to confront and cross-examine his accuser. The
Supreme Court set aside the boy's conviction and ruled that where a
substantial punishment is involved, a juvenile is entitled to DUE PROCESS
of law.[87] As a result, it was clearly and firmly established that the Bill of
Rights is not for adults alone, juveniles have constitutional rights, too.

Whether or not a juvenile retained his constitutional rights when in
school remained an open question. School officials found themselves being
bombarded with lawsuits and demonstrations challenging school RULES
involving everything from restrictions on content of school NEWSPAPERS
to dress codes. The COURTS divided in their decision as to whether or
not students had constitutional rights. Finally, the Supreme Court of
the United States settled the issue. During its 1968 term, the Supreme
Court, for the first time in 25 years, reviewed a case involving student
freedom of expression. In holding that students do have constitutional
rights, the Supreme Court said:

> **First Amendment rights applied in light of the special char-
> acteristics of the school environment, are available to teachers and
> students. It can hardly be argued that either students or teachers shed
> their constitutional rights to freedom of speech or expression at the
> schoolhouse gate.[88]**

As the Court said, students have constitutional rights, but these rights
are not absolute. The school has the power and the duty to make rules
governing student conduct and to enforce such rules. School officials'
rights to enact rules are recognized by all courts, for as one court explains:

---

[87] In re Gault, 387 U.S. 1 (1967).
[88] *Tinker v. Des Moines Independent Community School District*, 393 U.S. 503, 506 (1969).

> It cannot be seriously disputed that the interest of the State in maintaining an educational system is of such importance that the State is in fact charged with the duty to further and protect the public school system. Nor can it be denied that rules and regulations governing student conduct are required to maintain an orderly educational program. School officials of necessity have thus been given a wide latitude of discretion in formulating rules and regulations to prescribe and control student conduct within the school.[89]

Although the court in the above quoted case recognized the school's authority to prescribe rules, it held for the student. It held for the student because school *rules must be reasonable and must be weighed against the student's rights.* In this case, the court found that the school officials had not met the burden of justifying the rule.

Early case law had held that the school had authority to enact rules and discipline students and the courts would not interfere with the wide discretion granted the school authorities. Now the courts are saying that school officials' rules must be reasonable and school officials have the burden of articulating facts sufficient to demonstrate reasonableness. How the courts will handle cases involving student rights versus school rules or punishment is explained by a federal circuit court:

> It is always within the province of school authorities to provide by regulation the prohibition and punishment of acts calculated to undermine the school routine. *This is not only proper in our opinion but is necessary.*
>
> Cases . . . which involve regulations limiting freedom of expression and the communication of an idea which are protected by the First Amendment, present serious constitutional questions. A valuable constitutional right is involved and decisions must be made on a case by case basis, keeping in mind always the fundamental constitutional rights of those being affected. Courts are required to "weigh the circumstances" and "appraise the substantiality of the reasons advanced" which are aserted to have given rise to the regulations in the first instance. . . . The constitutional guarantee of freedom of speech 'does not confer an absolute right to speak' and the law recognizes that there can be an abuse of such freedom. The Constitution does not confer 'unrestricted and unbridled license giving

---

[89] *Sims v. Colfax Community School District,* 307 F.Supp. 485, 487 (U.S. Dist. Ct. Iowa, 1970).

immunity for every possible use of language and preventing the punishment of those who abuse this freedom. . . .

"In each case [courts] must ask whether the gravity of the 'evil,' discounted by its improbability, justifies such invasion of free speech as is necessary to avoid the danger."

In *West Virginia State Board of Educ. v. Barnette,* . . . involving a school board regulation requiring a "salute to the flag" and a pledge of allegiance, the Court was careful to note that the refusal of the students to participate in the ceremony did not interfere with or deny rights of others to do so and the behavior involved was "peaceable and orderly." [90]

The courts are recognizing student rights, but will allow reasonable rules to incidentally infringe on these rights. What is reasonable will depend on the facts. In addition, different judges may tend to see or give greater weight to various facts and judicial distinctions. However, there are certain judicial criteria which all judges are forced to consider; and there are certain legal standards and rules which have been clearly established for cases involving student rights. The following explanation of the various individual student rights point out the established legal principals, and also explains the kinds of circumstances which must exist in order for rules restricting rights to be found legally reasonable. (See also EXPULSION OF STUDENTS.)

Freedom of Speech and Assembly

The right to freedom of speech derives from the First Amendment, which provides in part: "Congress shall make no law . . . abridging the freedom of speech, or of the press. . . ." In the late 1960's, several students chose to express their opposition to the war in Vietnam by wearing black armbands to school. When the school officials heard of the proposed protest, they quickly enacted a rule prohibiting the wearing of armbands. This rule was announced at a school assembly, and students were told that any student refusing to remove his armband would be suspended from school. The protest took place as planned. A boy named Tinker and two other students were suspended. They sued the school district, and asked the court to grant an INJUNCTION prohibiting the school from punish-

90 (Citations omitted) *Blackwell v. Issaquena County Board of Education,* 363 F.2d 749, 753-4 (5th Cir. 1966).

ing them for exercising what they alleged was a protected right of free speech.

The *Tinker* case was appealed all the way to the Supreme Court, where it was established that the protections of the First Amendment are available to students. The Court stressed the fact that the state has the right to regulate the school's CURRICULUM, but said:

> School officials do not possess absolute authority over their students. Students in school as well as out of school are "persons" under our Constitution. They are posessed of fundamental rights which the State must respect. . . . In our system, students may not be regarded as closed-circuit recipients of only that which the State chooses to communicate. They may not be confined to the expression of those sentiments that are officially approved. *In the absence of a specific showing of constitutionally valid reasons to regulate their speech, students are entitled to freedom of expression of their views.*[91]

The Supreme Court set forth the test to be used in determining whether or not the reasons for regulating students' speech are "constitutionally valid:"

> [T]he student's right of free speech may be restricted where it can be demonstrated that the speech "materially and substantially interfere[s] with the requirements of appropriate discipline in the operation of the school."

Some disturbance is to be expected any time a person challenges someone else's preconceived ideas or seeks acceptance of an opposing viewpoint. The Supreme Court says that this minor disruption must be tolerated. It is only where school officials can show that the speech has caused or in all likelihood will cause a *material and substantial* disruption that they may lawfully restrict student speech.

Three cases involving symbolic speech may help to illustrate the "disruption test." In the *Tinker* case, the students wore black armbands in protest of the war in Vietnam. There was no actual disruption and the court held for the students. Subsequently, in 1970, several Mexican-American students in Texas wore brown armbands in expressing their displeasure with school policies and practices. Although the protest was

---

91 (Emphasis added) *Tinker v. Des Moines Independent Community School District,* 393 U.S. 503, 511 (1969).

against the school, there was no disruption and the court ruled in favor of the students.[92] In a similar case, several students of Mexican descent wore black berets in what they termed was an expression of their Mexican culture, unity of Mexican-Americans, and a symbol of dissatisfaction with the treatment given Mexican-Americans. The students were suspended, and the court upheld the suspension.[93] The reason for the court's action was that there were several instances of disruption caused by wearers of the black berets: loud talking, blocking passage of other students, a disturbance in the lunchroom, and other acts of insubordination.

Not all manners of dress are considered to be symbolic speech. To be entitled to the protections of the First Amendment, a symbol must symbolize a specific idea or viewpoint. A symbol is a way to transmit ideas, and unless it represents a particular idea, it is meaningless.

From the above cases, and many others which have not been cited, certain rules for specific situations have evolved:

1. Where the students' speech collides with the rights of others, it may be restricted.

2. Unpopular language may be allowed, but "fighting words" and obscene language are not.

3. If the student shows gross disrespect for the principal or the teacher, it is not protected speech.

4. Discussion of all ideas relevant to the subject matter is permitted in the classroom, but this is subject to the teacher's responsibility to maintain order, and right to guide the discussion.

5. Symbolic speech which is not materially disruptive must be allowed; but the equivalent spoken idea in the middle of an unrelated class discussion need not be tolerated.

6. Any speech, including spoken words, armbands, or buttons, which mock, ridicule, or are intended to disrupt the educational process because of race, religion, or national origin, are not permissible.

---

[92] *Aguirre v. Tahoka Independent School Dist.*, 311 F.Supp. 664 (U.S. Dist. Ct. Tex., 1970).
[93] *Brown v. Louisiana*, 383 U.S. 131, 141-142 (1966).

7. Distribution of armbands, buttons, etc. in halls or class-rooms during class may be prohibited.

8. The classroom is not a political forum. The teacher is responsible and accountable for providing students with suitable instruction. Therefore, control of the order and direction of the class and the scope and manner of treatment of the subject matter rests with the teacher, who has a right to be free of distraction and disruption by dissident students. As a result, disruption of the classroom and insubordination may be forbidden. There ideally should exist a procedure whereby students can present their grievances about an instructor in a proper format and at a proper time.

The age, intelligence, and experience of the students is relevant to the consideration of when the speech will create a material and substantial disruption. The students are accountable for speech which is in fact disruptive, and may be punished accordingly. In addition, they are obligated to respect the right of other students to pursue their studies in a relatively tranquil atmosphere.

Although the rules applying to symbolic speech and spoken words are applicable to speech in the form of demonstrations and picketing, school publications and underground newspapers, these three kinds of speech present special problems. With each form of speech there are some additional legal issues and rules to be considered.

Demonstrations, Sit-ins, and Picketing

Demonstrations, sit-ins, and picketing are in essence speech in the form of "idea/action." Student activism in the early 1970's turned much more passive that the militant civil disobedience which struck the nation's colleges and universities in the late 1960's. As a result, most schools were spared from the difficult decisions and problems which are inherent in "idea/action" type of speech.

However, there were many schools which did have student demonstrations. In one case, a group of black students conducted a library sit-in. They were seeking integration of the faculty. This case went all the way to the U.S. Supreme Court, where it was held that:

[The rights of free speech and assembly] are not confined to verbal expression. They embrace appropriate types of action which

certainly include the right in a peaceable and orderly manner to
protest by silent and reproachful presence, in a place where the
protestant has every right to be. . . .[94]

This case established the rule that peaceful demonstrations may not be
totally prohibited on school premises. The students have a right to present
their grievances before the school. However, school officials have a right
and a duty to protect all students within the school, to prevent disruption
of the educational process, and to protect the school PROPERTY. As a
result, the courts have ruled that school officials may enact regulations
governing the time, place and manner of conducting demonstrations and
sit-ins. These are "conditions," not "prohibitions," on the speech. These
regulations will be found legally reasonable where they are necessary to
protect the safety of the students in the school or to protect school property
or the normal operations of the school. Besides setting aside a time and
place for demonstrations, the school may enforce the following rules:

1. Students engaging in demonstrations may not prohibit others
    from moving freely in the school hallways or other areas of
    the building.

2. Students may not engage in destruction of property, riotous
    action, or other unlawful acts.

3. Demonstrations which deprive others of the right to pursue
    their studies in a relatively tranquil atmosphere are not per-
    mitted, and persons who do engage in such action may be
    punished.

4. All students have the right to be interviewed on campus
    by military recruiters or by representatives of other legal
    organizations which are invited by the school. Any student
    or group may protest against the organization but may not
    interfere with the other students' right to be interviewed.

Demonstrations which violate the school's reasonable rules are not
protected by the First Amendment, and the demonstrators may be punished. Although some of the demonstrators may not have directly participated in the disruptive conduct, they are equally responsible for the actions
of the splintered voices of their group.

---

[94] *Brown v. Louisiana*, 383 U.S. 131, 142 (1966).

School officials should be careful to distinguish the cause of any disruption which occurs. Students engaging in a peaceful demonstration have a right to be protected from the harassment and disruptive conduct of other students who do not agree with the demonstrators' views. Unless the demonstration was calculated to cause disruptive confrontations with other students, or such disruption could reasonably have been foreseen, the demonstrators are not responsible for the unforeseen reaction of their fellow students.

School Publications

A great many schools encourage and finance the publication of student newspapers or literary magazines. What is printed in these publications is the responsibility of the author, the student editors, and to some extent the faculty advisor.

Many faculty advisors are charged with the duty to "censor" items to be printed in school publications. Idealistically, the faculty advisor should serve as an advisor to the students with regard to such things as style, grammar, format, and suitability of materials. But the final decision on whether or not the item is in fact printed should be the student editor's responsibility. If the material is objectionable or disruptive, the student editors and the author should be held accountable.

Nevertheless, faculty advisors remain accountable in nearly all schools. The rule is that the faculty advisor may not be dismissed, demoted, removed from the advisory position, or in any other way punished for allowing the printing of material which is constitutionally protected. For example, if the faculty advisor is told that no articles may be printed which are critical of school policies and that he or she will be held responsible, can he or she be punished if a constructively written article critical of the school policy requiring tardy slips is allowed to be printed? The answer is "no." As long as the students have a constitutional right to print the article, the teacher may not be punished. In fact, the advisor would be violating the students' rights if he or she did as instructed and prohibited the printing of the article. School officials have no right to require a teacher to perform an act which the school officials have no legal right to do themselves.

Many of the same rules which govern freedom of speech are applicable to freedom of the press. Limited review of school financed publications is permitted, but this does not allow school officials broad censorship powers.

The school officials' commitment to publish is also a commitment to respect and comply with the law governing freedom of the press. The school may not be forced to finance student publications, but where it chooses to open up school publications as a forum for the dissemination of ideas, broad censorship is not legally permissible. Limited review is allowed, but the students have a right to express their criticisms and ideas when such expression will not materially and substantially affect the discipline and operation of the school.

In addition to the aforementioned principles, material which is libelous or clearly obscene may not be published in school newspapers or literary magazines. Also, where the student newspaper is supported by compulsory student FEES, it would be desirable to have rules providing for a right of reply by any person who is criticized in its publication or who disagrees with its editorial policy or treatment of a given event. It would be advisable to have student publications indicate that the opinions expressed are not necessarily those of the school or of the student body. Constructive criticism of school policies or personnel is allowable, but articles which are more in the nature of personal invectives or attack may be prohibited. (See also DEFAMATION; OBSCENITY.)

Underground Newspapers

"Underground newspapers" is meant to include all those publications which are printed at the students' own expense and off school premises. Publications printed at the students' own expense are subject to the same rights and restrictions of school printed publications. However, the students would have the additional right of freedom to determine the kinds of topics to which the publication shall be devoted. For example, if the school chooses to authorize printing of a literary magazine, it may restrict printable materials to poetry, lithographs, short stories, etc. The school officials would have no right to tell students who are printing a newspaper at their own expense that the students may only print poetry or short stories.

Underground NEWSPAPERS may not be totally prohibited on the campus. The students have a right to distribute and publish an underground newspaper so long as it does not unreasonably interfere with the normal school activities. Reasonable, nondiscriminatory rules governing the time, place, and manner of distribution of such publications have been upheld by the courts. Also, the school may require that the materials be submitted for prior approval. However, if the school enacts restrictions which are overly broad or burdensome, they may be seen as an impermissible prior restraint on the students' freedom of speech.

Rules requiring prior approval of the underground newspapers must include:

1. An *expeditious* review procedure.
2. An explanation of who has the authority to approve or disapprove of the material, and how the material may be submitted for approval.
3. A specific statement of the type of publications allowed.
4. A clear and specific statement of the kinds of things which are prohibited and which justify censorship.

In approving underground newspapers, idealogical censorship must in all cases be avoided. Material which is libelous, clearly obscene, or which would reasonably lead school officials to forecast a material and substantial disruption with the educational process or the rights of others may be denied approval.

Always remember, the courts require stricter tests to be complied with where the issue is one of prohibiting speech before it occurs. Whether it is a rule banning armbands, prohibiting demonstrations, requiring prior approval of underground newspapers, or preventing discussions critical of school policies or personnel, the courts will be strict in requiring school officials to enunciate and show reasonable grounds which have led them to forecast a material and substantial disruption. On the other hand, where speech has taken place, and it results in a material and substantial disruption, all courts will uphold the reasonable disciplinary measures taken to punish the responsible students.

Appearance

It would be easy to blame all of the school's problems involving challenges to their dress codes on the Beatles. After all, their "long" hair inspired thousands of adoring youthful fans to let their locks grow, too. Many of these fans were still in school, and the rule was, "The hair goes or the student goes." One of the first cases involved three members of a "rock and roll" band who were suspended for wearing a "Beatle type hair style." The case received national publicity. The court upheld the school's rule.[95]

Nevertheless, though the Beatles had an immediate effect on school APPEARANCE rules, challenges to dress codes were not previously unheard of. In fact, in 1923, one 18-year-old high school girl lost in her challenge of a school rule which prohibited the wearing of "transparent hosiery," "low-necked dresses" and "face paint or cosmetics." [96]

By the late 1960's and early 1970's, the legal issues changed. A long line of cases was forming which ruled that:

1. Students have constitutional rights.

2. School officials have the power and the duty to enact reasonable rules, but they must be able to demonstrate the reasonableness.

3. The students' rights must be weighed against the reasons necessitating the school rules.

School officials are now required to demonstrate the reasonableness of the rules. This is required even before the courts are forced to rule on whether or not the student has a constitutionally protected right to govern his or her own appearance.

Several courts have held that rules prohibiting male students from having hair extending beyond the collar of their shirts or below the ear are unreasonable. In 1973, the Oregon Court of Appeals explained that such a rule is unreasonable because it regulates the students' appearance 24 hours a day, seven days a week, while the student is only in school a small fraction of that time. However, the court went on to say that rules prohibiting metal-plated cleats on shoes and bells on pants are reasonable because this type of dress is damaging or disruptive and the student is not being adversely controlled to an unreasonable extent.[97] By the early 1970's, even when faced with the constitutional issues, the majority of courts were holding that a student has a constitutionally protected right to control the length of his or her hair. Nevertheless, some state courts have upheld various school dress codes. In judging the validity of a dress code, the

---

[95] *Ferrell v. Dallas Independent School District*, 261 F.Supp. 545 (U.S. Dist. Ct. Tex., 1966), aff'd, 392 F.2d 697 (1968), cert. denied, 393 U.S. 856 (1968).

[96] *Pusley v. Sellmeyer*, 250 S.W. 538 (Ark., 1923).

[97] *Neuhaus v. Federico*, 505 P.2d 39 (Ore., 1973).

controlling state decisions must necessarily be reviewed before a final determination of legality could be made.

However, as previously suggested, certain restrictions on student appearance are found to be reasonable by all courts:

1. Rules which are necessary to protect the *safety* of the students are uniformly upheld. Examples: prohibiting the wearing of long hair near machinery in "shop" classes without a hair net or other protections; young students who ride bicycles to school can be prohibited from wearing bellbottoms or other kinds of clothing which are likely to get caught in the bike chain.

2. Rules necessary to protect the *health* of the students are upheld. Example: rules which require students to keep their hair clean are reasonable. At the beginning of the 1973 school year, the superintendent of the Montoursville, Pennsylvania school district was forced to order the district's three schools closed so the 2800 pupils could get their heads checked by doctors. Lice had been found on the heads of some pupils before school opened. A program, screening pupils with dirty or lice infested hair, had been started, but it couldn't keep up with the lice.

3. Appearance which doesn't conform with the *rudiments of decency* may be regulated. Example: Dress which calls attention to anatomical details may be regulated.

4. Appearance which causes a *material and substantial disruption* may be restricted. Example: turbans or berets may make it difficult for students seated behind to see. Where this is the case, the student wearing the disruptive headgear could be required to sit nearer to the back of the room.

It is also possible that certain athletic or special classroom activities may present special safety hazards. Where this is the case, appearance rules should be enacted to help protect the students' safety. However, rules going beyond the demands of the activity are subject to question.

Freedom of Association

The right to freedom of association is found within the First Amendment, which states in part: "Congress shall make no law . . . abridging . . .

the right of the people to peaceably assemble." This is also part of the basis for protecting a student's right to demonstrate.

Students should be free to organize and participate in voluntary associations of their own choosing, but this is subject to school regulations assuring that such associations are neither discriminatory nor operated in a manner which interferes with the rights of others. Under this rule, state statutes and school rules may lawfully prohibit students from joining fraternities, sororities, and SECRET SOCIETIES.

Some groups are condoned and encouraged by the schools. If the school aids in the financial support of the group, it may reasonably require an accounting procedure and a list of officers or other persons responsible for the overall conduct of the association.

Freedom of Religion

Freedom of RELIGION is also a right which derives from the First Amendment. This amendment requires compliances with a two-pronged test: "Congress shall make no laws respecting an establishment of religion or prohibiting the free exercise thereof. . . ." As a result, the state must remain neutral.

Students may refuse to stand and sing the National Anthem where such a refusal is based on religious belief. Moreover, school authorities may not examine the reasonableness or sincerity of such belief. Students have the right not be instructed in religion unless such instruction is presented in an objective manner, e.g. the Bible as literature or a comparative religion class. As a result, PRAYERS and BIBLE READING in the schools have been declared unconstitutional.

In addition, students may not be compelled to participate in a FLAG SALUTE. This decision was made by the U.S. Supreme Court in 1943, when it was faced with the question of whether or not public school students who were Jehovah's Witnesses had a right to refrain from saluting the flag as a part of a required school exercise. The Supreme Court said, "To sustain the compulsory flag salute we are required to say that a Bill of Rights which guards the individual's right to speak his own mind, left it open to public authorities to compel him to utter what is not in his mind; . . ." [98] The Supreme Court did not sustain the compulsory flag

---

[98] *West Virginia State Board of Education v. Barnette*, 319 U.S. 624 (1943).

salute. (See also PLEDGE OF ALLEGIANCE; PRIVATE AND PARO-
CHIAL SCHOOL AID.)

Freedom from Unreasonable Search and Seizure

The Fourth Amendment provides in part that people have a right "to
be secure in their persons, houses, papers, and effects against unreasonable
searches and seizures. . . ." Although searches of students' lockers and
desks have resulted in several court cases, most courts have ruled that
school officials have the right to search this property as well as search the
student in many instances. For example: Where a vice-principal searched
a student's locker without a warrant and without consent, the marijuana
seized in the search was held to be admissible as evidence in a juvenile
delinquency hearing.[99] In another case, a student was searched to see if he
had stolen a dime. The search was upheld.[100]

The reasons given for upholding such searches have been:

1. School officials are not acting as governmental or police
   agents in conducting the searches.
2. Searches are necessary to maintain discipline, health, safety,
   and welfare of the students.
3. School personnel are acting "IN LOCO PARENTIS."
4. School lockers and desks are not in the exclusive possession
   of the student, and he or she therefore has no reasonable
   expectation of PRIVACY.
5. Parents have a right to expect safeguarding of their children
   and school officials have a duty to search if necessary.

The validity of several of the aforementioned arguments is questionable,
and courts of the future may extend the right to freedom from unreasonable searches and seizures to students. School officials would be wise to
enact written guidelines for conducting searches. Nevertheless, as long
as they are acting in good faith and for a proper motive, searches school
officials conduct will be valid; any contraband seized may be used as a
basis for disciplining the students; and in most cases, such evidence will
also be admissible in any criminal proceedings brought against the student.

---

[99] *In re Donaldson*, 75 Cal. Rptr. 220 (1969).
[100] *Marlar v. Bill et al*, 178 S.W.2d 634 (Tenn., 1944).

The motive behind the searches should be to protect the health, safety, and welfare of the students and to protect the school. If school officials conduct indiscriminate searches or act as agents for the police, the student will be protected under the Fourth Amendment, and evidence seized in such searches will be available for use in punishing or disciplining the student only where the seizure has complied with the legal provisions for reasonableness under the Fourth Amendment. (See also SEARCH AND SEIZURE.)

Miscellaneous Rights

Expulsion and suspension of students frequently involves the student's right to a fair hearing and due process of law. Married students, pregnant students, and student mothers also may cause some additional legal questions to arise in the school. The right of female students to participate in athletic activities is also at issue in many areas of the country. For an explanation of the law regarding these issues, see the following sections:
Due Process Rights—see DUE PROCESS; EXPULSION OF STUDENTS.
Required Expulsion Procedures—see EXPULSION OF STUDENTS.
Married Students' Rights—see MARRIED STUDENTS.
Pregnant Students' Rights—see PREGNANT STUDENTS.
Student Mothers—see MARRIED STUDENTS; PREGNANT STUDENTS.
Girls' Participation in Sports Activities—see ATHLETICS, sex discrimination in.

Students: 1. *Absence.* 2. *Assignments.* 3. *Automobiles.* 4. *Cheating.* 5. *Cleanliness.* 6. *Emancipated.* 7. *Homework.* 8. *Liability.*
Note: This book covers a great deal of material relating to students which has been explained under separate topic headings. See the Categorical Index at the beginning of this book and the word index at the end.
1. *Absence.* There are COMPULSORY EDUCATION laws governing students in nearly all states, and these laws must be followed. In order to enforce the law, it is reasonable for the district to require notes, in case of absence, from the child's home; and for long absences, a note from a doctor. Excused absences include those which are caused by illness, bereavement, and emergency situations. If vacations are taken by the child's family during the middle of the school year, notice should be given to the school ahead of time, and arrangements should be made for the

student to do the necessary assignments and to make up any important lessons that were missed.

2. *Assignments.* The grade level to which a student is assigned is within the discretion of the local school board. In assigning a student to a grade, the board must consider his or her age, intelligence, ability, and training. Once the grade level is determined upon these considerations, the parent has no grounds to object. It is permissible for the board to assign students to special classes where it is necessary. The parent cannot preclude the child's attendance without being guilty of failing to allow the child to attend school.

In addition to grade assignment, the school board has wide discretion in determining what school the child shall attend. The school that is nearest the child's home is not necessarily the school that he or she has the right to attend. If that school is overcrowded, or if there is some other valid reason for a student transfer, the courts will not substitute their opinion for that of the board. This is true except in exceptional cases. As one text states:

> Because school boards have the authority to assign pupils, and because no pupil has a vested right to attend a particular school, it does not follow that in all circumstances the assignment of a particular pupil to a particular school will not be examined by the courts. An example from North Carolina is illustrative. There a school board attempted to transfer a high school girl who had taken Latin during her freshman year, was a member of the school band, and generally received high grades. Her parents desired that she continue to have the competition and challenge offered by the expanded curriculum, particularly in foreign languages, at the school to which she had been assigned. It was shown that she planned to enter the field of medicine and that additional foreign language study would be helpful to her. She expected to go to college which required for entrance a minimum of two units in two foreign languages or three units in Latin. The school to which the girl was assigned for her sophomore year had no course in Latin, nor did it have a band. . . . When the board, after [a] hearing refused to reassign the girl to the original school, the parents sought relief in the courts. The Supreme Court of North Carolina, emphasizing that the statute placed all emphasis on the welfare of the child and the effect upon the school to which reassignment was requested, ordered her reassigned. [In re *Reassignment of Hayes,* 135 S.E.2d 645 (N.C., 1964.] It

was the judgment of the court that under the facts such reassignment was [not] warranted. Reutter and Hamilton, *The Law of Public Education*, Foundation Press, Mineola, New York, 1970, pp. 118, 119. (See also DESEGREGATION.)

3. *Automobiles.* School districts may expend money for the purpose of building PARKING LOTS for student vehicles. Students may drive their AUTOMOBILES to school, but once the auto is on school premises, it is proper for the school to make RULES regarding their use or disuse during the school day. It is reasonable to stipulate that students may not loiter in the student parking lot, that students park in only designated areas, and that automobiles are to be driven at a slow rate of speed. It is also proper to enforce the rules by taking away the privilege of using the parking lot.

4. *Cheating.* Cheating on examinations is sufficient grounds to fail a student or to deny a student his or her DIPLOMA so long as there is sufficient evidence to prove such conduct. If there is insufficient evidence, the student must be passed or graduated no matter what the suspicions might be.

5. *Cleanliness.* It is proper to insist that students be clean and healthy prior to entering school. If a child is unclean to the degree that he or she should not associate with the other students, the student may be sent home. While it is not legally required, hopefully some outside assistance would be obtained in such instances in order to help the situation at the child's home. There are child abuse and neglect statutes in all states, and if the situation warrants, social service agencies may be called upon to investigate. There would be no liability for DEFAMATION if there is good faith in the teacher's or administrator's actions because the condition directly relates to the educational process and would thus be within the scope of the teacher's or administrator's duty. (See also VACCINATION.)

6. *Emancipated.* An emancipated student is one who is free from parental or guardian control. Even though that student might be a minor, it is possible for him or her to become emancipated. When this occurs, the student may choose his or her own RESIDENCE or domicile. This could have some effect on the student's right to attend school within a particular school district without paying non-resident TUITION. (See also COMPULSORY EDUCATION; MARRIED STUDENTS.)

7. *Homework.* Teachers may assign students homework, and discipline students who do not satisfactorily complete the assignments. The homework must be reasonable and may not substantially interfere with the

student's private life. For example, it would be reasonable to require a two-hour homework assignment; however, it would not be reasonable to require that the assignment be completed only between the hours of 7:00 to 9:00 p.m.

8. *Liability.* A student is liable for his or her own torts. However, most students are "judgment proof." Although a person may be able to obtain a judgment against a minor who wrongfully injures another, that individual would have no money from which to pay. Because minors commit torts, and because they are generally judgment proof, most states have enacted legislation making the minor's parents liable for their children's conduct. This type of vicarious liability is limited, however. Parental liability generally is limited to an amount of less than $500 in many states, but as high as $2000 and even more in a few states. Anything over this amount remains as the sole obligation of the minor. An injured party may take a minor and his parents to small claims court for injuries that are not too serious. For those that are more serious in nature, a higher court is necessary.

Subpoena. A subpoena is a legal process which compels a person to appear and give testimony before a court or hearing body. A "subpoena deuces tecum" is a process by which the court or authorized hearing body commands a person to produce certain documents or records.

Substantive Law. Substantive law is the law which deals with an individual's rights, duties, and liabilities. Adjective law is the law which regulates procedure. (See DUE PROCESS.)

Substitutes. See TEACHERS, substitutes.

Subversive Organizations. See ANTI-SUBVERSIVE LAWS; ASSEMBLY; CONSTITUTIONAL RIGHTS OF TEACHERS AND ADMINISTRATORS; LOYALTY OATHS.

Summer School. Summer school sessions may be conducted, and TUITION may be charged, because summer school is in excess of the state requirements of providing students with a free education. If tuition is charged, the activity becomes proprietary in nature, and there should be no GOVERNMENTAL IMMUNITY in those states where the distinction between proprietary and governmental acts makes a difference.

See also: COMMON SCHOOLS.

Superintendent. The local school district superintendent has the responsibility of advising the local board about the operation and management of the schools. He or she also has the responsibility of making certain that school board policy is implemented and educational objectives are achieved.

On the one hand, the superintendent is practically a member of the board. At least he or she is the board's chief confidant, and has the delegated responsibility of evaluating whether or not the educational objectives are being met. The local board must rely on the superintendent's judgment and recommendations in making many of the board's major decisions. On the other hand, the superintendent is an employee without TENURE but with the delegated responsibility of exercising independent professional judgment in the everyday operation of the schools.

There are always judgments by various groups as to just what should be taught and how it should be done, who should be hired and what methods and materials should be used. Because these judgments sometimes conflict, it is necessary for the board to clearly set forth the superintendent's rights, duties, and responsibilities in relation to the board, to teachers, and to students. Policies should state which duties and responsibilities the superintendent may delegate to other administrators and, in turn, which of those duties and responsibilities should be delegated to teachers and to students. Formal, concise, and clear procedures must be established in order to ensure that these functions are properly executed.

The superintendent is the voice of the local board to the teachers— and the voice of the teachers to the board.

Sometimes the superintendent's authority is not clear; however, it is clear that included within the superintendent's authority is the following:

1. He or she is in charge of the day-to-day operation of the schools.

2. He or she is in charge of evaluating whether or not the educational objectives of the board are being carried out.

3. The superintendent must make certain that teachers are evaluated pursuant to the law or to local school board policies.

4. The superintendent is in charge of investigating whether or not a teacher is competent, or if a teacher should be dismissed. This should be done through the administrative staff. (See also DUE PROCESS.)

5. The superintendent must advise the board which applicants should be hired to fill vacant teaching positions.

6. It is the superintendent's duty to attend all school board meetings, and to advise and give his or her opinion on all issues except his or her own salary.

The superintendent is not charged with the responsibility of knowing the individual needs of every student, nor should he or she be expected to know which teaching methods best fit a particular classroom situation. Those duties should be left with classroom teachers and administrators.

As far as liability is concerned, much depends upon whether the superintendent is considered an "officer" of the board or an "employee." Generally, the superintendent is considered an officer of the school board. This means that he or she enjoys the same immunities as local board members and will be indemnified or immune for acts done within the scope of his or her authority. (See GOVERNMENTAL IMMUNITY; SCHOOL BOARD, liability.)

If the superintendent is considered an employee of the board, there can be personal liability for tortious acts done within the scope of his or her duty. Of course, if the superintendent is outside the scope of his or her duty, there will be personal liability regardless of whether or not he or she is considered an employee or an officer.

Sometimes the question will arise as to whether or not the super-intendent is liable for the tortious acts of subordinates. The general rule is that there is no liability. That is, there is no liability unless the super-intendent somehow participated in the wrongful conduct or had reason to know that such conduct was probable. If that were the case, the super-intendent might be considered negligent for not foreseeing certain injuries and enacting rules for their prevention. In such an instance, he or she would be liable for his or her own NEGLIGENCE but not for the negligence of a subordinate.

Superintendent of Public Instruction. See CHIEF STATE SCHOOL OFFICER.

Supervision. Every teacher must supervise the activities of the students within his or her charge. The extent of this supervision depends on the facts and circumstances surrounding the activities. Whether or not a person has properly fulfilled his or her duty of supervision is a QUESTION

OF FACT for the jury to decide. (See ABSENCE FROM CLASS; NEGLIGENCE.)

A student is not on the schoolgrounds by choice. He or she is there because state law requires this. Therefore, it is up to the school to provide a safe environment within which the student can learn. It follows that in order to have a safe environment the students must have supervision.

Where a large group of young people is gathered, teachers and administrators should be able to foresee the possibility of an injury. The gathering must be supervised in a reasonable and prudent manner. Assigning one teacher to supervise several groups on a large playground is generally not REASONABLE AND PRUDENT. A teacher assigned to the cafeteria, sitting down in a spot where he or she cannot see what is happening, is not reasonable and prudent. If a teacher is a vocational instructor, he or she cannot sit in the office while students are working with dangerous instruments such as band saws. The teacher must get out and try to supervise as much as possible. If he or she does so, and a student is injured, it would be difficult to find the teacher liable.

Before leaving this section on supervision, it should be mentioned that supervisory duties may be imposed upon teachers if the duties are not arbitrary and are not unreasonable. (See CONTRACTS.) Supervisory duties should either relate directly to the teacher's classroom duties or be equally assigned to all teachers. For example, an English teacher could be expected to direct a play, or a music director could be expected to supervise a "pep" band. Physical education teachers could be expected to coach, and shop teachers could be expected to put on demonstrations of how to construct whatever the students are building. The supervisory duty may, at times, extend into the evening or even on weekends. The only limitation is that the duty be reasonable and not arbitrary.

Many of the "extra" supervisory duties are the subject of school negotiations. Generally, there is no legal requirement that a teacher is entitled to extra pay for each extra duty. In order to solve these problems, the local board could adopt a policy whereby teachers are given compensation to supervise extracurricular activities. (See ASSIGNMENTS, nonclassroom.)

Supplemental Contracts. See CONTRACTS.

Suspension of Students. See EXPULSION OF STUDENTS; STUDENT RIGHTS.

Suspension of Teachers. See DUE PROCESS; TEACHERS, dismissals.

T

Teacher Aide. A teacher's aide must meet the standard of care of the ordinary teacher in the same or similar circumstances. Teachers have a higher standard of care for the SUPERVISION and safety of their students than the ordinary man on the street. If this care is entrusted to a teacher's aide, the aide must be instructed how to supervise and how to maintain safety just like the ordinary teacher. If the aide does not meet this standard, the aide will be personally liable. Whether or not the teacher or administrator will be held liable along with the aide depends on the circumstances. If the aide was properly instructed and given proper directions, there would generally be no vicarious liability. However, if the teacher or administrator knew or should have known that the aide was incapable of meeting the necessary standard, but ignored this fact and assigned the aide supervisory duties anyway, that in itself constitutes NEGLIGENCE and both could be held liable.

In addition to adequate instruction of the aide, there is a duty on the part of the teacher or administrator to supervise the aide and make certain that he or she is properly performing the assigned duties. This does not mean that the teacher or administrator must constantly be with the aide. It does mean, however, that the aide must be watched in a REASONABLE AND PRUDENT manner.

All of this holds true for parent volunteers and student tutors. Everyone is liable for his or her own torts. It does not matter that the parent is a volunteer or that an older student is tutoring another. These persons should be covered with insurance, either on their own or paid for by the district. All supervisory duties within the school or at school sponsored, activities such as field trips must meet the standard of care of the reasonable and prudent teacher. RULES of safety should be communicated, and should then be enforced.

Teachers: 1. *Assignments.* 2. *Disability.* 3. *Dismissals.* 4. *Grading.* 5. *Outside Employment.* 6. *Substitutes.*

Note: The preceding areas are covered in this section. A great many other areas relating specifically to teachers are covered under individual topic headings. For a listing of these areas, consult these topic headings and the word index at the end of the book.

1. *Assignments.* Generally a teacher's contract states that the teacher is to "teach in the elementary or secondary schools within —————— district." The contract seldom states that the teacher shall "teach the sixth grade at Lincoln Elementary." Because of this, teachers generally may be assigned to any grade level for which he or she is qualified, and at any school within the district, even after a final contract has been signed. Usually, the teacher and administrator have verbally agreed that the teacher will teach at a certain grade level in a certain school. However, this agreement is not binding. That is, it is not binding unless this agreement is *specifically written into* the contract that is later signed. The law considers the verbal agreement "preliminary negotiations," and it considers the final contract the full embodiment of all the terms. In order to forestall problems, teachers should negotiate that their CONTRACTS specifically state at what grade level and at what school the teacher shall be assigned. Provisions should be made wherein a transfer can take effect only under certain conditions after specific procedures are followed. Once this is done, the ambiguity of many contracts will be removed.

See also: TRANSFERS.

2. *Disability.* A teacher who is disabled may take his or her accumulated SICK LEAVE, and thereafter may be dismissed if the disability prevents him or her from performing for a substantial period of time. The

dismissal, however, is not automatic. The teacher is entitled to a hearing and DUE PROCESS rights. If the disability is not permanent and if the disability does not substantially interfere with performance of teaching duties, the teacher could not be dismissed.

3. *Dismissals.* Every year there are a great many cases that go before the COURTS in regard to teacher dismissals. Other cases are settled out of court, or are dropped because one of the parties does not want to experience the anxiety of a hearing and eventual lawsuit. The following basic principles involving teacher dismissals should be understood:

1. The teacher is entitled to DUE PROCESS and fundamental fairness. This is true whether or not the teacher has TENURE.

2. The teacher may only be dismissed for specific reasons. There must be *objective proof* that these reasons exist, or else the teacher has a right to retain his or her position.

3. Statutory dismissal procedures must be followed. If they are not followed exactly, any dismissal would be improper and would be reversed.

There is a need to distinguish between dismissal and NONRENWAL of a teaching contract. A dismissal is the removal of a teacher *during* his or her contract term. A nonrenewal occurs after a contract term has ended or is soon to end, and before another contract is signed. A tenured teacher has a continuing contract, and any discharge of that teacher at any time would be considered a dismissal.

Prior to any dismissal, a teacher is generally evaluated a number of times. During a dismissal proceeding there are usually attempts to use EVALUATIONS indicating negative performance as evidence against the teacher. The purpose of an evaluation is not to build evidence against the teacher. Instead, the evaluation process is used to "improve" teacher effectiveness. Therefore, if an evaluation is for the specific purpose of determining whether or not a teacher is going to be dismissed, the teacher must be notified *in advance* of such a purpose. All evaluations used for this new purpose, and all other evidence that is to be used against the teacher, should be in the teacher's file and should be open for his or her inspection.

Dismissing a teacher is not difficult if there are adequate grounds. If adequate grounds exist, if the teacher is afforded due process, and if dismissal procedures are followed, a dismissal will be upheld by the courts. The biggest problem, therefore, is in determining what constitutes "adequate grounds." Generally, reasons for dismissal are outlined in state STATUTES, and, in addition to the specific reasons stated, there is usually a "catch all" ground saying "for other good and just cause." This brings the teacher into a gray area of ambiguities. Although these ambiguities do exist, there are some general guidelines that can be followed.

First of all, a teacher may only be dismissed if what he or she has done or is not doing affects his or her classroom or teaching effectiveness. The primary inquiry is the effect on students within the classroom. Can the teacher teach? Are the students learning? These are the important considerations, and there are a few others. There are three legal duties placed upon the shoulders of teachers. All teachers must be able to:

1. Instruct;
2. Supervise; and
3. Provide a safe environment for his or her students.

If the teacher fulfills these duties, there will seldom be grounds for dismissal.

One of the most common grounds cited as a cause for dismissal is "incompetency." To say the least, "incompetency" is vague. In some states, incompetency is the sole grounds for dismissal, and almost any reason could fall within its meaning. Because of this vagueness, some measures and standards should be developed to define its limits, and to help as guidelines for educators.

The "competent" teacher is a person who has the intelligence and ability to communicate knowledge of the "average and ordinary" teacher. The burden of proving incompetency is on the school board. If a teacher rightfully possesses a teaching CERTIFICATE, that is prima facie evidence of competency; and that evidence, therefore, must be rebutted by the school board. Proof of incompetence must be shown by a "preponderance of the evidence." The court will look to see if there is objective proof, based upon something more than HEARSAY, that would lead one to believe the teacher is incompetent. This means that an isolated instance of incompetence will not be enough to dismiss a teacher. In order to obtain objective proof, there would generally need to be a pattern of behavior established indicating an inability to perform.

In order for proof to be admissible, it has to be trustworthy. If a case is being built against a teacher, the administrator should write down everything that could be of importance in relation to any incidents that occur. The administrator should communicate the problems or incidents to the teacher. There must be complete honesty. The evidence being built should not stem from personality conflicts or philosophical differences. Improper motives should not be behind the instigation of dismissal proceedings.

The teacher involved would be well advised to keep a journal and build a "file" of his or her own. If an incident occurs, the teacher should write down everything that can be remembered. Who was there? What happened? What was said? What was felt? Exactly when did it happen? What other things were happening at the same time? Where did it happen? Where were the other parties positioned? How did the incident occur? Could it have been prevented? What steps had already been taken to prevent it? These questions are important and will be asked if the time comes for a hearing. But more importantly, if these questions are asked and personally answered while the teacher's memory is fresh, when the time comes for a trial the attorney will have something to work with besides vague generalizations based on memory alone.

In addition to incompetency, most state statutes list "immorality" as a proper ground for dismissal. The term "immorality" has been having a difficult time in some courts in recent years. What constitutes immorality? In a 1973 Oregon case, the Federal District Court ruled that a teacher could not be dismissed for "immorality" because the term was unconstitutionally vague. *Burton v. Cascade School District, Union High School #5,* 352 F.Supp. 254 (U.S. Dist. Ct. Ore., 1973). Although most courts will probably continue to uphold immorality as a basis for dismissal, they will require that in order to sustain a dismissal based upon alleged "immorality," the school district must be able to show that the conduct complained of has affected the teacher's fitness and ability to perform his or her teaching duties.

Conviction of a FELONY is generally a proper ground for dismissal. What acts constitute a felony depends upon the federal and state laws.

Conviction of a felony is grounds for dismissal, even though that crime may not be a felony in another jurisdiction.

Conviction of a crime involving "MORAL TURPITUDE" is also grounds for dismissal, even if such crime is not a felony. This surely seems as vague a term as "immorality." Are child molesting, dope pushing, indecent exposure, and rape crimes involving moral turpitude? Yes. On the other hand, is conviction of drunk driving or fighting in a public place proof of moral turpitude? No.

The real issues to be determined in the above examples are: "Does the crime or conduct substantially interfere with the welfare of the school?" Does the conduct have a direct relation to the teacher's fitness in the classroom? Does it affect his or her performance? If he or she is not effective and cannot perform because of his or her alleged "immoral" conduct or crime conviction, the teacher can be dismissed. On the other hand, if the teacher can perform, and if the alleged "immoral" conduct or crime conviction does not affect the classroom or the teacher's performance, then he or she should not be dismissed. (See also CONSTITUTIONAL RIGHTS OF TEACHERS AND ADMINISTRATORS.)

Another common ground for dismissal of a teacher is "insubordination." Basically, this means not following the reasonable rules of one's administrator. The insubordination must relate to teaching performance and the classroom. An administrator could not tell a teacher not to frequent a particular restaurant and dismiss the teacher for disobeying. The RULES must relate to the teacher's position, and cannot violate any constitutional or contract rights. Furthermore, the rules of the administration must be communicated to the teachers and must not be arbitrary. If a teacher feels that an administrator's rule is unreasonable, breaking the rule will not solve the problem. Should a teacher want to question the authority of an administrator where a particular rule is concerned, he or she should follow appropriate GRIEVANCE procedures.

In addition to insubordination, statutes frequently refer to "physical or mental disability" as a grounds for dismissal. The physical or mental disability of a teacher simply gives the school district a right to break its contract without being liable. The school district would of course have to bear the burden of proving that the teacher is in fact physically or mentally disabled such as to prevent him or her from being able to adequately fulfill the required teaching duties.

Another ground which is frequently used as a grounds for teacher dismissals is what is termed "inadequate performance." Unlike "incompetency," which is defined as meaning inability to perform, "inadequate performance" is like saying that although the teacher has the ability to perform, he or she simply has failed to do so. The teacher must be shown to have failed to exert the required effort, and generally this requires a showing of a consistent pattern of conduct.

See also: DUE PROCESS.

4. *Grading.* It is within the teacher's discretion to have measures and standards by which a student's grade is determined. These measures and standards must be reasonable and communicated to the students. They may not be imposed arbitrarily or without some flexibility allowing for emergency situations within the student's family or personal life. A teacher may not be dismissed simply because he or she is a "difficult grader" or because his or her standards are more difficult for many students to achieve. The question is really a matter of degree. How reasonable is the grading criteria and is that criteria effectively communicated to the students? Furthermore, are the students given a reasonable chance of meeting the necessary criteria? If so, the grading is proper.

5. *Outside Employment.* A teacher may secure employment outside of his or her teaching duties. However, that employment may not interfere with the teaching position. If the teacher is continually late for school, or if the teacher leaves early, there would be a direct interference and the teacher could be dismissed for neglect of duty. Fatigue could be an indirect cause of neglect of duty and that could also become grounds for dismissal. However, merely taking a part-time job would not be improper.

6. *Substitutes.* Substitute teachers must meet the same standards of care and intelligence as the REASONABLE AND PRUDENT teacher in the same or similar circumstances. The substitute teacher's liability for NEGLIGENCE is the same as the ordinary teacher, and the substitute must follow the same RULES and perform the same duties as the regular classroom instructor. In other words, the only distinction made between the substitute teacher and the regular teacher is the length of time in the classroom. Legally, they are in the same position in almost all school situations.

Tenure. Tenure is a job security device. Tenure does not guarantee continued employment, but it does provide that a tenured teacher or administrator may not be removed from his or her position without specific or good cause. In addition, the school board is obligated to follow certain procedures in order to establish whether or not such cause exists. (Both teachers and administrators may obtain tenure status under most state laws. However, in the remaining part of this section, the term "teachers" will be used, and it is meant to include "administrators," unless otherwise noted.)

The concept of tenure was developed in the late 1800's, in an effort to guarantee that good teachers would not be subjected to arbitrary, capricious, or discriminatory dismissals. By the early 1970's, nearly 40 states had statewide tenure laws. There are differences in the amount of protections granted under these laws, but they all are aimed at trying to protect good teachers while at the same time allowing for dismissal of incompetent teachers. In addition, some states have what is known as a CONTINUING CONTRACT LAW or ANNUAL OR LONGTERM CONTRACTS.

Teaching is a public office which among other problems at one time found itself subjected to abuse by politicians. Tenure was an effective means of preventing politics from entering into teacher appointments or removals. This was noted and explained in one of the reports in the American Historical Association's investigation of the social studies in the schools:

> Although teachers in Colonial times had no legal claim to permanent tenure, in practice they often held office for life. Then, at about the same time the schools fell under public control and Jacksonian democracy came into power with its sense of popular "possession" of public offices, its spoils system, its theory of rotation in office. Teachers' tenure became precarious. All too often the position was handed about as a petty favor to friends of those in power. After all, anyone could teach school. Towards the end of the century, training for teachers had become so common that "anyone" could not always satisfy requirements. Demands for the merit system in politics were accompanied by a new attitude toward teaching and a realization that good teachers could not be procured and kept, under the old methods of filling positions. In 1875, President Eliot of Harvard wrote, "Permanence of tenure and security of income are essential to give dignity and independence to the teacher's position." In 1885, a committee of the National Education Association rendered an exhaustive report on tenure. It urged reform because "The public school system should be independent of personal or partisan influence and free from the malignant power of patronage and spoils." (Footnotes omitted); Beale, H. K. *Are American Teachers Free?* Scribner, 1936, pp. 465-466.

Tenure laws have frequently been criticized, but over the years, the kinds of objections raised have not changed significantly. As long ago as 1936, Howard Beale wrote in a historical report of the Commission on the social studies:

> The objections to security of tenure are twofold. Many superintendents oppose it because consciously or unconsciously they desire to retain their power over teachers. They are accustomed to giving orders. They fear an independent teaching staff. All over the world in a great variety of organizations there is a welling up of new ideas, a revolt against long-established leadership. This is happening in American education. The superintendents, being human, cherish their power over others and know that adequate tenure laws will deprive them of the more arbitrary exercises of it. Autocrats—and many superintendents are just that in relation to their teachers—usually struggle against limitations upon their autocracy. Besides, superintendents who often have to cringe before school boards or powerful elements in the community seek recompense in making teachers do the same before them. Then, too, the whole psychology of school administration has been built upon the issuance and carrying out of mandates. Superintendents talk to their teachers of "cooperation" but they usually mean "obedience." True cooperation with teachers is not an outstanding virtue of administrators. Even the superintendent who is not inclined to be dictatorial regards himself as "responsible" for the schools. The public often holds him responsible. Power, he feels, must accompany responsibility. Teacher tenure will diminish his power and make him less effective in his responsibility. One superintendent revealed the attitude of a whole class of administrators when he replied to a recent inquiry about the Indiana tenure law, "The effect has not been good here. It has tended to make the teachers more independent." The N.E.A. Committee on Tenure answered this sort of superintendent in 1934 when it declared, "The military conception of education, which contemplates blind and unreasoning obedience of all orders and regulations from official sources, and control of teachers through fear, has as little place in American education as has the same plan of management in the American classroom."
>
> The other reason for opposition to tenure laws is fear that they will operate to retain in office not only the good teacher of unconventional views, but also the incompetent or lazy teacher. One often hears that it is only the incompetent teachers who are concerned

about tenure. Obviously unfounded as investigation makes this
charge, it has wide credence among superintendents and the public.
There are, of course, incompetents who prefer agitating to teaching
and who therefore urge tenure laws to protect their own incompetence. One Indiana superintendent testifies that "some tenured teachers have developed an attitude that no further supervision of their
work is desirable." The problem of protecting the schools against
incompetence, laziness, or indifference and at the same time making
the good teacher secure is a difficult one. The probationary period of
one to several years, during which presumably a teacher's qualifications can be amply tested before permanent tenure is granted, is one
device to meet this problem. Another is the list of specified grounds
upon which teachers may be dismissed after a hearing. This appears
in all tenure laws. Even with these provisions for dismissal it is often
complained that, under the present tenure laws in New York, Chicago, and California, tenure is so secure that it is extremely difficult
to get rid of a teacher for poor teaching and indifference. These
complaints sometimes come from superintendents who do not believe
in security of tenure anyway. Yet often they come from good teachers
who desire protective legislation but desire improvement in tenure
laws to the point where they will protect only the good teacher. In
Chicago, for instance, Lillian Herstein declares, "In our city our
tenure is so safe that it is difficult to get rid of incompetent teachers."
Advocates of tenure laws are aware of this danger. But, with Miss
Herstein, they believe it wiser to prevent the removal of the few
incompetent teachers who are not ousted under tenure, than to endanger the independence of thought and teaching of the good teachers
who without tenure laws could be cowed and repressed to the detriment of their service to the community.

In Indiana, where a tenure law has been in force since 1927, an
enquiry was recently conducted, which brought from superintendents
some unfavorable and some favorable comments and which led the
investigator to conclude, "This inquiry would seem to indicate that in
Indiana the benefits of tenure have outweighed the detriments. It
would also seem to show that on the whole superintendents are not
handicapped in their work by tenure. It would also appear that most
teachers respond professionally to increased freedom and to protection from lay and school board interference and domination." One
Indiana superintendent wrote, "Tenure has prevented the replacement
of experienced teachers by local inexperienced teachers." Another
declared, "Our entire force would have been removed had we not had

tenure." Still another averred, "Tenure has prevented a raid on our schools by politicians, job-seekers and tax-reductionists." And another, "Our tenure teachers are very cooperative and agreeable. While some of our teachers have taken tenure to mean security in their positions and have lapsed in progressive spirit and initiative, the others have taken tenure to mean freedom from worry about political changes and have used all their energy in making their work efficient. It has enhanced their eagerness and initiative." One reported, "Since the passage of the tenure law teacher-superintendent relationship and cooperation have been decidedly improved." (Footnotes omitted); Beale, H. K. *Are American Teachers Free?* Scribner, 1936, pp. 475-478.

Tenure laws do have room for improvement, but they have definitely been in the best interests of the school system. Frequently, the COURTS have explained the intended purpose of tenure laws:

> While tenure provisions . . . protect teachers in their positions from political or arbitrary interference, they are not intended to preclude dismissal where the conduct is detrimental to the efficient operation and administration of the schools of the district. . . . Its object is to improve the school system by assuring teachers of experience and ability a continuous service based upon merit, and by protecting them against dismissal for reasons that are political, partisan or capricious. *Pickering v. Board of Education*, 225 N.E.2d, 16 (Ill., 1967).

By protecting teachers in this manner, tenure acts to free teachers from special interest and pressure groups, and allows them to exercise their initiative. In effect, the ultimate purpose of tenure laws is to improve the educational system and to benefit students.

In most states, tenure can only be attained after successful completion of a probationary period. The most common requirement is satisfactory service for three years plus renewal for a fourth. Substitute, intern, and student teaching are usually not counted as being a part of the probationary period. At the end of the probationary period, tenure is automatic in some states, but in many others, recommendation by the superintendent plus affirmative action by the school board is required. In a few states, the probationary period may be extended in order to give a teacher whose work has not met the district's tenure standards an additional opportunity to improve the quality of his or her service.

During the probationary period, most state laws provide that the teacher may be dismissed without cause at the end of the school year, or with cause if the dismissal is during the school year. In many states, the reasons for NONRENEWAL of the teacher's contract at the end of the year are not required to be given. Where reasons are required or are provided, it is for the purpose of pointing out the teacher's inadequacies to help him or her in future employment, and is not meant to force the school board to prove cause. (See also DUE PROCESS.)

Once a teacher has attained tenure, he or she may be dismissed only for what is often termed "cause." For an explanation of the causes which are required to lawfully dismiss a tenured teacher, see TEACHERS, dismissals. In determining whether or not the required cause does in fact exist, the school board is required to strictly comply with certain designated dismissal procedures. Failure to comply will generally result in the teacher having a right to REINSTATEMENT plus DAMAGES. For an explanation and outline of the required procedures, see DUE PROCESS.

Tenure status does not give a teacher a vested right to a particular position or to a particular school. SCHOOL BOARDS have the discretionary power to reassign or transfer teachers where such action is made in good faith and with proper motives. The transfer must be to a position of equal pay and status and within a reasonable distance of the other position, or the transfer may be considered tantamount to a DEMOTION. (See also TRANSFERS.) In addition, ABOLITION OF POSITIONS for financial reasons may be valid grounds for terminating a tenured teacher's contract.

Tenure status may be voluntarily relinquished by resignation. Tenure generally terminates automatically when a teacher reaches age 65. Tenure status also may be affected by amendments or even repeal of the state tenure laws. Such a law may be changed without its being found unconstitutional because the COURTS hold that no contract to keep the tenure law intact exists between the state and the teacher.

Some states have tenure in some districts but not in others. Although the constitutionality of such laws has been challenged on the grounds of DISCRIMINATION and EQUAL PROTECTION, they have been upheld. However, where the exclusion of some counties from a tenure law was in effect intended as a means of racial discrimination, the law has been found unconstitutional. *Alabama State Teachers Association v. Lowndes County Bd. of Ed.*, 289 F.Supp. 300 (U.S.Dist.Ct.Ala., 1968).

With the advent of COLLECTIVE BARGAINING, tenure laws are being subjected to renewed challenges. Some people feel that job security should be a negotiable item and there is no longer any necessity for the state to grant this "fringe benefit" by statute. Through collective bargaining, many of the tenure protections could be provided for in contract AGREEMENTS. Nevertheless, it is doubtful that the tenure laws will be repealed. They provide too great a benefit for the students and the school system—as well as for the teachers themselves. However, to remain viable in modern times, tenure laws should require:

1. A probationary period;
2. A method of evaluating teachers;
3. Tenured teachers who are unable to adequately perform their teaching duties may be dismissed;
4. A review of the school board's decision on whether or not cause for dismissal exists should be limited to checking to see if the required due process procedures were followed, and if substantial reliable evidence existed to support the decision; and
5. Other penalties besides complete dismissal should be examined and allowed as alternatives.

Textbooks, adoption of. See ANTI-EVOLUTION STATUTES, CURRICULUM; SCHOOL BOARDS.

Textbooks, free. Many state laws require school districts to provide free textbooks for students attending public schools. This is a proper expenditure of school FUNDS. The more controversial question arises in connection with state laws which require school districts to provide free textbooks for *all* students attending school, including those attending a private or parochial school. As a general rule, this kind of law is constitutional, and it is held not to be in violation of the Establishment of RELIGION clause. For example, in 1968, the Supreme Court of the United States upheld a New York program of providing free textbooks to students attending private and parochial as well as public elementary and secondary schools. The Court recognized this "aid" as being secular in nature, and the benefit to the private and parochial schools as being indirect. *Board of Education v. Allen*, 392 U.S. 236 (1968).

The constitutionality of this form of aid may be challenged where DISCRIMINATION is involved. In 1973, the Supreme Court was faced with a Mississippi textbook program in which the state purchased textbooks and loaned them to students attending both public and private schools, without regard to the fact that some of the private schools had racially discriminatory admission policies. The Court found the law unconstitutional because it aided the establishment of schools which might discriminate. The Court explained that the granting of textbooks to sectarian schools for secular subjects does not significantly advance the religious functions such as to make the law unconstitutional, but this must be distinguished from aid to schools which are discriminatory. *Norwood v. Harrison*, 93 S.Ct. 2804 (1973).

See also: CHILD-BENEFIT THEORY; PRIVATE AND PAROCHIAL SCHOOL AID.

Threats. See ASSAULT.

Torts. A tort is a civil wrong. It is a wrong committed against someone's property or person. When a tort has been committed, the person who has been wronged may seek DAMAGES by suing the wrongdoer.

See also: ASSAULT; BATTERY; DEFAMATION; FALSE IMPRISONMENT; MENTAL DISTRESS; NEGLIGENCE; TRESPASS TO PERSONAL PROPERTY.

Tracking of Students. See INTELLIGENCE TESTING.

Transfers. Transfers of teachers are not always seen as punitive acts. As a result, good faith transfers do not require a formal DUE PROCESS hearing. As one court explained:

> It is conceivable that many teachers are transferred by county boards of education, not because of inefficiency, misconduct or unfitness, but rather because of the mere fact that they are competent, effective teachers, and that, therefore, a proper administration of the county public school system dictates the basis of transfers to places and positions where the teacher's special qualifications will better promote the entire public school program of the county.

State ex rel Withers v. Board of Ed. of Mason Co., 172 S.E.2d
796, 803 (W.Va., 1970).

Many teachers are also transferred because of personality conflicts or because of unsatisfactory service. These transfers are also upheld by the
COURTS because transfers are not intended to punish the teacher, they
are meant to give him or her a chance to improve his or her performance.

As previously stated, transfers which are not punitive in nature do not
require a hearing, but this is subject to one very important rule:

> **The transfer must be in a position of equal pay and status, and in
> the same general location. In addition, it must be to a position within
> the teacher's area of certified qualification or the area specified in his
> or her contract.**

If the transfer does not conform to this rule, the teacher must be granted a
hearing prior to the transfer, or the courts will not uphold it.

TENURE status may not be affected by transfer to a new position. As a
result, the teacher cannot be forced to go through another probationary
period in order to obtain tenure. However, though tenured as a teacher, if
transferred to an administrative position, the person retains his or her
tenure as a teacher, but where STATUTES allow, the person can be forced
to undergo a new probationary period before tenure is acquired as an
administrator.

In order to comply with the requirements of DESEGREGATION of
the school faculty, the school board may be forced to transfer tenured or
nontenured teachers to effect integration.

See also: ABOLITION OF POSITIONS; DEMOTIONS.

Transportation. State STATUTES frequently prescribe requirements for
the operation of school transportation systems. Such requirements often
include: safety standards, colors, identification markings, taillight warnings, liability insurance, and minimum qualifications for school BUS
DRIVERS. In addition, most state statutes specify who has the right to
school transportation, and who may be transported at the school board's
discretion.

It has been clearly held that it is constitutional to authorize the expenditure of public FUNDS for the transportation of students. As a result,
school districts may own and operate their own school buses, may contract
with private operators for bus transportation, or may even reimburse
parents for providing students the necessary transportation.

Some states require school districts to provide transportation, while several others make it optional or make it mandatory only under certain conditions. If the state laws make it mandatory for school districts to provide transportation, all children must be treated equally. Therefore, it has been held that even if transportation of some students would involve a much greater expense, this is not a sufficient reason to deny transportation. However, there is a split of authority as to whether or not traffic hazards may be considered in establishing transportation policies. Judicial authority exists to support both arguments, but all COURTS agree that the legislature validly could provide for consideration of such things, if it chooses to do so.

Some statutes mandate transportation only for students who live within various designated distance limitations. These limitations are easily susceptible to varying interpretations and therefore, lawsuits, where they are stated in terms of "unreasonable," "remote" or "inaccessible." In these instances, by questioning the reasonableness of the board ruling, the courts will determine whether or not the school board has abused its discretion. The result will depend on the individual facts and circumstances, and the court will consider such things as age of the pupils, weather conditions in the area, traffic hazards and conditions, and width and surface of the road required to be traveled.

In cases of transportation of private and parochial school students, the legal issues generally center on the constitutionality of spending public FUNDS in support of RELIGION. Although furnishing transportation to private and parochial school students benefits their schools to some extent, such expenditures have been upheld on the basis of the CHILD-BENEFIT THEORY. This theory holds that where the main benefit inures to the child, the secondary benefit to the school can be disregarded, and such an expenditure will be upheld. It should be noted that unless the state statutes explicitly require it to do so, the school board cannot be *compelled* to furnish transportation to private or parochial school students. In addition, some state laws forbid SCHOOL BOARDS from providing such transportation.

See also: PRIVATE AND PAROCHIAL SCHOOL AID.

Trespass to Personal Property. Trespass to personal property is the intentional taking or interfering with the use, possession, or physical condition of the personal property of another without authority to do so. This is an intentional tort. There are seldom any suits brought for this tort as the result of school activities. Nevertheless, it is one of the most common torts committed by teachers, administrators, and students. At the end of every school year, teachers can be seen emptying various and sundry articles from their desks and closets. These articles—squirt guns, comic books, and cigarettes—all have been confiscated from students, and all are wrongfully detained. The personal property of a student is his or her own to keep. A teacher or administrator cannot interfere with that possession unless the property in question is interfering with the educational process. Even when it is interfering with the educational process, the teacher or administrator only has the authority to retain temporary possession. Thereafter, the property must be returned to its rightful owner.

Trespass to personal property is not usually particularly serious. The articles involved are often valued at less than a dollar and no one complains over their confiscation at any great length. However, it is still wrong to keep what is not one's. The teacher, therefore, may not detain the property for an unreasonable period of time, nor may he or she damage the student's property. Usually at the end of the school day, it is proper to return the goods to their owners. The teacher may instruct the students not to return the articles in question to school, but if they are returned, there is still no right to keep them. If the students bring the squirt guns or other "banned" articles back again, the remedy is not to keep the property but to resort to other disciplinary measures.

In referring to the wrongful detention of personal property, we are talk-contraband (property which is illegal to possess) to school, the teacher or ing about personal property which is legal to possess. If a student brings administrator has the legal right and duty to take the property and turn it over to the proper authorities. This type of property should not be given back to the student because he or she has no right to possess what is illegal. Cigarettes, pocketknives, lighters, and things of that nature are not necessarily illegal to possess. It may be illegal to sell cigarettes to minors, but in nearly all states, it is not illegal for a minor to possess them. Lighters and certain pocketknives lawfully can be possessed.

There are times when, although a teacher knows that he or she has no right to deprive a student of his or her property, the teacher considers it to be dangerous or wrong to return the confiscated articles to the student. Under these circumstances it is reasonable to inform the child's parents that the school does not allow students to carry knives, cigarettes, etc. at school.

School officials could also ask the parents to come to discuss the matter, and return the "banned" articles at that time. If the student continues to bring the "banned" but legal articles to school, harsher disciplinary measures should be taken. However, keep in mind that there is no right to permanently deprive the owner of possession of legal items.

See also: SEARCH AND SEIZURE.

Tuition. Tuition is a payment charged for instruction. The legal residence of a student is the RESIDENCE of his or her parents or legal guardian. A student is entitled to attend school in the district of his or her legal residence without paying tuition.

Nonresident tuition. Here, the issue is whether or not a child living in one school district may attend school in another district without paying tuition. Some state STATUTES cover this problem, but where no such statutes exist, the local school board has the discretion to do as it wishes. The board does not have to allow a nonresident to attend the district's schools, in the absence of statutes to the contrary, and therefore, may condition admittance upon payment of a reasonable tuition.

Summer school tuition. Summer school, as used in this context, is meant to refer to a session of school which is offered in excess of the minimum school program. Although summer school tuition is charged by most school districts, and is required to be charged by a few state statutes, its legality has not been effectively challenged in the courts. The constitutions of most states require their state legislatures to provide free and uniform systems of public schools. No provision is made in state constitutions for summer schools. Statutes and district provisions requiring summer school tuition may very well be in conflict with some state constitutions requiring free schools.

Tuition reimbursements. Tuition reimbursements to low-income parents of private school students, tax credits to middle-income parents, as well as other tuition reimbursements for students attending private schools have been found unconstitutional by the U.S. Supreme Court. (See PRIVATE AND PAROCHIAL SCHOOL AID.)

College Tuition. The state may charge tuition for students attending state colleges. One of the more controversial issues has been the charging of out-of-state students a higher tuition than resident students are charged. Such a difference in the amounts payable has been upheld by the COURTS. However, once a student establishes a residence in the state, the out-of-state tuition fee may no longer be charged. A state may not permanently classify a student as being out-of-state merely because his or her residence was not within the state at the time of admission. As the Supreme Court of the United States said when it struck down Connecticut's regulations which permanently classified students as "out-of-state" if their residence was not in Connecticut when they applied for admission:

> **. . . [A] permanent irrebuttable presumption of nonresidence . . . is violative of the Due Process Clause, because it provides no opportunity for students who applied from out of State to demonstrate that they have become bona fide Connecticut residents.** *Vlandis v. Kline,* **93 S.Ct. 2230, 2237 (1973).**

In making a determination of whether or not a previously out-of-state student has become a bona fide resident, the state may consider all relevant factors, such as voter registration, state in which tax returns are filed property ownership, whether or not the student remained in the state year-round, driver's license, marital status, vacation employment, car registration, etc.

See also: FEES.

U-Z

Underground Newspapers. See NEWSPAPERS; STUDENT RIGHTS.

Uniforms. See CURRICULUM; RULES.

Union Security. Union security in the public schools really should be termed organizational security. Organizational security is the protection of the employee organization's status by provisions in an AGREEMENT establishing a closed shop, AGENCY SHOP, or maintenance-of-membership.

Closed shops in the public schools may constitute an illegal DISCRIMINATION against the right all citizens have to apply for government employment.

See also: DUES CHECKOFF.

Unions. See ASSEMBLY; COLLECTIVE BARGAINING; CONSTITUTIONAL RIGHTS OF TEACHERS AND ADMINISTRATORS; UNION SECURITY.

Unwed Mothers. 1. *Students.* See EQUAL PROTECTION; PREGNANT STUDENTS; STUDENT RIGHTS.

2. *Teachers.* See CONSTITUTIONAL RIGHTS OF TEACHERS AND ADMINISTRATORS; EQUAL PROTECTION; MATERNITY LEAVE; TEACHERS, dismissals.

Vaccination. Vaccinations may be required as a condition of school attendance. If the parent objects, he or she would be in violation of COMPULSORY EDUCATION laws. The right to require vaccinations extends to private and parochial schools. In other words, if the state statute requires vaccinations for smallpox or diptheria, all schools must follow that directive, including the private or religious institutions.

In the absence of state statutes, a vaccination may be required in emergency situations such as an epidemic. Even without an emergency situation, it has been held in some states that schools may give vaccinations and may require students to be vaccinated. These states include among others: Missouri, New York, North Carolina, Texas, and Arkansas.

See also: MEDICAL SERVICES.

Vice-Principal. The vice-principal is part of the administration and is not a part of the teaching staff while carrying out his or her administrative functions. He or she is considered an employee and not an officer of the school board. The vice-principal reports directly to the principal and is generally in charge of specific areas such as student discipline. The vice-principal is liable for his or her own acts, but not the acts of teachers unless the vice-principal knew or should have known of the potential tortious conduct.

See also: GOVERNMENTAL IMMUNITY; NEGLIGENCE; PRINCIPAL.

Vocational Programs. Money may be allocated to vocational programs without violating any constitutional provisions. Vocational education is a proper educational endeavor, but it is, by its very nature, one of the more hazardous activities carried on within the school system. Because of this, vocational education teachers need to be very cognizant of RULES of safety. Before any student is allowed to use a machine, rules of safety must be communicated and understood. Students not only should be required to pass an examination regarding each machine or activity to be pursued, but rules of safety must be impressed upon them and, if they later violate rules of safety, they should be disciplined immediately.

Many vocational classes are overcrowded, and the students, lacking proper supervision, are inclined to present disciplinary problems. In addition, many machines, torches, and various and sundry instruments are present which can cause serious damage to students. As with all teachers, the vocational education teacher has a duty of SUPERVISION. Due to the nature of the class, this duty of supervision is even higher than that of the ordinary teacher. If the classroom is overcrowded, the duty cannot be properly fulfilled. Therefore, if this situation exists, it is recommended that the teacher notify the administration of the hazardous condition. The teacher should keep accurate records of incidents relative to safety, and, if he or she properly documents the situation, the classload should be lowered without difficulty. If the classload is not lowered and the teacher has acted in a REASONABLE AND PRUDENT manner under the circumstances, liability for any injuries would shift to the ones responsible for letting the hazardous condition exist.

In many places, the machines or instruments used are hazardous in themselves in that they do not meet the minimum standards of safety as set forth in state statutes or state administrative standards. If a student is injured in this situation, he or she would have two causes of action. One would be for NEGLIGENCE and the second would be for violation of state law. Realistically, this would almost impose strict liability automatically, and the school district and the teacher would have few, if any, defenses. Therefore, in such a situation these machines, etc., must be replaced or the class should be cancelled.

See also: GOVERNMENTAL IMMUNITY; NEGLIGENCE.

Vouchers. Educational voucher plans have been suggested as a means of providing the consumer of education with a greater variety of choice. The basic form of a voucher plan is to provide each student's parent or parents with a voucher which could be used for admission into any school which is accredited and is participating in the voucher system. The schools would then present their vouchers to the state board of education for reimbursement. Public, private, parochial, and experimental alternative schools would all be eligible for possible accreditation and participation in the voucher system.

Proponents of the voucher system argue that this would: provide a greater freedom of choice, encourage competition and resulting upgrading of education, equalize educational opportunities, ease school district problems, and provide the consumer with an opportunity to seek an educational system which is capable of fulfilling individual needs. Opponents of the voucher system feel that it would: facilitate segregation and DISCRIMINATION, constitute a violation of the constitutional requirement of separation of church and state, and pose a threat to teachers' rights and the stability of public school systems.

Parochial schools would probably have to be allowed to participate in the voucher system because failure to include them would perhaps be an unconstitutional discrimination against religion because the state is required to remain neutral. But, from a realistic standpoint, parochial schools would be allowed to participate, not because of the Constitution, but because of the tremendous pressure being exerted to increase the forms of aid to alleviate the financial problems being faced by parochial schools. If parochial schools are forced to close, many states and local school districts would face a serious financial crisis by being required to absorb the thousands of parochial school students into an already crowded public school system. As a result, the main question to be answered is whether or not a voucher system would violate the First Amendment's establishment of RELIGION clause by being viewed as an impermissible state aid in support of religion.

The state cannot levy taxes to support religious activities or institutions. Just as the Supreme Court has found tax credits to be an impermissible form of aid, so it would appear that voucher plans in their basic form are unconstitutional. Several various theories have been used to uphold certain other forms of indirect state aid to parochial schools (CHILD-BENEFIT THEORY; EXTERNAL BENEFIT THEORY, and FUNDAMENTAL INTEREST THEORY). These theories could *perhaps* be used to validate a voucher system, *if* such a system were carefully designed and drafted.

Bills for voucher systems in the basic form have been introduced in the legislatures of several states. Whether or not voucher systems will become law throughout the country remains for the future to decide. Whether or not such systems, upon becoming law, will be able to withstand a constitutional challenge remains for the courts to decide. The weight of judicial reasoning suggests that such systems would constitute an unconstitutional establishment of religion. In fact, an Ohio law relating to a voucher system has already suffered a defeat in the courts. *Wolman v. Essex,* 342 F.Supp. 399 (U.S. Dist. Ct. Ohio, 1972).

Waiver. Legally, a waiver is the foregoing of a legal right, and once that right is waived, it can no longer be recaptured. Waiver can be important in many cases. Many cases turn on just this point. For example, in contract NONRENEWAL cases, the local board must give the teacher notice of nonrenewal on or before a certain date. If the notice is not given, the teacher may accept his or her contract on or before a certain date thereafter. If the contract is not accepted properly, the right is waived and there will be no liability.

Witnesses. Witnesses are people who testify at an administrative hearing or a court trial. In order to prove one's case, a person may call witnesses with personal knowledge on certain facts or issues. That witness may then be cross-examined by the opposing party. One of the fundamental rights of DUE PROCESS is that a person has the right to confront witnesses against him or her, and this also means the right to cross-examine.

Workshops. Workshops are "in-service" type programs specifically designed to help educators become more aware of certain areas within education. Teachers may be required to attend a certain number of workshops, but this is negotiable The number must be reasonable and so must the time. Workshops may be used as credit for continuing education requirements set up by the local board, but this will depend upon adopted school board policies.

See also: CERTIFICATION; SCHOOL BOARDS.

General Index

A

Ability grouping, 155-156
Abington School District v. Schempp, 37, 202*n*
Abolition of positions:
    consolidation of districts, 13, 14
    decreasing population growth rate, 13
    discrimination, 13
    financial reasons, 292
    greater services at less expense, 13
    if abolished in fact, 13
    initial staffing of new district, 14
    legal arguments, 13
    not a demotion, 15
    one school replacing two, 14
    principal, 14
    reasons bona fide, 13
    reorganization, 14
    tenure, 13, 14
Absence:
    compulsory education, 57-58
    leave, 75, 159-160
    students, 274-275
    teacher, 15
Academic freedom, 16-17, 60, 61, 62, 67-69, 260, 261, 262-265, 267-268
Acanfora v. Montgomery County Board of Education, 151
Accidents:
    absence of teacher, 15
    negligence (*see* Negligence)
Accountability:
    achievement tests, 18
    evaluations, 120-121

Accountability: *(cont.)*
    legislation, 17-18
    malpractice, 163-164
    merit pay, 174
Achievement tests, 18
Acquisition of property
    (*see* Buildings; Property)
Activity funds, 18
Administrative agencies:
    burden of proof, 43
    checks or balances, 19
    courts, 91
    delegation of responsibility, 19
    due process, 107
    extent of judicial review, 19-20
    legal problems, 18
    school boards, 18
    scope of authority, 18
    standards, 18, 19
    state and federal government
        creations, 18
Administrators:
    constitutional rights of teachers
        and administrators, 62-77
    principals, 196-197
    superintendent, 278-279
    vice-principal, 301
Agency shop, 20, 300
Agent, 20, 141
Agreement:
    grievance, 147
    mediation, 169
    salary schedules, 228
    scope of bargaining, 238
    severance payments, 243
    textbooks, free, 293